The MAILBOX®
SUPERBOOK™
GRADE 2

Your complete resource for an entire year of second-grade success!

W9-BZQ-724

Editors:
Darcy Brown, Cynthia Holcomb, Sharon Murphy

Contributing Editor:
Susan Hohbach Walker

Contributors:
Katherine Bateman, Rebecca Brudwick, Marsha Carr-Lambert, Elizabeth Chappell, Robin Works Davis,
Michele Gunther, Nicole Iacovazzi, Susie Kapaun, Lisa Kelly, Martha Kelly, Pamela Kucks,
Cheryl Sergi, Cheryl Stickney, Maureen Swigon, Carol Troutman

Art Coordinator:
Cathy Spangler Bruce

Artists:
Jennifer Tipton Bennett, Cathy Spangler Bruce, Clevell Harris,
Kimberly Richard, Rebecca Saunders, Barry Slate, Donna K. Teal

Cover Artist:
Jim Counts

www.themailbox.com

The Education Center, Inc.
Greensboro, North Carolina

ABOUT THIS BOOK

Look through the pages of *The Mailbox® GRADE 2 SUPERBOOK™*, and discover a wealth of ideas and activities specifically designed for the second-grade teacher. We've included tips for starting the year, managing your classroom, maintaining parent communication, and motivating your students. In addition, you'll find activities for reinforcing the basic skills in all areas of the second-grade curriculum. We've also provided reference materials for every subject, literature lists, arts-and-crafts ideas, holiday and seasonal reproducibles, and bulletin-board ideas and patterns. *The Mailbox® GRADE 2 SUPERBOOK™* is your complete resource for an entire year of second-grade success!

Library of Congress Cataloging-in-Publication Data

The mailbox superbook, grade 2 : your complete resource for an entire
    year of second-grade success! / editors, Cynthia Holcomb, Sharon
    Murphy ; contributing editor, Susan Hohbach Walker ; contributors,
    Katherine Bateman ... [et al.] ; art coordinator, Cathy Spangler
    Bruce ; artists, Jennifer Tipton Bennett ... [et al.].
        p.   cm.
    ISBN 1-56234-198-7 (pbk.)
    1. Second grade (Education)—United States—Curricula—Handbooks,
manuals, etc.   2. Teaching—United States—Aids and devices—
Handbooks, manuals, etc.   3. Education, Primary—Activity programs—
United States—Handbooks, manuals, etc.   4. Classroom management—
United States—Handbooks, manuals, etc.   I. Holcomb, Cynthia.
II. Murphy, Sharon (Sharon V.)   III. Bateman, Katherine.
LB1571 2dM35   1998
372.1102—dc21   98-5187
                                                           CIP

Manufactured in the United States
10 9 8 7 6 5 4

TABLE OF CONTENTS

BACK TO SCHOOL

BACK TO SCHOOL

On Your Mark, Get Set...

The first few days before school can be a flurry of activity as you attend to the many details of getting your room ready, making lesson plans, and securing materials. Stay on top of things with the checklists on pages 14 and 15. Duplicate a copy of each form and fill in the tasks you need to accomplish. With a quick glance you will be able to see what progress you have made, and what tasks still lie ahead as the big day draws near!

Set The Stage

Each school year brings with it a new beginning, new students, and new adventures in learning. Set the stage for back-to-school fun with a special look for your classroom. Peruse the list below for theme ideas; then put your imagination to work in designing a door decoration, a welcome-back bulletin board, a student-helper chart, a birthday display, and nametags that incorporate the theme.

"Dive Into A New Year"
Use a small plastic swimming pool, swim rings, and beach towels to decorate your room with a display that really makes a splash!

"Catch Second-Grade Excitement!"
Pitch a display of baseballs, gloves, and mitts to make the new school year a big hit!

"More Fun Than A Barrel Of Monkeys"
Create a swingin' scene with these curious creatures to set the stage for an exciting new year.

"We'll Have A Whale Of A Year!"
These magnificent mammals will welcome your new second graders in a big way!

"Nuts About A New Year"
Let a display of frisky squirrels and animated acorns show your new students that "nut-thing" is better than a new second-grade year!

"Welcoming A Bright Bunch Of Students"
A smiling sun character surrounded by sunglasses will get your year off to a shining start.

"Put Your Best Foot Forward"
Make tracks for a great new year with a display of funny footprints and snazzy sneakers.

Summer Similarities

This back-to-school correspondence provides the background for a first-day activity. A week before school begins, program the questionnaire on page 16 with questions relating to summer (see programming suggestions on this page). Then mail each student a copy of the questionnaire and a welcome note instructing the student to bring the completed questionnaire to school on the first day. Prior to the activity, construct a large graph programmed with information from the questionnaire. On the first day, read each question aloud. If a student answered *yes,* write his name on the corresponding section of the graph. The completed graph will give each child an opportunity to find friends with similar interests. Your students may be surprised at how much they have in common.

Programming Suggestions:

➤ Did you go on a vacation?

➤ Did you go swimming?

➤ Did you climb a tree?

➤ Did you play an instrument?

➤ Did you go to the movies?

➤ Did you meet a new friend?

➤ Did you go to the library?

Vacation	Swimming	Climb Tree	Play Instrument	Movies
Maggie	Justin	Eli	Holly	Matt
Jacob	Joseph	Bobby	Maggie	Enriqué
Alyssa	Bobby		Jacob	Alyssa
Michael	Shammar			Michael
	Eli			
	Enriqué			
	Alyssa			
	Michael			
	Beau			
	Holly			

Robin

Connecticut

Mount Rushmore

PERSONALIZED POSTCARDS

Ease students' first-day jitters by giving them an early glimpse at some of your interests. During the summer, collect a class supply of postcards that reflect something about you. For example, gather cards with a scene from your home state, from a vacation spot you visited, or of an animal or flower you like. Prior to the first day of school, mail a postcard to each of your students. Include a personal message about the upcoming school year, and ask each child to bring her postcard on the first day of school. During the first-day introductions, ask each student to share her postcard and to tell the class something about you. Sharing bits of information about you will make your students feel special and in-the-know on the first day of school.

COOL COUPONS

Place coupons on your students' desks to greet them as they take their seats on the first day of school. Program a copy of the coupon on page 17 (see programming suggestions on this page); then photocopy a class supply to distribute. Your students will enjoy redeeming the coupons, and you will have an opportunity to meet each student one-on-one. Continue using the coupons throughout the year when students earn special rewards.

Incentive Ideas
- a sticker of choice
- one pencil
- 15 minutes of free time
- sit by a student of choice during lunch
- skip an assignment
- read a story to the class

Cool Work Coupon!
Dana

Cool Work Coupon!
Stan
(student's name)
is entitled to
skip an assignment
(reward)

Get-Acquainted Interviews

Use this fun and informative process to help students get better acquainted. Pair students; then give students ten minutes to question their partners—finding out as much as possible about each other. At the end of the interview time, ask a general question such as, "What is your partner's middle name?" Give each student a chance to answer the question, and let his partner confirm or deny the answer. After asking several questions, your students will feel well acquainted with their partners and other classmates, and you will know more about your students, too!

Sample Questions

What is your partner's favorite color?
What is your partner's favorite food?
What pets does your partner have?
How many brothers and sisters does your partner have?
How old is your partner?
When is your partner's birthday?
What is your partner's favorite school subject?
What is a sport your partner likes to play?
What is your partner's favorite book?
What is your partner's favorite movie?
How does your partner get to school?

Back-To-School Simon Says

Try this twist on Simon Says for a great way to get to know your students. Have your students stand; then say a traditional Simon Says phrase, and add a request for information. For example, "Simon says, stand on one foot and tell me your favorite food." Say the phrases as quickly as possible and occasionally omit the words "Simon says" to keep students alert. Simon says, "Have fun!"

Information, Please

Here's a beginning-of-the-year method for lining students up. It not only keeps students quiet and orderly while they get in line, but it helps you become familiar with their interests. Before you have your students get in line, ask a personal question such as, "What is your favorite color?" Call on each student to answer the question. After each child answers, have her line up. Students will quietly listen to their classmates' answers, and before you know it, everyone is in line and ready to go!

TAKE-HOME TREATS

After the first day of school, send your students home with special messages and treats from you. Create one of these novel notes for each of your students, and attach the appropriate treat. Distribute them to your students as they leave for the day to let them know how special they are. These treats will be such a hit that you'll want to share them on other important occasions throughout the year.

I'm so happy to have you in my class. You're a "beary" special student!

I'm glad you're in my class! I'm nuts about you!

salted PEANUTS

You're one terrific human "bean"! I'm lucky to have you in my class.

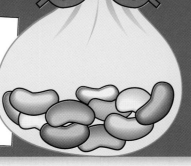

Here's a treat for a great job today! Keep up the good work.

vanilla
chocolate
strawberry
bubble gum
chocolate chip

Ice-Cream Memories

Take your students from warm summer days back into the classroom with this cool graphing activity. As each child gets settled on the first day of school, give him a copy of the ice cream and cone patterns on page 18. Ask each student to think about snacking on a cool, creamy ice-cream cone on a warm summer day. Have each student color and decorate his ice-cream pattern to represent his favorite flavor of ice cream. Next create a graph on a large piece of poster board. Write students' favorite ice-cream flavors along one side of the graph. Post the graph on a display titled "What's The Scoop?" After students cut out and assemble their ice-cream cones, have one student at a time attach his cone to the display; then have him mark a square on the graph to correspond to his favorite flavor. The resulting graph will help keep summer memories alive in your classroom.

Paper-Bag People

Use this clever activity to help students get to know one another. During the first week of school, give each student a paper lunch bag and a variety of scrap materials. Ask each student to transform his paper bag into a puppet that looks like himself. Provide a copy of page 19 for each student, and ask him to fill in the information. Then have each child cut the completed form on the solid line and glue it to the back of his paper-bag puppet. Have students use the finished puppets to introduce themselves to their classmates; then place the puppets in a center for students to explore on their own. These puppet people will help your students get acquainted without the usual inhibitions.

Name: Sam

Favorite Color: green

Favorite Book: Jumanji

Things I Like To Do:
ride bike

in-line skate

A Place I Like To Go:
beach

GRAND BANNERS

Celebrate the start of the school year by displaying this grand student-made banner. Give each child a large triangle cut from a 12" x 18" sheet of white construction paper. Have each student write his name on the triangle as shown; then have him decorate the resulting pennant with pictures or symbols that represent his interests. When the student finishes the decorations, have him fold in half a colorful, 4" x 12" construction-paper strip and glue it to the top of his pennant as shown. (Be sure a small space is left between the pennant and the fold.) Thread heavy yarn through each pennant to create a banner. String the banner from your classroom ceiling or wall to represent the grand students in your class.

Colorful Welcome

Welcome your students back to school by preparing this colorful door display. Create three large sunflowers using green construction paper for leaves and black for the flowers' centers. Also make a class supply of yellow flower petals. Mount the leaves and flower centers on your classroom door. Label the flowers' centers as shown. As each student arrives on the first day of school, have her write her name on a petal and attach it to a flower on the door. By the time all your students have arrived, the colorful greeting will be complete.

LABEL IT

Take time before school begins to create these simple label lists. The early effort will save you time as you label students' materials on the first day of school. Purchase sheets of address labels, and print each student's name on an entire sheet. When it's time to label student workbooks and supplies, just peel and stick a label to each item. Extra labels come in handy for a first-day graphing activity or simple nametags.

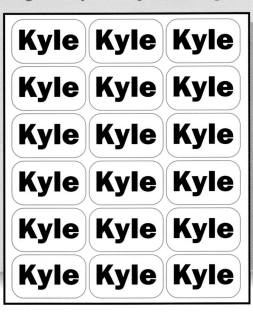

Noteworthy Nametags

After the initial investment, these practical nametags can be used again and again. Purchase clear plastic clip-on nametags from an office supply store, and slip in a personalized name card for each student. When each child arrives at school, you can easily attach the nametag without damaging clothing. Store the tags in a visible location for students to put on each morning as needed. When students go to another teacher's class, have them put their nametags on for easy identification. If a substitute teacher is in your classroom, the tags will easily be available for her use, too.

Motivating Magnet

Encourage students to display schoolwork at home by having them create these unique take-home magnets early in the school year. To make a magnet, each child traces a head pattern (page 20) onto poster board and cuts it out. Next he cuts out the label (page 20) and glues it to the head as shown. He then glues on two wiggle eyes and a one-inch pom-pom to create the facial features. If desired, have the student add yarn or paper hair to his creature before hot-gluing a magnet to the back. Students can proudly display their school papers at home using their self-made magnets.

Andy   Becky   Kim   Zoe

ABC Lineup

Besides helping you learn your students' names, nametags can be used to play this fun alphabetizing game early in the year. Give each child a nametag to wear; then place your students in groups of four or five children. Ask each group to arrange itself in alphabetical order. After checking each arrangement for accuracy, regroup students for another round. Your students will enjoy learning their classmates' names while they practice a valuable skill. For a fun finale, have the whole class form a large group and arrange themselves alphabetically.

Buggy About Books

Foster a love of reading early in your school year with this project. During the first weeks of school, have each child bring a favorite book to share with the class. Have each student describe his book for his classmates. (If time allows, invite him to read it aloud.) Next have each student write his name and his book's title and author on a six-inch construction-paper circle. Then have him draw a small illustration to depict a scene from his book. Mount the circles on a classroom wall to create a caterpillar display as shown. Your students may be so buggy about books, they'll want to add to the display all year.

Amahd
Old Bear
by
Jane
Hissey

Lou
Jennie's Hat
by
Ezra Jack Keats

Shonna
Amelia
Bedelia
by
Peggy
Parish

Katie
The Napping House
by
Audrey Wood

Little
Ka

First-Day Checklist

Room Preparations

_____	☐
_____	☐
_____	☐
_____	☐
_____	☐
_____	☐
_____	☐
_____	☐
_____	☐
_____	☐

Teaching Preparations

_____	☐
_____	☐
_____	☐
_____	☐
_____	☐
_____	☐
_____	☐
_____	☐
_____	☐
_____	☐

Communications (office, parents, etc.)

_____	☐
_____	☐
_____	☐
_____	☐
_____	☐

First-Week Checklist

M

☐
☐
☐
☐

T

☐
☐
☐
☐

W

☐
☐
☐
☐

T

☐
☐
☐
☐

F

☐
☐
☐
☐

Comments

Fun-In-The-Sun Questionnaire

Circle One

_____ yes   no

_____ yes   no

_____ yes   no

_____ yes   no

_____ yes   no

_____ yes   no

_____ yes   no

_____ yes   no

Remember!

Please bring this completed form with you on the first day of school. We will have fun graphing this information!

Cool Work Coupon!

_____
(student's name)

is entitled to

_____
(reward)

Cool Work Coupon!

_____
(student's name)

is entitled to

_____
(reward)

Cool Work Coupon!

_____
(student's name)

is entitled to

_____
(reward)

Patterns
Use with "Ice-Cream Memories" on page 10.

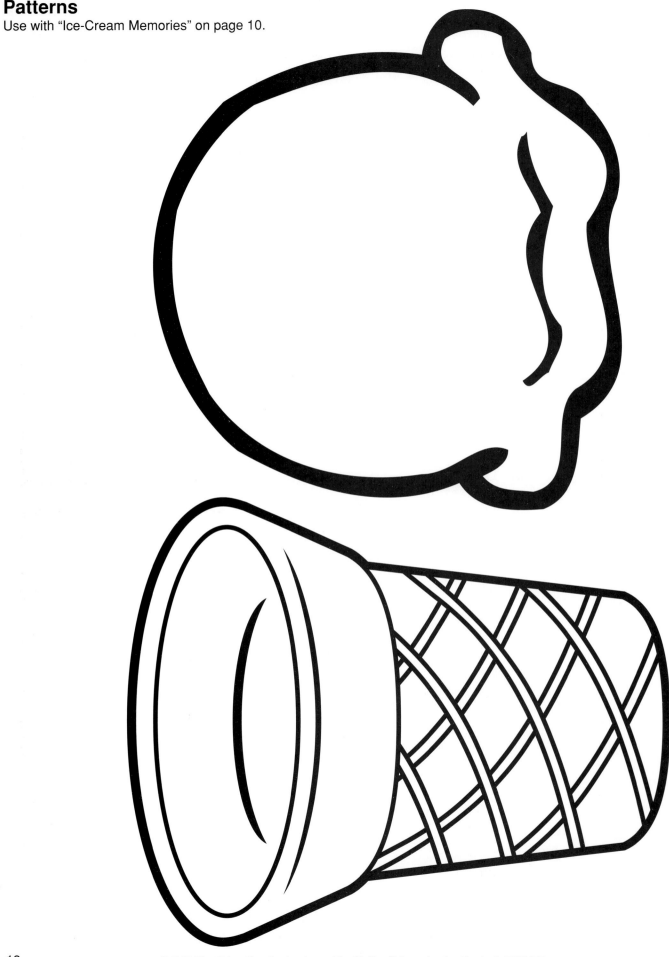

Patterns

Use with “Paper-Bag People” on page 10.

Name: ____________________

Favorite Color: ____________________

Favorite Book: ____________________

____

Things I Like To Do:

____

____

____

A Place I Like To Go:

____

Name: ____________________

Favorite Color: ____________________

Favorite Book: ____________________

____

Things I Like To Do:

____

____

____

A Place I Like To Go:

____

©1998 The Education Center, Inc. • *The Mailbox® Superbook • Grade 2* • TEC451

Patterns

Use with "Motivating Magnet" on page 12.

label

head

label

head

©1998 The Education Center, Inc. • *The Mailbox® Superbook* • *Grade 2* • TEC451

BULLETIN BOARDS

Bulletin-Board Bonanza

Bulletin boards are a vital part of the classroom. In addition to adding a decorative touch, bulletin boards can also be used as good-work exhibits, as informative displays, and as interactive teaching tools. Try some of the following suggestions to create distinctive displays in your classroom.

Background Paper With Pizzazz

Let the theme of your bulletin board inspire your choice of background paper. Gift wrap comes in a variety of designs that can enhance a bulletin-board display. Use birthday wrap to cover a board that features students' birthdays, or holiday wrap to add spark to a seasonal display. Wrapping paper also comes in many colors and patterns that are not available in standard background paper choices.

Create other interesting displays with the following background ideas:
newspaper
road maps
calendar pages
fabric
wallpaper
colored cellophane
plastic tablecloths
bedsheets

Distinctive Lettering

The title on a bulletin board can be a work of art in itself! Try cutting letters from these materials:

wallpaper samples
sandpaper
greeting cards
foil
magazine pages
posters
paper bags

Keep It On File

Take a picture of each bulletin board before you take it down. Store the photos in an album or in an appropriate file. You'll have a wonderful collection of bulletin-board ideas to choose from in the coming year, as well as a handy reference showing each completed display.

Borders That Beautify

If you're looking for just a touch of color to add to a bulletin board, use items from the list in "Background Paper With Pizzazz" to create borders for a board covered with a solid-color background. Make your own border by tracing several strips of precut border onto the new material. For added durability, laminate the strips before cutting them out.

Interesting borders can also be made using
doilies
cupcake liners
dried leaves
die-cut shapes
adding-machine tape that students have decorated

Create a colorful display with these student-made crayon characters. Have each student write his name and complete the sentence about his favorite color on the crayon pattern (page 36). Next have him color the pattern with his favorite color, cut it out, and add construction-paper legs, arms, and facial features. Display the completed creations and the title on a bulletin board covered with black background paper. What a striking back-to-school display!

After discussing the qualities of a good friend, have your students create these delightful buddy cutouts for a friendship display. Have each student cut out a buddy pattern (page 36), place it on a folded sheet of paper, and trace. After cutting on the resulting outline, the child unfolds the paper and colors one of the buddies to resemble himself and the other to resemble a friend. He then writes a message of friendship across the cutout before displaying it on a colorful board.

Enlist your students' help in creating this fun and functional helper display. Have each student cut out and personalize a construction-paper pattern (page 36), then decorate it to resemble himself. For each classroom job, program an enlarged construction-paper copy of a hat pattern (page 37) with a job description. Staple the hat cutouts to the board; then pin one student cutout below each job description. Pin the remaining cutouts around the border of the board. Each week assign new jobs using an established method of rotation. Hats off to classroom helpers!

Bring the beauty of fall foliage indoors! Cover a bulletin board with white background paper. Paint a bare tree shape and add desired background details. Then have students trace their hands atop sheets of red, orange, brown, and yellow construction paper and cut out the resulting shapes. Attach the handprints to the bulletin board as shown. Add the title and a border, and enjoy the autumn scene!

Set the stage for Halloween safety with this "purr-fect" seasonal display. Cover a bulletin board with black background paper. Add a construction-paper moon and fence. After a discussion about Halloween safety, have each student write one safety rule on a copy of the cat pattern on page 38. Then have her color it and cut it out. Display the completed kitties along the fence to encourage a safe Halloween.

Encourage positive behavior with this terrific turkey. Enlarge, color, and cut out the turkey pattern on page 38 before mounting it on a bulletin board. Store a supply of colorful construction-paper feathers (page 38) in a pocket attached to the board. Then be on the lookout for good deeds. When a student performs an act of kindness, write his name on a feather and staple it to the turkey. Challenge the class to earn a predetermined number of feathers for the turkey. What are you thankful for? Good deeds!

This winter display looks good enough to eat! Have each student cut and glue white construction-paper circles to create a snowman. Pop a supply of popcorn. Have each student spread a thin layer of glue on his snowman and attach pieces of popcorn. If desired, tint a small amount of the popcorn with colored tempera paint for students to use to create eyes and buttons. Staple the completed creations and the title to a bulletin board covered with blue paper. Let it snow!

Celebrate the Hanukkah season with this sparkling display of good work. Give each student two large triangle shapes with the center sections cut out. Show the students how to glue the shapes together to form stars. Then have each student wrap yellow, white, and blue pieces of tissue paper around the eraser end of a pencil, dip them in glue, and apply them to his star. When dry, attach each star to a bulletin board along with a sample of each student's best work.

Spread holiday cheer by displaying each student's best work. Have each student decorate an eight-inch white construction-paper square to resemble holiday gift wrap. Then assist each student in attaching a length of curling ribbon to her package. Mount the packages on a bulletin board along with the title and a sample of each student's best work.

Create a "tree-mendous" display with this student-made bulletin board. Have each student use crayons or markers to decorate a white, six-inch paper plate with a holiday design. Starting at the top, work your way down the tree, stapling one additional paper plate in each row. After the plates are in place, add the title and a construction-paper trunk. Top it off with a bright yellow construction-paper star. Happy Holidays!

Ring in the New Year with steps in the right direction! Give each student a copy of one of the patterns on page 39. (Be sure to distribute an equal number of patterns facing each way.) Have each student write a self-improvement goal for the new year on the pattern. Staple the completed forms to a bulletin board as shown. Add the title, and step up to a new year!

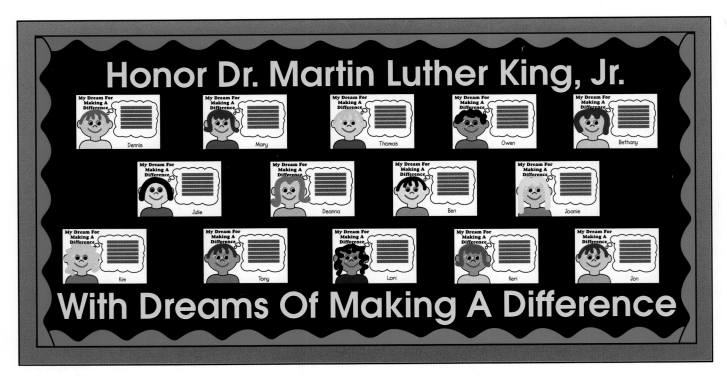

Honor Dr. Martin Luther King, Jr.'s dreams to make a difference. Distribute a copy of the form on page 39 to each student. Have the student draw his likeness on the form and write his dream for making a difference. Display the completed forms and the title on a bulletin board as a tribute to Dr. King.

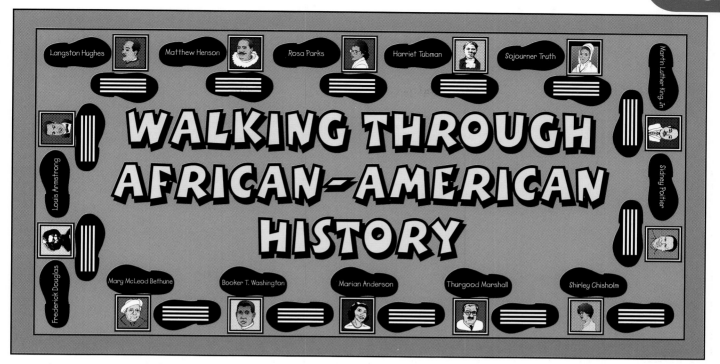

Use this display to walk your students through African-American history. Have each student trace his footprints on black construction paper and cut them out. Then have each student use a white crayon or paint pen to write the name of a famous African-American on one footprint. Next have him write a sentence about that person on his other footprint cutout. Trail each footprint pair around the bulletin board along with a photo of the corresponding person. Add the title, and you're ready to celebrate African-American history!

Celebrate Valentine's Day with hogs and kisses! Use the patterns on page 40 to create the needed templates for the hog and kiss projects shown. To make a hog, a student traces the heart templates onto construction paper and assembles the head and body of the hog as shown. Then she attaches facial features made from construction paper. To make a kiss, she traces the candy pattern onto tagboard, cuts it out, and wraps a piece of slightly wrinkled foil around it. Staple the completed projects to a bulletin board for valentine fun!

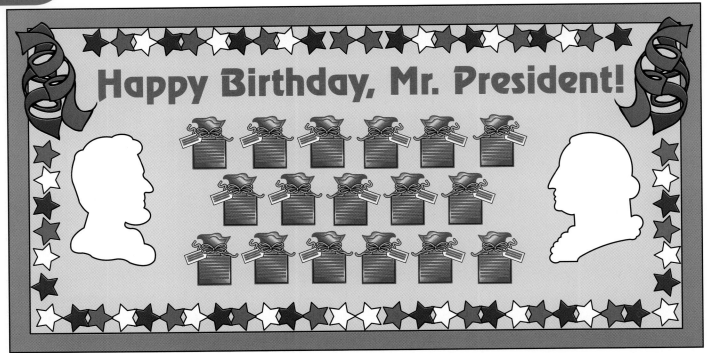

Pay tribute to two famous presidents with this colorful display. After sharing literature about Presidents Washington and Lincoln, ask each student to name a birthday gift each president might have enjoyed. Have each student write about a gift on a tagboard copy of the box pattern on page 41. Help each student "wrap" his box with colored cellophane, tie it at the top with curling ribbon, and attach a gift tag. Staple the completed projects, the title, and enlarged copies of the presidential profiles on page 41 to the board.

This whimsical March bulletin board will bring plenty of smiles! Have each student decorate a paper plate in her own likeness. Then distribute a copy of the form and leprechaun pattern on page 42 to each student. Instruct the student to color and cut out the leprechaun, then glue it to the top of the paper-plate project. Then have her complete the form. Staple the projects on a bulletin board, add the title, and watch for smiles!

Welcome spring with this colorful display. On a copy of the balloon pattern on page 43, have each student write a message about spring. Next have her personalize the basket pattern, then color and cut out both patterns. Hole-punch the holes on the balloon and basket, and lace a 30-inch string through them in numerical order, taping the ends in place. Staple the completed balloons to a blue bulletin board decorated with clouds; then add the title and soar into spring!

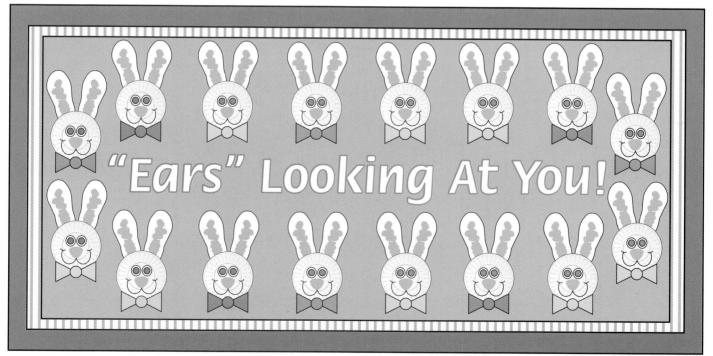

A little fancy footwork puts the finishing touch on this seasonal bulletin board. Have each student use crayons to decorate a paper plate to resemble a bunny's face. Next have him make the bunny's ears by tracing his foot onto two sheets of white construction paper. Instruct the student to color the inside of the ears pink before cutting them out and gluing them in place. Provide colored construction paper for students to use to accessorize their bunnies with colorful bow ties. These bonny bunnies make a super seasonal display!

Motivate students to read, read, read with this magical display. Mount an enlarged color copy of the magic-carpet pattern (page 44) on a bulletin board. Have each student complete a copy of the lamp pattern (page 44) by writing the title of a favorite book and drawing a picture from the story. Staple the completed projects to a bulletin board. Add the title, and let the magic begin!

Get your students hooked on books with this awesome aquatic display. Using the patterns on page 45, duplicate a class supply of colorful fish. Distribute a fish to each student, and instruct her to write the title of a good book and a sentence or two about the story. Arrange the completed cutouts on a bulletin board decorated as shown. Invite your students to peruse the display for a bite on a new book.

Show off students' good work with this sizzling display. Duplicate a class supply of the chili-pepper pattern (page 46) onto red construction paper. Program each pattern with a student's name. Then enlarge, duplicate, and color an additional copy of the pattern, and mount it in the center of the bulletin board. Staple to the board an example of each student's best work topped with her personalized pepper. Add the title and a red border. Wow, what a hot bulletin board!

Put your students' best work in the "spot" light! Cut a length of white bulletin-board paper to fit your board. Before stapling it to the board, invite each student to draw several spots on the paper with a black marker. Add the title and border; then post examples of students' best work. The resulting display will really hit the spot!

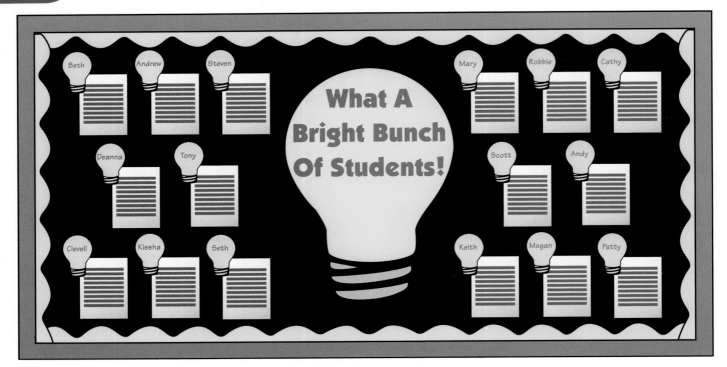

Brighten your classroom with a display of your students' best efforts. Personalize a yellow construction-paper copy of the lightbulb pattern on page 46 for each student. Then enlarge and color an additional copy of the pattern. Write the title on the large lightbulb before mounting it on the board. Attach a sample of each student's work topped with his personalized lightbulb. What a bright bunch of students!

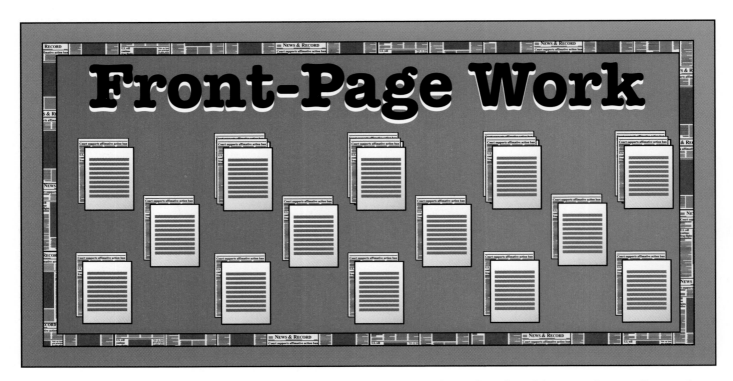

Read all about it! This easy display will spread the news about hardworking students. Cut a class supply of 8 1/2" x 11" pages from newspaper. Staple them to the board to highlight student work as shown. Add a border cut from newspaper and a bright title. What a display of newsworthy work!

Have a ball with this end-of-the-year display. Cover a bulletin board with white background paper. Add a strip of brown paper to resemble sand and a strip of blue paper cut to look like waves. Give each student a 12-inch white construction-paper circle. In the center of the circle have each student write about his favorite experience in second grade; then instruct him to color the circle to look like a beach ball. Staple the colorful creations to the board. Add the title and a cheery sun character for a bouncy end-of-the-year display.

This simple display is just right for ending the year. Have each student trace his hand on colored construction paper and cut out the resulting shape. Provide markers so students can write their summer plans on their cutouts. Staple the completed handprints to a bulletin board. Add the title and a border, and your display is complete. Hooray for summer!

Pattern
Use with "What A Colorful Class!" on page 23.

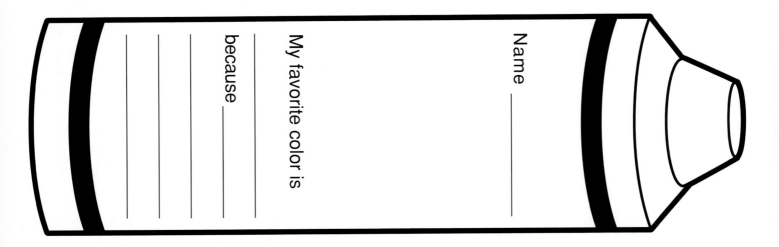

Name _____

My favorite color is _____

because _____

Pattern
Use with "Focus On Friendship" on page 23 and "Hats Off To Helpers!" on page 24.

place on fold

place on fold

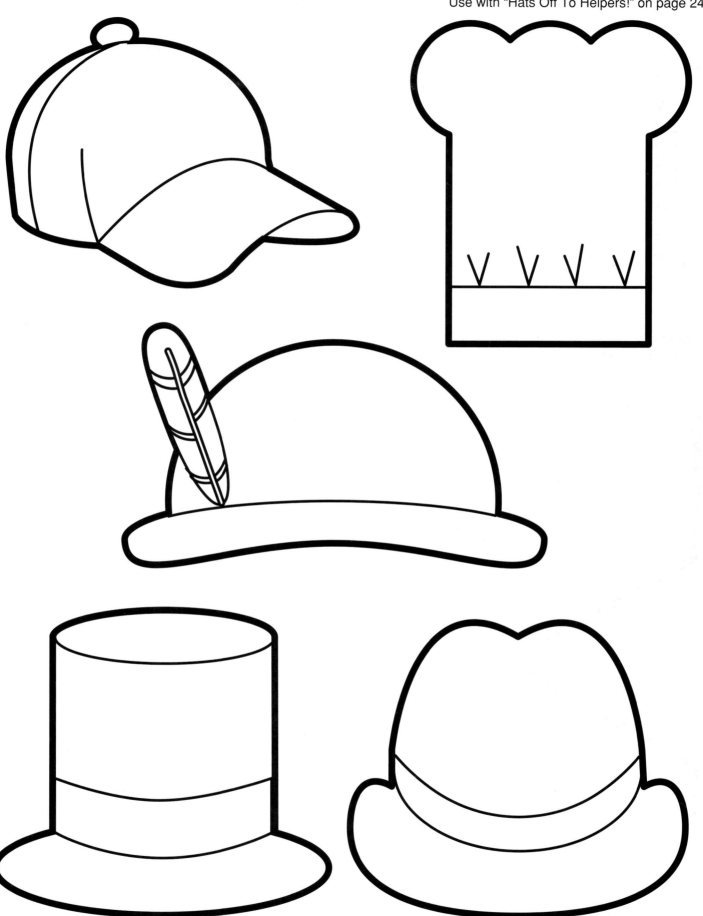

Pattern

Use with "Have A 'Purr-fectly' Safe Halloween!" on page 25.

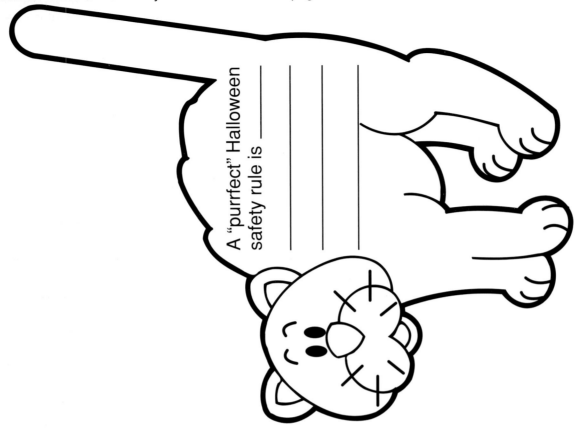

A "purrfect" Halloween safety rule is _____

Patterns

Use with "Give Thanks For Good Deeds!" on page 25.

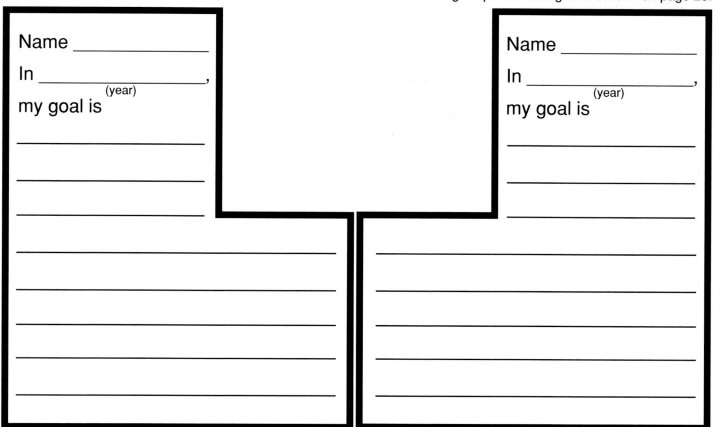

Name _____

In _____,
      (year)
my goal is

_____

_____

_____

_____

_____

_____

_____

Name _____

In _____,
      (year)
my goal is

_____

_____

_____

_____

_____

_____

_____

Pattern
Use with "Honor Dr. Martin Luther King, Jr...." on page 28.

My Dream For Making A Difference

Name _____

Patterns

Enlarge and/or reduce patterns as needed to use with "Hogs And Kisses For Valentine's Day" on page 29.

I would give President

_____ a

I saw a little leprechaun;
He hopped upon my head.
He smiled and winked and tipped his hat,
And this is what he said:

_____

_____

_____

_____

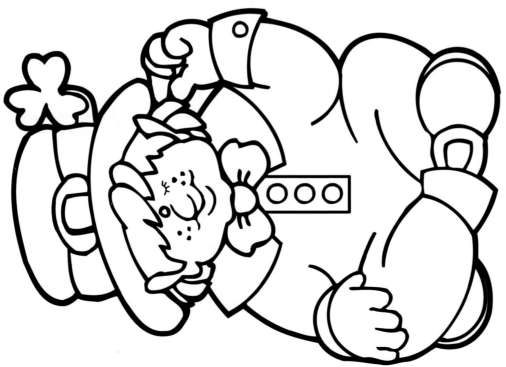

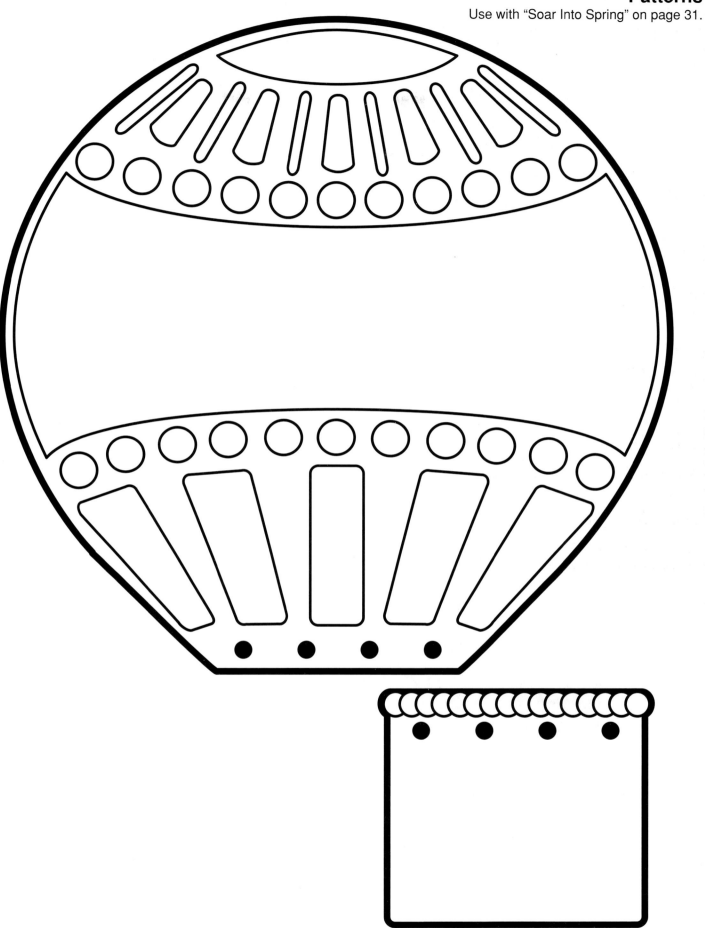

Patterns

Use with "Reading Is A Magical Experience!" on page 32.

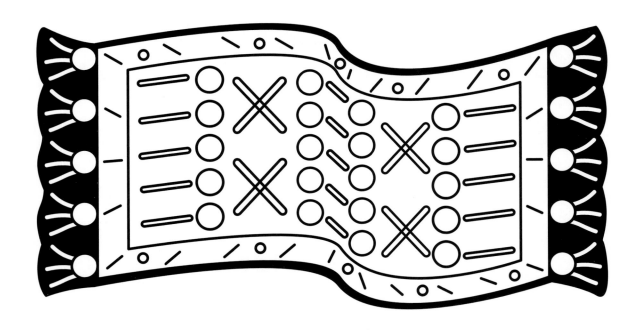

Title _____

Name _____

 • *The Mailbox® Superbook* • *Grade 2* • TEC451

Name _____

Name _____

Pattern

Use with "Red-Hot Chili Papers" on page 33.

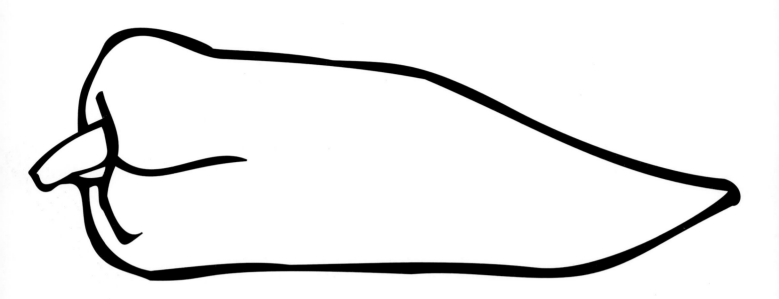

Pattern

Use with "What A Bright Bunch Of Students!" on page 34.

©1998 The Education Center, Inc. • *The Mailbox® Superbook • Grade 2* • TEC451

CLASSROOM MANAGEMENT

Classroom MANAGEMENT

BE PREPARED!

Be prepared for unexpected situations by keeping an emergency kit on hand. In addition to the basic first-aid kit, stock a drawer or box with the following items:

- A SEWING KIT
- A SCREWDRIVER AND HAMMER
- A PACKAGE OF ASSORTED NAILS
- RESEALABLE PLASTIC BAGS IN ASSORTED SIZES
- A FLASHLIGHT
- NAIL SCISSORS AND CLIPPERS
- TWEEZERS
- A SMOCK OR AN OLD, OVERSIZED SHIRT
- SAFETY PINS
- AN EMERY BOARD OR A NAIL FILE
- MATCHES OR A LIGHTER
- A BALL OF STRING
- PACKING TAPE

Curriculum Organizer

Keep your monthly curriculum organized with this helpful hint. Set up four hanging files and label each with a week of the upcoming month. At the beginning of the month, map out the activities and lessons you plan to teach during the next four weeks. (If desired, use the reproducible on page 58 to help with planning.) File the plan sheet, along with all the books, worksheets, and resources needed, in the appropriate week's folder. Then organize for the upcoming week by removing the items from the folder and transferring them to a set of five stackable trays labeled *Monday* through *Friday*. Place the appropriate materials in the tray labeled with the day that you will be using them. This plan will keep you prepared and organized for the week ahead!

To further organize and prepare for the next school year, keep a copy of the plan sheet filled out for each week. Clip copies of reproducibles, overhead transparencies, book lists, and other information pertinent to the lessons to each plan sheet. When the next school year rolls around, you will have copies of your previous lesson plans to refer to, as well as access to all the materials needed for each lesson.

WALL-POCKET STORAGE

Have a collection of necessary materials close at hand by hanging a wall-pocket organizer by the chalkboard. Store items—such as extra chalk, flash cards, reward stickers, and hall passes—in the pocket. When you need an item during instructional time, you'll find it right at your fingertips!

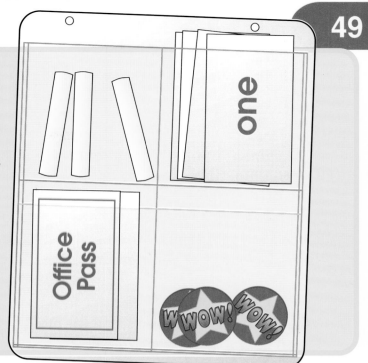

Extra Storage Space

Create additional storage space in closets and cabinets by attaching stick-on pockets to the inside of the doors. These see-through pockets are great for storing flash cards, lunch forms, tardy slips, and daily reminders. You'll have access to the items you use most in a space-saving place!

Storing Display Items

Store posters, maps, charts, and bulletin-board displays with this simple and accessible method. Separate the items into the desired categories (by months, topics, or themes), and place each category into a see-through trash bag. Fold the top of each bag over a wire hanger and secure it with clothespins. Hang the bags in a closet or storeroom. When looking for a particular item, you'll be able to spot it hanging neatly in a bag.

And More Storage…

There is no end to the number and types of items that need to be organized in your classroom! Keep clutter-free by utilizing some of the following storage ideas:

- Use a silverware tray to hold paintbrushes, colored pencils, and markers in your art center.
- Ice-cube trays and egg cartons make handy organizers for storing tiny craft items or game pieces. They also work well for holding small amounts of tempera paints.
- Cardboard tubes from wrapping paper or paper towels are perfect for storing charts, maps, and posters. Roll up the poster and place it inside the tube. Then label the tube's contents before putting it away.
- Use margarine tubs and whipped-topping tubs to hold paints, clay, or small manipulatives.
- Cardboard shoe organizers are just the thing for holding sets of papers or serving as cubbyholes.
- Check craft stores for plastic, multidrawer containers. Use the drawers for holding sequins, buttons, pom-poms, beads, and other small craft items.

Just Clip It!

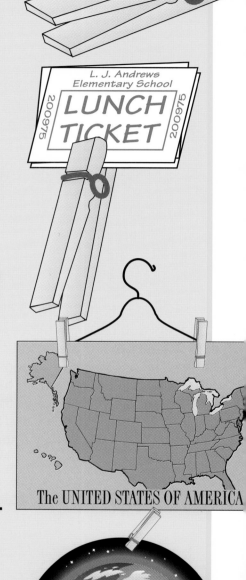

Spring-type clothespins can be used in a variety of ways in the classroom. Keep a supply on hand for the following uses:

✳ Program a set of clips to be used as passes to the office, nurse, and restrooms. When a student needs to leave the room, he clips the appropriate clothespin to his shirt.

✳ When a paper clip is too small for the job, use a clothespin! It can hold a large stack of papers, a supply of lunch tickets, or a set of flash cards.

✳ Display a chart or poster in a jiffy by using a clothespin and a wire clothes hanger. Clip the poster to the clothes hanger; then hang it from the corner of the chalkboard or from a small nail placed in the wall.

✳ Suspend several lengths of monofilament line from the ceiling. Attach a clothespin to the end of each length. Use the clothespins to hold student artwork or decorative displays.

✳ Program clothespins with the names of students. Use the programed clips for emergency nametags, to label art projects and materials, and as manipulatives in graphing activities.

✳ Glue a magnet to the back of several clothespins. They can be placed on filing cabinets as message holders, or they can be attached to magnetic chalkboards to hold posters, charts, and displays.

✳ Some art projects require that pieces be held in place while the glue dries. Using a clothespin to hold the pieces allows you to attend to other tasks.

Pocket Organizers

Keep materials accessible at a glance with clear, plastic multipocket shoe bags. Look for inexpensive bags at discount stores and put them to work in your classroom.

- Hang a clear, multipocket shoe bag by your desk to organize the basics you need every day. Place the following items in the pockets, and you'll have your necessary materials on hand in one central place:

  lunch tickets
  medical forms
  office passes
  overhead transparency markers
  extra chalk
  reward stickers
  grading pens
  scissors that students may borrow
  rubber bands
  index cards
  a calculator
  a bottle of glue

- Place a shoe bag in your art center, and stock it with supplies needed for the current project. It will be easy for students to find each item, and cleanup will be a simple task as well.

- Store laminated, die-cut bulletin-board letters in the pockets of the shoe bag. Each pocket will hold a generous supply of letters and will protect them from becoming crumpled or bent.

- A see-through shoe bag can also serve as a classroom job chart. Use a permanent marker to label each pocket of the organizer with the title of a classroom job. Program a class set of index cards with students' names. To assign jobs, place a name card into a pocket. Jobs can easily be reassigned by removing the card from the pocket and replacing it with another card.

STUDENT-SUPPLY POCKETS

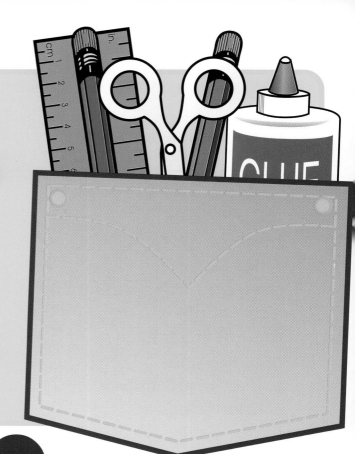

Does the time your students spend looking through their desks for supplies give you the blues? Here's an easy solution! Ask parents to donate old pairs of adult-size blue jeans. Cut the back pockets from the jeans, and use Velcro® to attach a pocket to the side of each student's desk. Have students place their pencils, scissors, crayons, and glue in the pockets, and the materials will be easily accessible for them!

Follow The Dots

Colored, self-stick dots come in handy for placing students in small groups. Select a color for each small group you wish to create; then place a colored dot on the corner of each student's desk. When it's time for students to work in small groups, children with the same-colored dots will work together.

Use the dots for these purposes as well:

* Dots come in handy when you need a group of student helpers—just call out a color and your helpers are chosen!

* Use the dots to target a certain group for personal attention, praise, or extra help. Designate a color dot for each day of the week. Be sure that every student in that color group gets to read aloud, answer a question, or receives extra words of encouragement on his designated day.

* Color-code student journals and workbooks for easy collecting and distributing. You can also help yourself keep up with writing journal responses by targeting a certain color to respond to each night.

Station To Station

Do you have work stations in your classroom? Then you know how easy it is for students to misplace their supplies as they travel from station to station. Eliminate this problem by placing a plastic lunchbox at each station. Stock each lunchbox with pencils, scissors, glue, and any other necessary items. All supplies will be on hand and ready to go when students visit. These boxes also make great portable centers when taking your students on field trips, outdoors, or to another classroom to work.

Students In The Know

Keep students informed of the daily schedule, your behavioral expectations, and their homework responsibilities with the forms on pages 60–63. When students are made aware of the routines and expectations, they are better prepared to succeed in the classroom. Parents will appreciate the written guidelines as well!

LUNCH COUNT MADE EASY

"Bear-ly" have time to take lunch count in the morning? Then enlist the help of these friendly bears! Duplicate and color the desired number of copies of the bear pattern on page 64. Label each pattern with an appropriate lunch choice. Staple the bears to a bulletin board and attach a construction-paper necktie to each bear. Next write each student's name on a spring-type clothespin, and clip it to a paper lunch sack stapled to the board. When each student arrives each morning, she attaches her clothespin to the appropriate tie. You'll be able to record the lunch count with a quick glance at the board, and reinforce graphing techniques and student responsibility, too!

Right-Hand Man

Need a special helper? Then turn to your right-hand man! Create this special classroom character from a white, cloth work glove. Fill the glove with fabric stuffing or cotton balls. Glue a wiggle eye to both the ring and middle fingers as shown. Add a red felt mouth and a cloth bow tie; then fit a small tin can inside the opening of the glove to make it stand up. Place the character on a different student's desk each morning to signify that he is your right-hand man for the day. Enlist the student's help in taking lunch count, delivering messages, and collecting papers for absent classmates. Each student will feel special when he has a turn to be your right-hand man.

Attendance Helpers

Enlist student helpers to assist you with routine daily tasks. Each week give a class attendance list to a pair of students. (If desired, use a copy of the form on page 59.) As other students arrive, have them report to the two helpers. One helper is responsible for checking off attendance and will report to you any absences for the day. The other helper makes a tally of how many students are buying milk or a lunch, and provides that information for the lunch count. Keeping track of these daily tasks will be easier for you, and it will help develop students' organizational skills.

SUPER SIGNAL

This bright idea will keep your classroom from sounding like a traffic jam! Duplicate a tagboard copy of the traffic-signal pattern on page 65. Use markers to color the lights the appropriate colors. Cut out a construction-paper arrow, glue it to a spring-type clothespin, and clip it to the traffic signal. Tell students that when the arrow points to the red light, it is time to stop what they are doing. When the arrow points to the yellow light, they need to listen carefully to directions. The green light gives students the signal to begin their work. Simply move the arrow to indicate the desired classroom behavior!

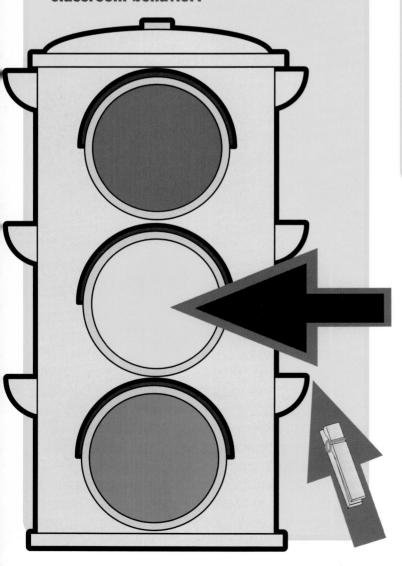

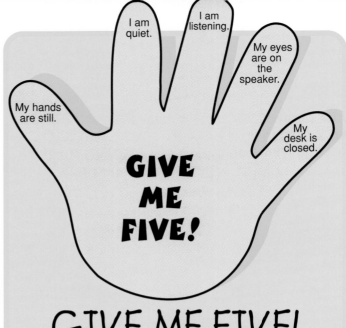

GIVE ME FIVE!

Give a high five for this attention-getting idea! Enlarge a tagboard copy of the pattern on page 66 and display it in the classroom. Discuss with your students the five skills of a good listener as outlined on the pattern. When you desire students to display these skills, get their attention with the phrase, "Give me five!" Each student checks the chart to make sure he is demonstrating the five tasks, then raises his hand to show he is ready. What a "hand-y" way to encourage listening skills!

Transition Time

Transition time between lessons can sometimes lead to off-task behavior. Encourage students to quickly and quietly prepare for the next lesson with this simple reward system. Tape an index card to each row of desks or table grouping. Each time a group of students prepares for the upcoming lesson in a timely and appropriate manner, reward them by placing a sticker on their index card. When a group has accumulated a predetermined number of stickers, reward members with a special privilege, such as lining up first, sitting at a special table at lunchtime, or visiting a learning center of their choice. Students will quickly see that with cooperation and teamwork, their best efforts will be recognized.

Book-Order Box

Students' book orders offer many good deals on quality literature, but collecting the order forms and money can take quite a bit of time. Eliminate the hassle with a box designated to collect the orders. Request that each student bring her money and order form to school in an envelope labeled with her name. (Place several blank envelopes by the box in case a student forgets!) Have each student place her order inside the box instead of handing it to you. Then, when you have a chance during the day, check the contents of the box to make sure all forms are properly filled out and the correct money is enclosed. When it's time to send in the order, you'll have all forms and money ready to go!

Good-Morning Message

Start the day in this on-task way. Each morning write a short message to your students on the chalkboard. Include in the message a short task for students to complete. Students will look forward to this morning challenge, and you will have time to read messages from parents, check homework assignments, and take care of last-minute preparations.

What a rainy day!

Draw a picture of a rainy-day activity and write a sentence about it.

Keep Those Canisters!

Keep a supply of 35mm film canisters on hand! They are the perfect containers for baby teeth lost at school, buttons that have come loose, earrings that have lost their backings, and other tiny treasures that need to be sent home. If desired place a self-stick dot on the container's lid, and label it with the contents and the child's name. The canisters are small enough to fit in a child's pocket, but large enough not to get lost.

Take Note!

Designate an area of your chalkboard for special reminders. Throughout the day, make note of homework assignments, notes to send to parents, or library-day reminders. At the end of the day, refer to the list to help students gather the papers and materials they need to take home. With this visual reminder, students will be less likely to forget an important note or assignment.

LIBRARY-SHELF MARKER

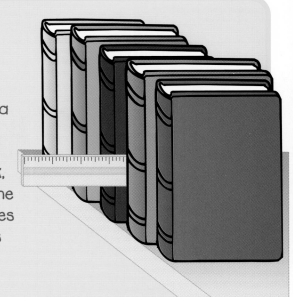

Keep your classroom bookshelves in good order with a supply of wooden rulers (or paint-stirring sticks). Place the rulers (or sticks) in a decorated container on top of your bookshelf. When a student wishes to look at a book, she marks its place on the shelf by inserting the ruler in the book's place. If she decides to keep the book, she removes the ruler and places it back in the container. If she wants to put the book back, its proper place is marked. Your shelves will stay neater with this minimal student effort.

Caught On Tape!

When a student is absent, it can be difficult for him to complete the missed work at home without the benefit of your oral instructions. If you are going to introduce a new topic, give detailed instructions, or read a book to your students as part of a lesson, why not record it on tape? You can send the cassette tape (along with the missed work) home to the student. You can even include a special get-well message on the tape—sure to bring smiles to a youngster sick in bed!

Heading Helpers

If your students are having difficulty putting proper headings on their papers, try this cooperative suggestion. Make an oversized display of the paper heading and post it in a prominent place. Encourage students to check their papers against the heading each time they start a new assignment. For an added check, have each student ask a classmate to proofread her heading before she turns in her work. This will also be a big help to new students coming into your classroom.

No More Nameless Papers!

Here's a gentle reminder for students to write their names on their papers before turning the papers in. Place a pencil and a colored highlighting pen by the turn-in basket. If a child has written his name on his paper, he highlights it before placing it in the basket. If he has forgotten to write his name, he uses the pencil to do so, then highlights it and turns it in. This simple reminder works wonderfully!

Challenge Activities

Challenge Activities

Keep a supply of activities on hand for those students who are early finishers. Make a copy of several challenging reproducibles that you don't plan on using in your daily lessons. Mount each reproducible on construction paper, and attach a corresponding answer key to the back. Laminate the pages and place them in a decorated box labeled "Challenge Activities." Store several wipe-off markers in the box as well. When a student has extra time, encourage her to select a reproducible, complete and check her work, and then wipe away the programming before returning the activity to the box. Place new activities in the box periodically to provide new challenges.

Classroom Supplies

Before you know it, it's time to order supplies for the upcoming year. Be prepared with an ongoing list of supplies that you ran out of or wish you had on hand during the current year. As the name of an item comes to mind, jot it down in the back of your lesson-plan book. When it's time to request supplies, your list of reminders will be waiting.

Cooperative Cleanup

End the day with a classroom cleanup session. Assign each student a small task, such as erasing the chalkboard, emptying the pencil sharpener, dusting the bookshelf, or picking up scraps of paper from the floor. Your room will be in tip-top shape for the coming day, and your students will take pride in their orderly classroom.

Thinking Ahead

Keep notes about each unit in your plan book for the upcoming year. At the end of each day, jot down a few comments about each lesson. You may decide that it would be better to teach geometry in the spring, or that the units on time and money need additional reinforcement. Also write down the names of any books, videos, or manipulatives that enhanced the lesson. When the next year rolls around, you will have an easier time planning lessons, gathering materials, and making supply lists.

Review skip counting before the lesson on cans.

Read *Inch By Inch* to introduce measurement.

Find applesauce recipe for Johnny Appleseed unit.

Lesson Plans For The Month Of _____
Week # _____

Subject	Topic/Skill	Materials

Notes: _____

_____

Class Information

	Name	Birthday	Parent Name	Home No.	Work No.
1.					
2.					
3.					
4.					
5.					
6.					
7.					
8.					
9.					
10.					
11.					
12.					
13.					
14.					
15.					
16.					
17.					
18.					
19.					
20.					
21.					
22.					
23.					
24.					
25.					
26.					
27.					
28.					
29.					
30.					

Note To The Teacher: Duplicate this page; then program it with the desired information.

Daily Schedule

Time	Activity	M	T	W	T	F

Note To The Teacher: Duplicate this page; then program it with the necessary information. If desired, enlarge and color the page before displaying it.

Our Classroom Rules

We have discussed the rules we need in order to have a positive learning environment. We agree to:

_____

_____

_____

_____

_____

_____

Note To The Teacher: Duplicate this page; then program it with the necessary information. If desired, enlarge and color the page before displaying it.

Homework Policy

Rewards:

Note To The Teacher: Duplicate this page; then program it with the necessary information. If desired, enlarge and color the page before displaying it.

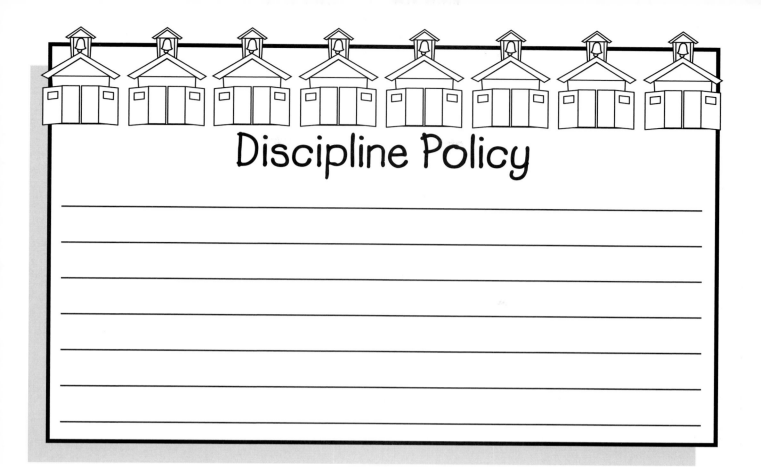

Discipline Policy

Severe situations will be handled by:

Note To The Teacher: Duplicate this page; then program it with the necessary information. If desired, enlarge the page before displaying it.

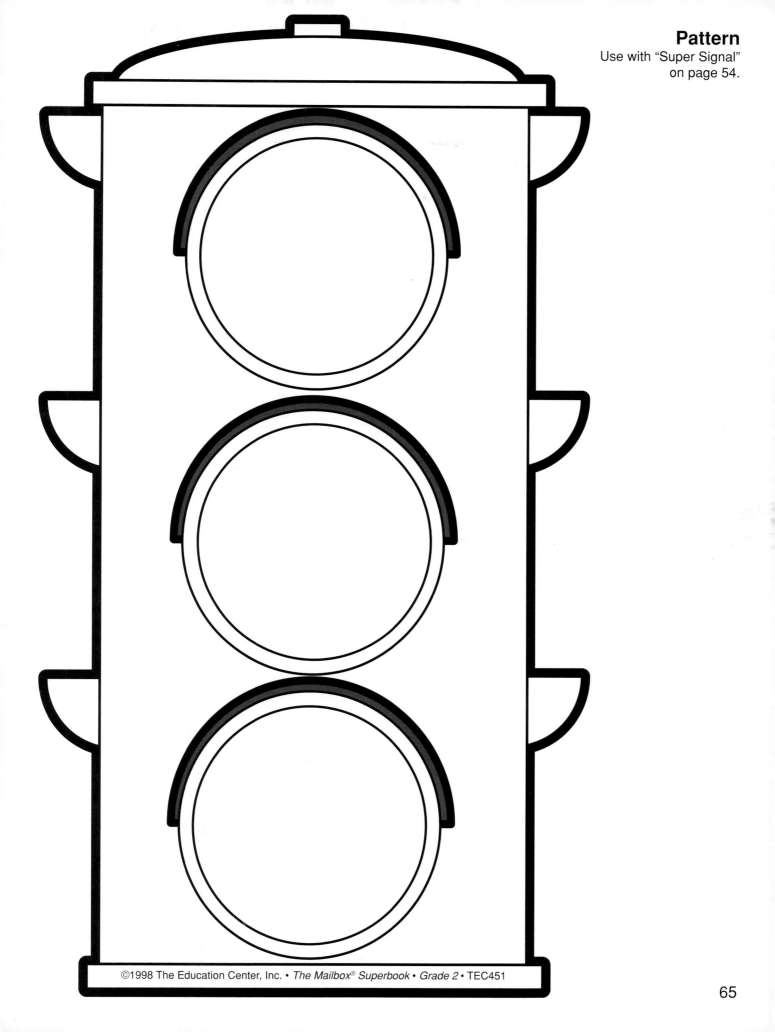

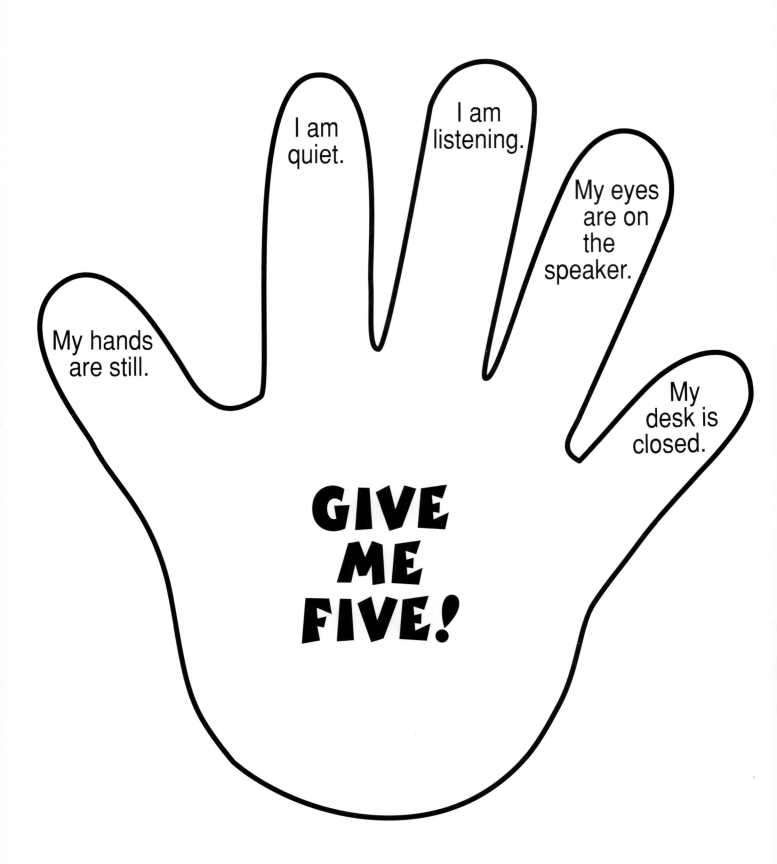

I am
quiet.

I am
listening.

My eyes
are on
the
speaker.

My hands
are still.

My
desk is
closed.

GIVE
ME
FIVE!

MOTIVATING STUDENTS

Motivating STUDENTS
Motivation In Motion

Set the stage for learning by creating a positive environment in your classroom. Your students will be more receptive to learning when they feel good about themselves. See the lists below for ideas about letting each student know how special she is and for reinforcing desired behaviors. Encourage each child to do her best, and watch the positive results!

Recognize students for

- helping a classmate
- making a new student feel welcome
- encouraging a fellow student
- cooperating
- using nice handwriting
- turning in neat work
- treating others with respect
- learning math facts
- being a careful proofreader
- learning the weekly spelling words
- turning in homework assignments consistently
- keeping an orderly workspace
- persevering with a difficult assignment
- following classroom rules consistently
- having a good attendance record
- trying, as well as making good grades

Reinforce positive behavior with the following privileges:

- sitting by a friend during a lesson
- choosing a classroom job for the week
- being first in line for a day
- designing a bulletin board
- choosing a game for the class to play
- selecting bonus words for the spelling list
- skipping a homework assignment
- selecting a musical tape to be played during art time
- eating lunch with the principal or other member of the faculty
- sitting at the teacher's desk for a day

Motivation By The Letter

Entice your students to use their best behavior with this teamwork approach. Begin by selecting a specific behavior that needs improvement. Then, as a class, decide on an incentive for reaching the goal. Use 1/2-inch graph paper to spell out the reward in large block letters. Post the graph paper in a prominent location. Each time you notice a student displaying the target behavior, invite him to color a square on the graph lettering. When all the letters are colored, celebrate with the reward!

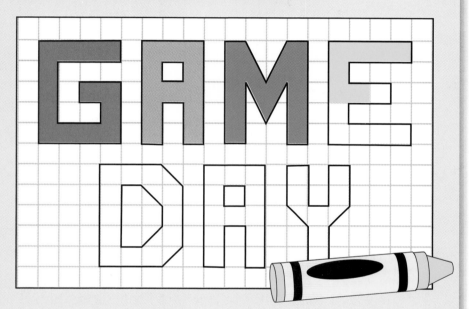

Funny Money

Cash in on good behavior with this motivational idea. At the beginning of each week, give a copy of a funny-money pattern from page 74 to a different student. Give the student a black marker to design the funny money of the week. Duplicate a supply of the money to use as rewards for good grades, appropriate behavior, completed assignments, or improved handwriting. At the end of the week, let students "spend" the funny money they have earned to purchase stickers, small treats, or special-privilege coupons.

Beat The Ice

Keep your students on task with a round of Beat The Ice. Get a large ice cube and a small bowl or towel to catch the drips. Challenge each student to complete a predetermined amount of his assignment before the ice melts. As the students work, hold the ice cube in your hands (over the towel or bowl), and gently toss it from one hand to the other. Congratulate all who finish before the ice cube melts with a cold but hearty handshake.

Instant Awards

Keep a supply of these little awards on hand to recognize individual achievements. Using colored paper, duplicate a supply of the awards on page 75. Each day, place several of the awards in your pocket or on the corner of your desk. When you spot a student demonstrating good behavior or trying his best at a task, present him with an award to show that you appreciate his efforts. What a nice way to say "Keep up the good work!"

Bloomin' Good Attendance

Motivate students to maintain good attendance with this bloomin' good idea. Draw a flowerpot in the bottom corner of your chalkboard. For each day that your class has perfect attendance, draw a flower in the pot. At the end of two weeks, reward the class with two minutes of free time for every flower in the pot. If desired, adapt the idea to reflect a holiday or seasonal theme, such as feathers on a turkey, cherries on a tree, or eggs in a basket.

Quiet As A Mouse

Encourage students to work quietly with this soft and fuzzy incentive. Collect a supply of small stuffed animals, or invite students to bring them from home. When it's time for students to work quietly at their desks, allow each child to place one of these silent, stuffed friends on his desktop. The stuffed animal may stay on the desk as long as the student remains quiet and on task. When the assignment is complete, the student returns the stuffed animal to the shelf until needed again.

Wall Of Fame

Show students that you appreciate their best efforts with a classroom Wall Of Fame. When a student makes significant progress in a certain subject, photograph her holding her good work. Mount the photo, along with a caption describing the achievement, on a bulletin board titled "Our Wall Of Fame." At the end of every grading period, allow students to take their photos home to share with their parents.

Orderly Desk Incentive

Keeping desks neat and orderly is a task that is easily overlooked in the busy course of the school day. Make sure that the desk situation stays under control with a weekly desk inspection. Inform your students of the day you will check for neat desks, and remind them to have their desks neat and orderly by that day. Then choose a time when the students are out of the room and inspect each desk. If it is in good shape, tape a "Clean Desk" banner to the desk. When students come back into the room, they will be eager to see whether they have earned the special award.

Magic Squares

Put a little magic into your classroom with this incentive idea. Use an invisible-ink marker from Crayola® Changeables™ to draw five stars in random squares on a large sheet of graph paper. Choose a reward for the whole class, such as having a snack or ten minutes of free time, and write it on a piece of paper. Place the reward in an envelope and display it by the graph paper. When a student exhibits appropriate behavior, allow him to color a square on the graph paper using a changeable-ink marker. If he uncovers a star, he opens the envelope and the class is rewarded. Students will be eager to cooperate to earn special privileges.

Turn in your homework on time.

No More Monkey Business!

This class-effort progress chart will help eliminate monkey business in your classroom. Set a goal for your students, such as a week of having everyone seated before the tardy bell rings or having everyone's homework turned in on time. Duplicate, color, and cut out the monkey pattern on page 76. Cover a bulletin board with background paper and use markers to draw a palm tree as shown. Divide the tree into a desired number of steps required to reach the goal; then write the goal on a paper strip and post it above the palm tree. Staple the monkey to the bottom step of the tree. Each time the class makes progress toward the goal, move the monkey to the next level of the tree. When the monkey makes it to the top, celebrate with an afternoon of stories, an hour of math games, or free time at learning centers.

Good-Deed Deputy

Encourage your students to look for their classmates' positive qualities with the help of a Good-Deed Deputy. Each day assign a different student to be the deputy. Throughout the day, he must be on the lookout for students who are doing their best work, helping other students, or performing good deeds. Give the deputy a special notebook to jot down each occurrence. Then take a few minutes before dismissal to have your deputy read his official report of the good deeds he witnessed during the day.

Pass The Paper

This quick and easy activity will make each student feel special. Have each child write her name at the top of a sheet of writing paper. When you say, "Pass the paper," each student hands her paper to the classmate on her right. The classmate writes a positive sentence about the student whose name appears at the top of the paper. Continue having students pass the papers until five or six statements have been written; then collect and distribute the papers to their owners. Repeat the activity once a week, starting the papers at a different location each time to ensure that everyone has a chance to write about each classmate.

The Sweet Smell Of Success

Simmer a batch of self-esteem with this recipe for positive feedback. Obtain a cooking pot with a lid and place it on your desk. Each time you witness a student succeeding either academically or socially, jot it down on a piece of paper and place it in the pot. (If desired, use vegetable- and noodle-shaped cutouts for this purpose.) At the end of the week, uncover the pot and read the notes aloud before giving them to the students to take home and share with their families.

Special Delivery

Children love to receive mail. Capitalize on this by writing a letter to each student several times during the year. Take time during each grading period to write notes about good behavior and academic accomplishments to send to deserving students. (Indicate in your gradebook which students receive notes; make sure each student receives equal attention!) Even though it will take a little extra time, the payoff in student motivation and increased self-esteem is well worth the effort!

April 6

Dear Chad,
    I am so proud of your spelling grades. You have studied hard this week. Keep up the good work!

Love,
Ms. Kelly

V.V.S. (Very Valuable Student)

Strengthen self-esteem by designating a V. V. S. (Very Valuable Student) in your classroom each week. During the week he is spotlighted as the V. V. S., the student is in charge of special events such as the following:

- selecting a book to read to the class

- choosing a topic for show-and-tell

- leading the line to lunch

- bringing a healthful snack to share with the class

- bringing pictures of his family to share with the class

To culminate the week, have each student draw a picture or write a message for the V. V. S. on a sheet of paper. (Be sure that you write a message, too!) Bind the pages into a booklet and staple it between two construction-paper covers. Then invite the V. V. S. to decorate the cover of his booklet. What a special tribute to a very valuable student!

Dear David,
I'm glad you were the V.V.S. this week! I loved the book you read to us.

Betsy

Pal Pouch

This special-delivery idea is ideal for birthday students, but it can be used at other times during the year to boost a student's self-esteem. Make a student feel extraspecial by hanging a Pal Pouch from her desk. To make a Pal Pouch, attach a decorated manila envelope to the back of the selected student's chair. Encourage the other students to place positive notes in the pouch throughout the day. Provide a special place for the student to sit and read her mail before dismissal. What a treat and a self-esteem booster!

In The News

What a thrill it would be for your students to see their pictures in the newspaper! If you are having a special event in your classroom, such as a play or special project, call the local paper. Many newspapers feature articles or photographs of school activities. Students will be proud that their work is considered newsworthy and will delight in showing the feature to their families and friends.

Patterns
Use with "Funny Money" on page 69.

©1998 The Education Center, Inc. • *The Mailbox® Superbook* • *Grade 2* • TEC451

CELEBRATE GOOD WORK!

You're The Apple Of My Eye!

BRAVO!

WAY TO GO!

Your Work Is Out Of This World!

AWARD-WINNING BEHAVIOR

ALL-STAR STUDENT

You Did A Whale Of A Job!

Note To The Teacher: Use with "Instant Awards" on page 69.

PARENT COMMUNICATION

PARENT COMMUNICATION

NEWSWORTHY EVENTS

A classroom newsletter is the perfect tool for letting parents know all the happenings in your classroom. Use the newsletter form on page 87 combined with the writing talents of your students to produce a periodical for parents to enjoy. Each week assign each newsletter topic to a different student. Encourage the student to interview classmates, talk with the school secretary, or confer with school staff members to gather information about his topic. After editing each student's article, have him, in turn, copy the information onto a newsletter form. Then duplicate and distribute classroom copies for students to take home and share with their families.

THE CLASSROOM GAZETTE

Teacher: Ms. Murphy   Date: 2/12/98

WHAT WE'RE LEARNING

STUDENTS IN THE NEWS

UPCOMING EVENTS

WHAT'S NEW AROUND SCHOOL

Keep Parents In The Know

Strengthen communication between home and school with the reproducible forms on pages 83–86. You'll find forms for making parents aware of homework and discipline policies, party information, and special material requests. In addition, there are forms for requesting school supplies, alerting parents of missing assignments, obtaining permission for field trips, and sending out special reminders. Reproduce the forms as needed to help maintain the vital parent-communication link in your classroom.

WANTED

Parents to help in the classroom

- Chaperone field trips
- Assist students in the library
- Prepare art projects (at school *or* at home)
- Organize class parties
- Supply materials for special projects, events, and celebrations
- Read a story to the class
- Share a skill or information with the class
- Work with students in class
- Create a bulletin-board display
- Assist students with computer skills

See Ms. Smith for details.

WANTED: Volunteers

Remind parents that they are a very important part of the learning process by inviting them to volunteer for various tasks in the classroom. Even if parents work, they may be able to take on some of the responsibilities listed. Parents will feel as though they are making significant contributions, and you will have much-needed help with classroom duties!

Student Snapshots

Do you keep a camera handy in your classroom? If so, use it to give parents an opportunity to feel part of their child's learning experience. Take photos of your students during special events or while they are working on classroom projects. Then, at the end of each grading period, send your favorite snapshot of each child to his parents along with his progress report. Parents will feel included in the special activities that they don't often get to see, and the student will have a keepsake of the event.

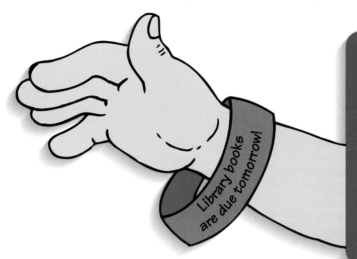

Library books are due tomorrow!

TAKE NOTE!

Make sure that important reminders get home with this easy method. Write the same short message on a strip of paper several times, duplicate the desired number of copies, and then cut them apart. Before students leave for the day, staple a strip around each child's wrist. Students will enjoy this unique way of taking home messages, and parents will appreciate the reminder.

Colorful Communication

At the beginning of the year, parents often receive an overwhelming amount of notes. Try this tip to make your classroom communications easily recognizable to parents. Duplicate your beginning-of-the-year information on one color of copy paper. As parents look through the many notes sent home during the first week of school, your correspondence will draw their attention. Continue to use this same color of paper on all homebound notes throughout the year. Parents will see the familiar color and know that the note contains important classroom correspondence.

LUNCH TO GO

In the excitement that surrounds field-trip preparations, one or more students often forget to bring a bag lunch for the event. Send a gentle reminder home to parents the night before the field trip with this unique memo. Have each student personalize and decorate a brown paper lunch bag. Send the decorated bags home with the students to remind parents to send sack lunches for the trip. What a handy reminder—the sack is already labeled with the child's name and is ready to be filled!

Amber

Welcome To Open House

Prepare for Open House with this spectacular display. In advance, ask each student to bring a favorite T-shirt from home. Next have each student use yarn, construction paper, markers, and other materials to create her likeness on a paper plate. Instruct each student to slip her T-shirt over the back of her chair and tape the completed paper-plate likeness to the chair as shown. (If support is needed for the paper plate to stand straight, tape a ruler to the back of the paper plate and then tape it to the back of the chair.) Next have each student write a riddle about herself on an index card using clues about her favorite foods, favorite activities, and interests. Punch a hole at the top of each card; then thread a length of yarn through the hole and tie the ends. Have each student place the riddle around the neck of her likeness. When parents arrive for Open House, have them find their child's desk by identifying the correct likeness and riddle.

I love vanilla ice cream with jelly beans. I enjoy playing soccer. Who am I?

THE IMPORTANT THINGS

What is the most important thing about second grade? Students will let their parents know with this Open House bulletin board. Prior to Open House, share *The Important Book* by Margaret Wise Brown (HarperCollins Children's Books, 1990) with your students. Distribute a copy of the pattern on page 88 to each student. Have each student color the front of the pattern, cut it out, and then fold it on the dotted line. On the inside of the pattern, have each student follow the format used in the book to tell what he feels is the most important thing about second grade. Display the completed projects on a bulletin board titled "What's Important About Second Grade?" The result is sure to bring smiles from all who see it!

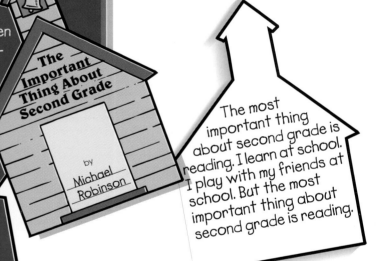

The Important Thing About Second Grade

by Michael Robinson

The most important thing about second grade is reading. I learn at school. I play with my friends at school. But the most important thing about second grade is reading.

PARENT LETTERS

Personalize Open House by having letters waiting for parents who attend the event. Several days before the big night, have each student write a letter to his parents telling them about his school-day routine, his friends, and some of the things he has learned. Have each student place his letter on his desk for his parent to read. Then, during Open House, encourage each child's parents to write a short note back to their child telling about their impressions of Open House. (If a parent is unable to attend, write a brief note to the child after the event so that each student will receive a response.) Students will be thrilled to find a response waiting for them the next day!

Sign Up!

Parents often want to use Open House as a conference time. Be prepared to avoid this situation by having a conference sign-up sheet available. If desired, also make use of this opportunity to have parents sign up for class parties, to volunteer in the classroom, or to come read to the class. Post copies of the forms on pages 89 and 90 so that parents can sign up for these important activities. Then, if a parent tries to involve you in an impromptu conference during Open House, you can gently lead him to the sign-up sheets and schedule a more appropriate time—and perhaps convince him to sign up for other activities as well!

Must-Sees In Our Classroom
- Morton (the hedgehog)
- science center
- class library
- computer station

The "Must-See" List

Make sure your Open House visitors hit all the highlights of your classroom by posting a "Must-See" list. Brainstorm with your students the special items and displays they want the visitors to see. Copy the list onto a sheet of chart paper and display it in a prominent location. When parents arrive that evening, have your students act as tour guides to escort them to all the must-see sights.

ATTENDANCE DRAWING

Thank all your visitors for coming to Open House with this special drawing. Place a decorated container, a pencil, and a supply of blank slips of paper by your classroom door. Instruct each visitor to write her name and phone number on a slip of paper and place it in the container as she enters the room. Then culminate your Open House activities with a special drawing. Randomly select three names from the container. Award each of the selected persons with a free lunch in the school cafeteria on the day of her choice. Be sure to inform the winners of the time your class goes to lunch, and encourage them to dine with your students. Not only is there a free meal in the bargain, but you will also be promoting positive parent-school relations!

Open House Video

Spend a few weeks before Open House making a video of your students in their daily routine. Record footage of your class working in groups, playing on the playground, eating in the cafeteria, and working independently. Arrange to play the video in your classroom on the night of Open House. If desired, the tape can be rewound and played several times throughout the evening. After Open House, the tape can be sent home with students whose parents could not attend the event. For added fun, save the tape and play it for your students at the end of the year—they'll be amazed at how much they've grown!

Preconference Preparations

Set the stage for a successful conference by planning ahead. A few days before each parent conference is scheduled, send home a copy of the form on the top of page 91. Request that the form be returned prior to the meeting time. This form allows the parent to think about specific topics to discuss, and it will prepare you for any concerns the parent may have.

It may be helpful to both you and the parent to see how a child views his performance at school. Prior to parent conferences, have each student complete a copy of the form on the bottom of page 91. Share the completed form with the child's parents to discuss how the student feels about his school experience.

With these preparations, you will be well equipped to discuss with parents the successes, the concerns, and the goals for each student. Be sure to keep documentation of the topics discussed during the meeting. If desired, use a copy of the form on page 92 to record the conference information. At the end of the conference, make a copy of the completed form to give to the parent. Your parent communication link will be off to a great start!

Correspondence Keeper

Keep track of your correspondence with parents during the year by labeling a file folder with each student's name. When you receive a note from a parent, place it in her child's file after you have read it. Also keep on file copies of notes you have sent home. If you need to refer to a specific note, you'll know exactly where to find it.

Thanks a million!

Dear Mrs. Dunlap,
Thank you for baking cookies for our Christmas party. Your contribution was a real treat.
Sincerely,
Mrs. Cody

THANK YOU, PARENTS!

A thank-you note is a perfect opportunity to maintain positive parent communication throughout the year. Buy a supply of thank-you cards to keep in your classroom. Send notes to parents for occasions such as:

- sending party supplies to school
- volunteering to help with a field trip
- calling other parents with reminders of school parties and events
- helping their child with skill reinforcement
- volunteering for bus, cafeteria, or playground duty
- grading papers
- making copies of reproducibles
- arranging for a guest speaker
- coming to Open House
- attending a conference

Homework Policy

Dear Parent,

Homework is an important part of your child's learning experience. Your child will benefit greatly from your support and encouragement of good work habits at home.

Please read the homework policy below and discuss it with your child. Then sign the lower portion of the form and return it to school with your child. Be sure to keep this portion of the form for future reference.

Homework Policy: _____

_____

_____

_____

Sincerely,

_____
teacher signature

_____
date

©1998 The Education Center, Inc. • *The Mailbox® Superbook • Grade 2* • TEC451

I have read the homework policy. I have also discussed the policy with my child.

_____
parent signature

_____
date

_____
student name

Behavior And Discipline Policies

Dear Parent,

Your child's success is very important. To create and maintain a positive learning environment for all students, I will follow the behavior and discipline policies below.

Please read them and discuss them with your child. Then sign the lower portion of the form and return it to school with your child. Be sure to keep this portion of the form for future reference.

Behavior Policy: _____

_____

_____

Discipline Policy: _____

_____

_____

Sincerely,

_____
teacher signature

_____
date

©1998 The Education Center, Inc. • *The Mailbox® Superbook • Grade 2* • TEC451

I have read and do understand the behavior and discipline policies. I have also discussed these policies with my child.

_____
parent signature

_____
date

_____
student name

83

It's A Celebration!

Dear Parent,
   We are celebrating _____

at _____ on _____ , _____.
        time   day   date

You can help with the celebration by _____
_____
_____
_____.

Thank you for your help!

                              Sincerely, _____
                                              teacher signature

Special Project Supplies

Dear Parent,
   We are working on a special project related to _____.
                                                          subject

Your child needs to bring the following items by _____ .
                                                              date

• _____
• _____
• _____
• _____

Thank you for helping!

                              Sincerely,

                              _____
                                   teacher signature

_____
date

Dear Parent,
    Your child needs the following school supplies:

_____ pencils
_____ paper
_____ crayons
_____ glue
_____ scissors
_____ other: _____
              _____
              _____
              _____

GLUE

COLORFUL CRAYONS

8 LARGE CRAYONS   8 LARGE CRAYONS

- -

_____
date

Dear Parent,
    Your child needs to complete the following assignments:

_____
_____
_____
_____
_____
_____

This work is due by: _____

Please sign and return this form.
Thank you for your help and support!

_____   _____
teacher signature   parent signature

We're Going On A Field Trip!

Dear Parent,

We are planning a trip to _____ on _____, _____.

Your child will need to bring:

• field-trip permission form (below)

• _____

• _____

• _____

• _____

Keep this note at home and post it as a reminder.

Thank you!

_____
teacher signature

_____ has my permission to attend the field trip on _____.

student

date

_____
parent signature

Don't Forget!

To:

From:

Just A Reminder!

To:

From:

THE CLASSROOM GAZETTE

Teacher:_____ Date:_____

WHAT WE'RE LEARNING

STUDENTS IN THE NEWS

UPCOMING EVENTS

WHAT'S NEW AROUND SCHOOL

Note To The Teacher: Use with "Newsworthy Events" on page 78.

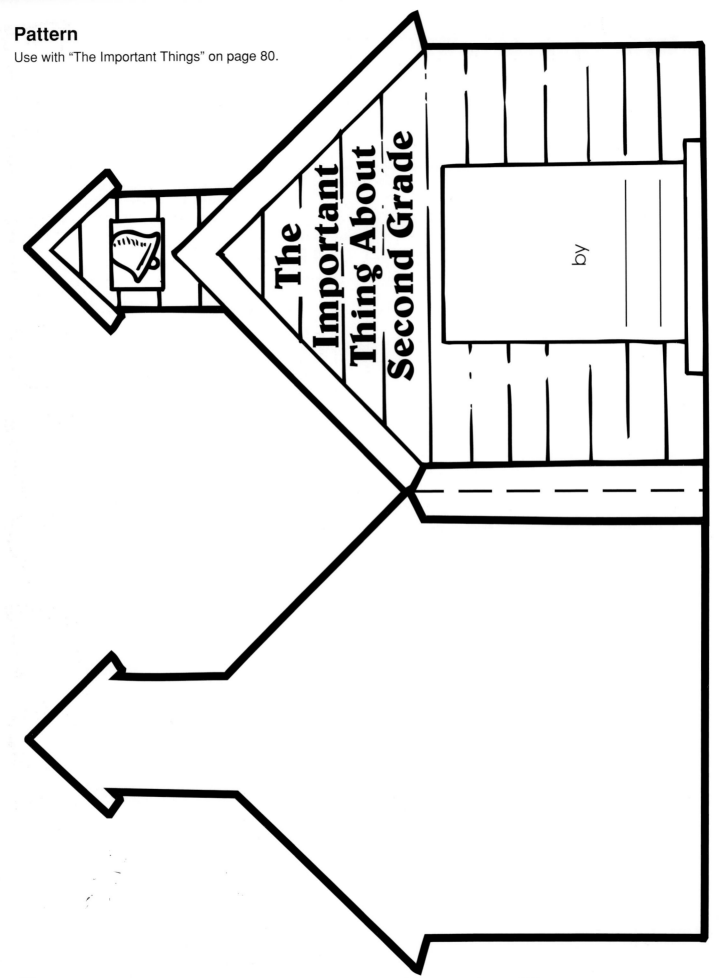

The Important Thing About Second Grade

by

It's Conference Time!

Please sign up for one of the times listed below.

Student	Parent	Date	Time

Note To The Teacher: Duplicate one copy of this form and program the necessary information. Then post for parents to sign.

Wanted!
Parent Volunteers
We need your help with the following parties and activities:

Event:	We will need:	Parent Volunteer(s):
	_____	_____
	_____	_____
	_____	_____
	_____	_____
Event:	We will need:	Parent Volunteer(s):
	_____	_____
	_____	_____
	_____	_____
	_____	_____
Event:	We will need:	Parent Volunteer(s):
	_____	_____
	_____	_____
	_____	_____
	_____	_____
Event:	We will need:	Parent Volunteer(s):
	_____	_____
	_____	_____
	_____	_____
	_____	_____
Event:	We will need:	Parent Volunteer(s):
	_____	_____
	_____	_____
	_____	_____
	_____	_____

Note To The Teacher: Duplicate one copy of this form and program the necessary information. Then post for parents to sign.

☆☆☆☆☆ Preconference Form ☆☆☆☆☆

Student's Name _____

Parent's Name _____

Date _____

My child's attitude about school is: _____

_____

I see strengths in my child's progress in these areas: _____

_____

I have concerns about my child's progress in these areas: _____

_____

Topics I would like to discuss: _____

_____

☆☆☆☆☆ Student Self-Evaluation ☆☆☆☆☆

Name_____   Date_____

- [ ] I do my best work.
- [ ] I use my manners.
- [ ] I follow the rules.
- [ ] I am kind to my classmates.

☺ Most of the time

😐 Sometimes

☹ Not very often

I think I am good at _____.

I would like to do better in _____.

My feelings about school are _____

_____.

Note To The Teacher: Use the forms with "Preconference Preparations" on page 82.

Our Conference Record

Student: _____

Persons In Attendance: _____

Date: _____

Level/Comments:	
Reading	
Spelling	
Writing	
Grammar	
Math	
Science	
Social Studies	
Work Habits	
Social Skills	

Student's Strengths:

_____

_____

_____

_____

Areas For Improvement:

_____

_____

_____

_____

Actions/Suggestions:

_____

_____

Additional Information:
(tests, cumulative records, observations)

_____

_____

_____

_____

_____

Follow-Up Plan:

Parent Concerns:

_____

_____

_____

_____

_____

_____

signed _____   _____
                    (teacher)   (parent)

Note To The Teacher: Use with "Preconference Preparations" on page 82.

ARTS & CRAFTS

ARTS and CRAFTS

Art projects are so much fun, but organizing the supplies can be a challenge. Arrange your materials in easy-to-use ways that make art time more enjoyable for you and your students.

- Keep balls of yarn and string tangle-free with a plastic funnel. Place the ball inside the funnel and pull the string out through the spout.

- Use baby-wipe containers to hold cotton balls, sponge shapes, paintbrushes, and craft sticks. The containers will stack neatly in your closet or cupboard.

- Make individual sets of paint by pouring leftover tempera paint into the cups of Styrofoam® egg cartons. Allow the paint to dry. Reuse the paint by moistening a paintbrush with water and running it over the desired color.

- Store seasonal craft supplies in clear plastic boxes. Felt, pipe cleaners, and glitter in seasonal colors will be easier to find when grouped together.

- Stock up on project materials when you find them on sale. Some items to keep on hand are:

clothespins	paper lunch sacks
coffee filters	paper plates
cotton balls	pipe cleaners
doilies	wiggle eyes
paper cups	

Other materials can be obtained by asking parents to send specific items to school. Use the form on page 108 to request donations for special projects.

STUDENT SUITCASES

Welcome the new school year with this get-to-know-me project. Have each student color and cut out an enlarged copy of the suitcase pattern on page 109. Then have her personalize the nametag on the suitcase. Next have the student cut pictures from discarded magazines of objects that are significant to her and glue them to the suitcase. Display the completed projects on a bulletin board titled "Look Who's Traveling Through Second Grade!"

APPEALING APPLE MOBILES

Transform wire coat hangers into a display of appealing apples. To begin, a student bends a coat hanger into an apple shape. He applies a coat of glue around the hanger. Then he places the hanger, with the hook extended, between two sheets of red, yellow, or green tissue paper and gently pats the layers together. When the glue is dry, he trims away any excess paper. To complete the project, he attaches construction-paper leaves and a stem. Suspend the colorful creations from your ceiling for a mouthwatering display. This project is easily adaptable for a variety of holiday and seasonal displays. Have your students use the technique to make the following:

- Fall leaves
- Halloween jack-o'-lanterns
- Christmas lights
- Mittens
- Valentine hearts
- Shamrocks
- Easter eggs
- Umbrellas
- Spring flowers

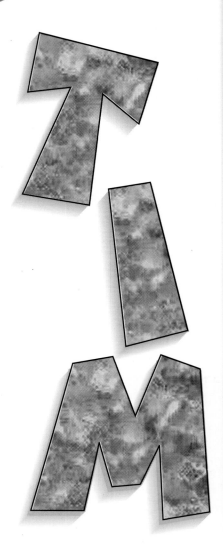

SPLATTERLESS SPLATTER PAINT

Get the look of splatter paint without the mess! Provide each student with a sheet of white construction paper, tempera paint powders, and access to a spray bottle filled with water. Have each student gently spritz his paper with water before using a spoon to sprinkle tempera powder over the area. If desired, have the student spray the paper a second time to moisten any dry powder. Lay the projects flat to dry; then display the colorful creations, or use them with one of the following variations:

• Have students cut shapes from their colored paper to use in seasonal pictures. The bright colors lend themselves to beautiful spring flowers, dazzling Easter eggs, and awesome Christmas ornaments.

• For an unusual look, have students cut basic shapes from black construction paper to glue atop their colored creations. The reverse image makes a striking display.

• Have each student cut his colored paper into geometric shapes, then arrange abstract designs with the pieces before gluing them atop a solid-colored paper.

• Use the colored paper to make die-cut letters. Give each student the letters needed to spell her name; then provide construction-paper pennants for each student to glue her letters to. Suspend the personalized pennants around the classroom for an eye-catching display.

PSEUDO SAND PAINTING

Students will get down to the nitty-gritty with this texturized project. Fill several resealable plastic bags with white cornmeal. Add a different color of food coloring to each bag. Seal each bag and gently knead the color into the cornmeal. Open the bags to allow the mixtures to dry. Have each student draw a design with glue on a sheet of black construction paper, then sprinkle the colored cornmeal onto the glue. After the glue dries, the student shakes off the excess cornmeal. Display these lovely creations on a bulletin board.

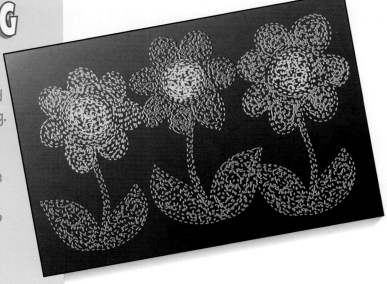

SPOOKY SPIDERS

Send shivers through your classroom with this display of spooky spiders! To make a spider, have each student follow the directions below.

Materials needed for one spider:
4 black pipe cleaners
2 wiggle eyes
one 2 1/2" section of a cardboard tube
glue
black tempera paint
paintbrush

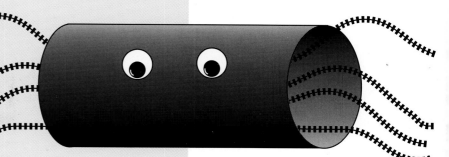

Steps:
1. Paint the cardboard-tube section with black tempera paint. Allow to dry.
2. Insert the four pipe cleaners through the tube so that equal lengths show on both sides.
3. Glue the pipe cleaners in place. After the glue dries, bend the spider legs in the desired positions.
4. Glue the wiggle eyes to the spider.

Display the completed spiders on a bulletin board covered with imitation spiderweb material. What a spooky display!

SMILING SCARECROW MAGNETS

Welcome the arrival of fall by having your students fashion these adorable scarecrow magnets. To make a magnet, each student traces a three-inch circle on a piece of tagboard, then cuts it out. Next she draws a face on the circle and glues several strands of raffia to the cutout to resemble hair. Next she cuts a hat from the remaining tagboard, colors it, and glues it atop the raffia. After the glue dries, she attaches a strip of magnetic tape to the back of her creation. Students can attach their magnets to metal objects in the classroom, or take them home for their families to enjoy.

THANKSGIVING WINDSOCKS

Brighten your classroom with a flock of turkey windsocks. To construct a windsock, each student rolls and staples a 9" x 12" sheet of brown construction paper to form a cylinder. Next she colors and cuts out a copy of the turkey's head and feet (page 110) and glues them to the cylinder as shown. Then she uses a copy of the feather pattern (page 110) to trace and cut out several red and orange construction-paper feathers, and glues them to the back of the cylinder. To complete the project, she staples a construction-paper strip to the cylinder for the handle and glues tissue-paper strips for the streamers. When suspended from the ceiling, these terrific turkeys will be a feast for the eyes!

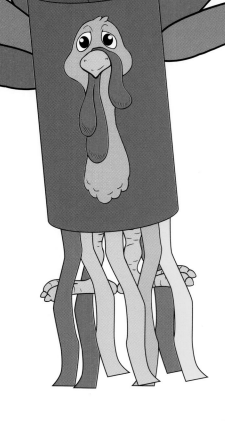

HANUKKAH LIGHTS

Hanukkah lights will shine as your students create these illuminating projects. Have each student place an eight-inch square of construction paper atop an eight-inch square of cardboard. Then have him cut out a copy of the dreidel pattern (page 111) and trace it on the center of the paper. Next have him use a pushpin to punch holes along the traced lines. After all holes have been punched, have each student remove his cardboard. Then tape the construction-paper squares to your classroom windows and watch as light streams through the tiny holes. Happy Hanukkah!

PRETTY POINSETTIAS

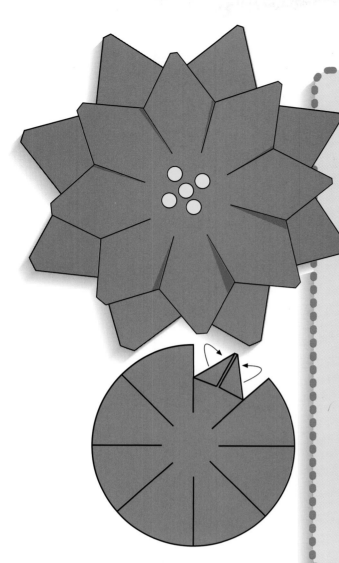

These pretty poinsettias add holiday flair to any classroom display. To make a poinsettia, a student folds both an eight-inch and a six-inch red construction-paper circle in half, then in fourths, and finally in eighths. The student unfolds each circle and cuts each fold line three-fourths of the way down toward the center. For each circle, he folds back the corners of each section tab (to form a point) and secures the corners with glue. (See the illustration.) Then he glues the center of the smaller circle atop the larger circle. For a final touch, he hole-punches yellow construction paper and glues the dots in the center of the resulting poinsettia. Display the completed projects for all to enjoy.

CHRISTMAS COUNTDOWN

Count down the days to Christmas with this colorful holiday bell. To make a bell, a student copies the poem shown onto a large self-adhesive label. Next she gathers as many paper strips (half green and half red) as there are days until Christmas. She then uses the strips to create a paper chain. Next she inverts a red, plastic cup and pokes a hole in what is now the top of the cup. Next have her thread the ends of a length of colorful ribbon through the hole—leaving a loop of ribbon at the top of the cup—and tie the two ribbon ends into a knot. Staple one end of the chain to the bottom of the cup, and then attach the poem as shown. Watch the excitement grow as students remove a link with each passing day. Let the countdown begin!

How many days until Christmas?
Here's a way to tell.

Take off a link each passing day
And when you reach the bell,

You'll know that Christmas Day is here,
And you've done your job quite well!

REINDEER BASKETS

These versatile baskets are sure to be a hit as party favors, gifts, or holiday decorations.

For each reindeer basket you need:
1 mini straw basket (large enough to hold 6 wrapped candies)
2 brown pipe cleaners
1 mini red pom-pom
1 medium-size brown pom-pom
2 wiggle eyes
one 12-inch square of cellophane
3 Hershey's® Hugs®
3 Hershey's® Kisses®
1 copy of the verse shown
glue
scissors
ribbon

Steps:
1. Glue the red pom-pom and wiggle eyes to the front of the basket.
2. Twist one pipe cleaner around each side of the basket handle and then shape it to resemble antlers.
3. Glue the brown pom-pom to the back of the basket for the tail.
4. Place the candies in the basket.
5. Place the basket in the center of a square of cellophane. Draw the opposite corners to meet in the middle and secure with a ribbon.
6. Attach a copy of the verse to the ribbon.

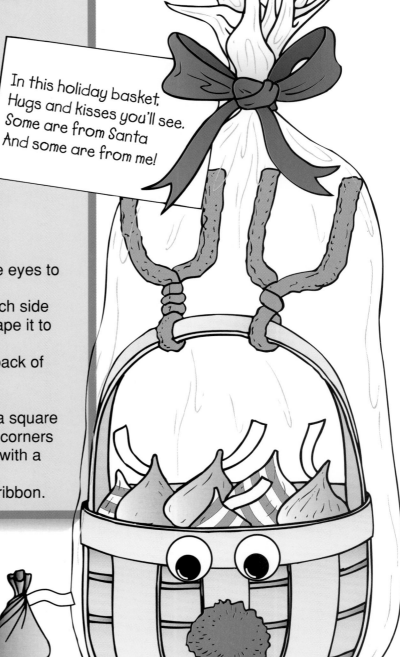

In this holiday basket,
Hugs and kisses you'll see.
Some are from Santa
And some are from me!

ABSTRACT ART

Splash some color into the new year with these creative collages. To create a collage, a student glues crinkled tissue-paper strips and confetti shapes onto an eight-inch white construction-paper square as desired. Encourage each student to arrange the materials on his paper to create an abstract design. When the collage is dry, the student frames his creation by gluing it to a nine-inch, colored poster-board square. Mount the colorful creations on a bulletin board for a dazzling New Year's display.

SPARKLING SNOWFLAKES

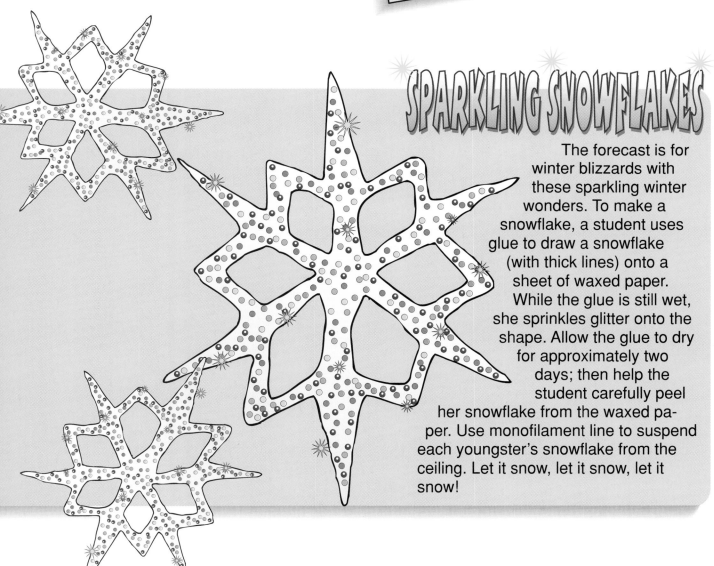

The forecast is for winter blizzards with these sparkling winter wonders. To make a snowflake, a student uses glue to draw a snowflake (with thick lines) onto a sheet of waxed paper. While the glue is still wet, she sprinkles glitter onto the shape. Allow the glue to dry for approximately two days; then help the student carefully peel her snowflake from the waxed paper. Use monofilament line to suspend each youngster's snowflake from the ceiling. Let it snow, let it snow, let it snow!

SHAMROCK VIEWERS

Celebrate the glory of green with these snazzy shamrock viewers.

Materials needed for one viewer:
two 8 1/2" squares of green construction paper
one 8" square of green cellophane
1 craft stick
1 copy of the shamrock, leprechaun, and pot-of-gold
   patterns on page 112
crayons
scissors
glue

On St. Patrick's Day
All the things that I had seen,
When viewed through my shamrock
Were a nice shade of green.

Steps:
1. Fold both pieces of construction paper in half.
2. Cut out the shamrock pattern and trace it onto the sheets of folded construction paper (as shown) and cut out each shape.
3. Glue the cellophane between the two resulting cutouts, trimming away any excess cellophane.
4. Glue the craft stick to the bottom of the shamrock.
5. While the glue dries, color and cut out the leprechaun and pot-of-gold patterns.
6. Glue the patterns atop the shamrock as shown.

Have students recite the poem on the pot of gold before looking through their viewers to see a world of green.

QUILTED CARDS

These unique cards are fun to make and a joy to receive! To make a card, a student traces a valentine-shaped template onto seasonal fabric and then uses fabric scissors to cut it out. Next she glues the bottom and sides of the shape to a sheet of poster board, leaving a two-inch opening at the top. When the glue dries, she stuffs the valentine with cotton balls and then glues the opening closed. To complete the card, she uses her best handwriting to pen a valentine greeting on the poster board. The result? A valentine card that is sure to warm the heart.

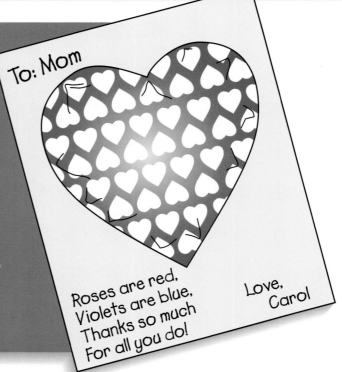

To: Mom

Roses are red,
Violets are blue,
Thanks so much
For all you do!

Love,
Carol

"EGGS-TRODINARY" EASTER EGGS

Create these elegant eggs for an "eggs-trodinary" Easter display. To make an egg, a student paints an oval inflated balloon with a diluted-glue mixture and covers it with colorful tissue-paper squares. Remind students to keep the tissue paper free of wrinkles as they cover the balloon with a double thickness. Then have students set the projects aside to dry.

When the paper is completely dry, have the student draw an egg-shaped opening on the balloon as shown. Then assist her in popping the balloon and cutting out her egg shape. Have students fill their "eggs-traspecial" eggs with cellophane grass, marshmallow bunnies, and jelly beans.

FABULOUS FLOWER PRINTS

A bouquet full of celery prints? It makes a surprisingly lovely display! To prepare, cut several stalks of celery about two inches above the base. Prepare two different pastel colors of tempera paint and pour each into a metal pie plate. To make the flower petals, a student dips a celery stalk into one color of paint and stamps its impression on a sheet of white construction paper. He continues in this same manner, alternating with the other color of paint. After the paint has dried, he uses crayons or markers to add stems, leaves, and a vase to his picture. Display the pretty prints for a lovely springtime scene.

REMARKABLE RAINBOWS

Celebrate springtime with these colorful creations. To make a rainbow, a student cuts a ten-inch construction-paper circle in half. Then he cuts an arch in the bottom of the half-circle to make a rainbow shape. Next he lightly pencils in six arcs and glues appropriate-colored construction-paper squares in the arcs of the rainbow. To complete the project, he glues cotton balls to both ends of the rainbow to resemble clouds. Decorate classroom windows, a bulletin board, or a doorway with these remarkable rainbow projects.

MOTHER'S DAY PLANTERS

These unique planters make wonderful gifts for moms and any other special person. In advance, gather a laundry-detergent scoop and two milk-jug lids for each student. To make a planter, a student glues a milk-jug lid to each side of her scoop as shown. After the glue dries, she places potting soil and a small plant inside the scoop. Then she sprinkles the soil with a few drops of water. For a finishing touch, she ties a length of colorful ribbon to the handle of the scoop. The receiver of this pretty planter is sure to feel showered with love!

LOVELY LADYBUGS

Attract lots of attention with a display of these inviting insects. To make a ladybug, a student paints two-inch squares of red tissue paper onto a nine-inch paper plate using a diluted-glue mixture. When the glue is dry, the student cuts a four-inch black construction-paper circle in half and glues one half to the plate (as shown) to create the ladybug's head. Next he glues two wiggle eyes to the head and several black construction-paper circles to the body. He tapes three black pipe-cleaner halves to his plate, and bends them to create legs. To create the wings, he uses a black marker to draw a line down the center of the ladybug. Wow! What a sight!

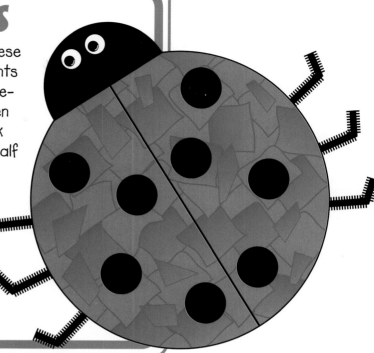

Dad,
You are
wonderful.
Thanks for
being my dad.
I ♥ you!

Love,
Jerome

TERRIFIC TIES

Dad won't mind getting another tie for Father's Day when it's one of these treasures! Have each child trace a tie-shaped template onto colored construction paper and then cut it out. Next have him glue pictures on the tie of his dad's favorite things cut from discarded magazines. After the glue has dried, assist him in taping a safety pin to the back of the tie. Then have him write a personal message below the pin. Dads will delight in wearing these terrific ties for a funny Father's Day snapshot or keeping them as special mementos.

RECIPES

Create a variety of art materials for your classroom with the following collection of recipes for glue, dye, paints, doughs, and papier-mâché.

Sparkle Paint

light corn syrup
food coloring
glitter

In each of several small containers, mix corn syrup, a few drops of food coloring, and glitter. Have students use the mixture to paint on construction paper, paper plates, tagboard, or any other heavy paper. Allow several days' drying time.

Pastel Paint

evaporated milk
food coloring

Pour evaporated milk into several small containers. Add a few drops of food coloring to each container and mix. When painted on construction paper, the paint has a creamy, pastel appearance.

Wet-Look Paint

1 part white liquid glue
1 part tempera paint

Mix the paint and glue together, and apply to paper with a paintbrush. This paint retains a shiny, wet appearance when dry.

Colored Glue

white glue
food coloring

Pour glue into a small container and add the desired amount of food coloring. Stir until the color is blended. Have students apply the color with a paintbrush to a variety of materials.

Easy Dye
rubbing alcohol
food coloring

Use this simple method to color pasta, rice, seeds, or dried flowers. Put a small amount of rubbing alcohol into a container with a tight-fitting lid. Add the desired amount of food coloring. Place the objects to be dyed inside the container and secure the lid. Gently shake the container for one minute. Spread the objects on paper towels to dry.

Cooked Play Dough
1 cup flour
1/2 cup salt
2 teaspoons cream of tartar
1 cup water
1 teaspoon vegetable oil
food coloring

Mix the dry ingredients. Stir in the water, oil, and food coloring. Place the mixture in a heavy skillet and cook over medium heat for two or three minutes, stirring frequently. Knead the dough until it is soft and smooth. Store in an airtight container.

Simple Papier-Mâché
1 part liquid starch
1 part cold water
newspaper torn into strips

Mix together the starch and water. Have each student dip strips of newspaper into the mixture before applying to a balloon, chicken wire, or another form.

Edible Dough
2 cups creamy-style peanut butter
1 cup honey
3 cups instant dry milk

Stir together the peanut butter and honey; then add the powdered milk a little at a time. When the mixture becomes stiff, knead it with your hands until it is thoroughly blended. Refrigerate the dough overnight. Provide each student with a piece of waxed paper and a small amount of dough. After the dough is molded into shape, students can eat their creations.

No-Cook Modeling Dough
2 cups flour
1 cup salt
water
tempera paint powder

Mix the ingredients, adding enough water to make the dough pliable. This dough will air-dry to harden, or can be baked at 300° for an hour, depending on the thickness of the object.

Dear Parent,
   For our upcoming art projects, we will be needing the supplies indicated below. If you are able to donate any of these items, please send the materials to school with your child. We appreciate your help!

____ aluminum foil
____ baby-food jars
____ buttons
____ cardboard tubes from paper towels or toilet tissue
____ coat hangers (metal)
____ (empty) coffee cans
____ cotton balls
____ craft or Popsicle® sticks
____ egg cartons
____ fabric scraps
____ glitter
____ magazines or catalogs
____ newspapers
____ paper plates
____ paper sacks
____ pipe cleaners
____ (empty) plastic margarine containers
____ (empty) plastic milk jugs
____ plastic six-pack rings
____ (empty) plastic soft-drink bottles
____ plastic drinking straws
____ ribbon
____ sandpaper
____ Styrofoam® packing pieces
____ (clean) Styrofoam® meat trays
____ sponges
____ wallpaper samples
____ wrapping paper
____ yarn

Other:

____ _____
____ _____
____ _____
____ _____

Sincerely,

_____
        teacher signature

Note To The Teacher: Duplicate one copy of this page and program the necessary information. Then duplicate copies for your students.

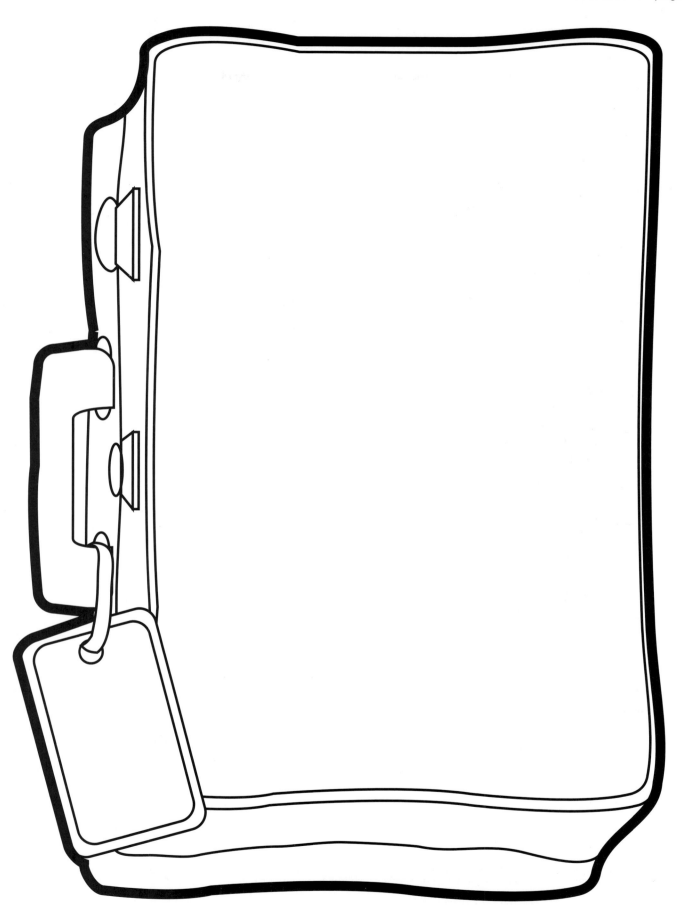

Patterns

Use with "Thanksgiving Windsocks" on page 98.

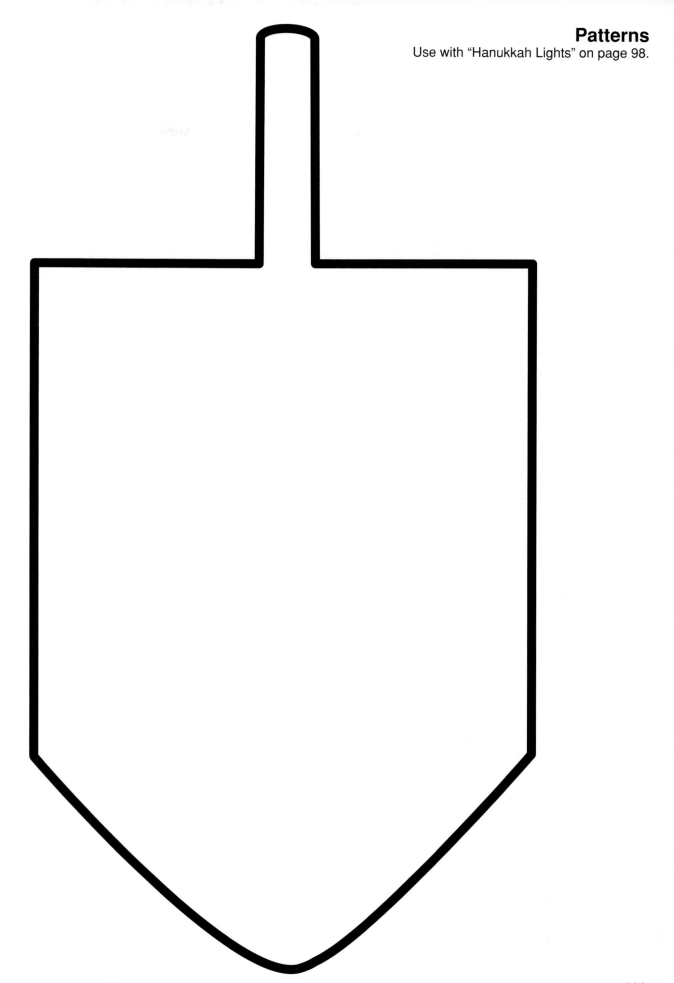

Patterns

Use with "Shamrock Viewers" on page 102.

Place on fold.

Place on fold.

On St. Patrick's Day,
All the things I had seen,
When viewed through my shamrock
Were a nice shade of green.

CENTERS

CENTERS

Center Setup

Learning centers provide excellent opportunities for students to practice a variety of skills in kid-pleasing ways. Every area of the curriculum and almost any skill can be reinforced through file-folder games, puzzles, partner activities, small-group projects, or individual tasks.

As you set up a center, decorate the area so that it is inviting to students. Place a sign or poster explaining the steps or rules of the activity. Centers should be designed so that students can complete each activity with little or no help from you. Have all the materials students will need at the center. Also include a method for students to check their own work and make any necessary corrections.

Design some centers for students to use during their free time. Encourage students to visit a center to complete an art project, explore a topic of study, or work a puzzle. Make these open centers available to students at any time.

Design other centers for additional skills practice and reinforcement, and have students visit the centers as part of an assignment. Schedule a time for each student or group of students to visit each center once a week.

An attendance container is an easy way to keep tabs on which students have visited a center. Place a colorfully decorated container at each center. Program a different craft stick with each student's name and the number or name of the center, and place the sticks in the container. When a student visits the center, she removes her stick and places it in a corresponding container on your desk. After all students have visited the center, transfer the sticks back to the original container. You'll be set to monitor attendance for the next center activity.

Center Suggestions

Center activities should be designed to meet the needs and curricula of your classroom. Basic centers can be set up at the beginning of the school year. As the subject matter and skill levels progress, adjust the activities accordingly. Include some of the following centers in your classroom:

Math Center:
Encourage students to use manipulatives or play games that reinforce basic skills.

Writing Center:
Supply students with writing prompts, journal topics, vocabulary lists, and supplies for creating student-made books.

Art Center:
Use seasonal themes, curriculum tie-ins, and a variety of materials for students to use in creative expression.

Game Center:
Keep a supply of purchased games, jigsaw puzzles, word searches, crossword puzzles, and game pieces at the center. Remember that many games help students develop problem-solving strategies.

Listening Center:
Have students use headphones to listen to classical music, a set of taped directions, or recorded stories. Drawing activities, writing assignments, or skill sheets can accompany each recording.

Reading Center:
Place a collection of books, magazines, newspaper articles, and poetry selections at the center. The collection may enhance a unit of study, spotlight a featured author, or promote seasonal selections.

Fraction Fun

Combine your students' artistic talents with this fraction-reinforcing center. Create task cards similar to the ones shown. Program the back of each card for self-checking; then laminate the cards for durability. Place the task cards, crayons, and a class supply of drawing paper at a center. A student visually divides a sheet of paper into sixths and numbers the squares from one to six. Next she reads a task card and completes the activity in the corresponding square. She then flips the card to check her work. She repeats this process with the additional cards. Periodically add new task cards to keep student interest high.

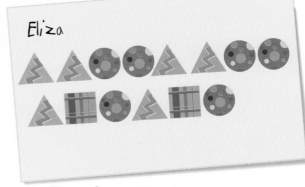

Eliza

Perky Patterns

Reinforce patterning skills with recycled materials. Cut a large supply of basic shapes—such as squares, circles, and triangles—from leftover gift wrap, wallpaper samples, or fabric. Place the shapes, glue, and a supply of paper at a center. A student uses the shapes to create a predetermined number of different patterns. She then glues the patterns onto a sheet of construction paper. Display the completed patterns on a bulletin board for an eye-catching display.

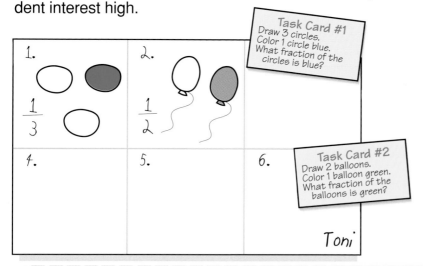

Task Card #1
Draw 3 circles.
Color 1 circle blue.
What fraction of the circles is blue?

Task Card #2
Draw 2 balloons.
Color 1 balloon green.
What fraction of the balloons is green?

Toni

MUNCHABLE MATH

Students can review a variety of math skills at this tasty learning center. Place a box of colorful breakfast cereal and a supply of three-ounce paper cups at the center. A student visits the center and fills one cup with cereal. Then she uses the pieces to complete a variety of tasks, such as

- estimating how many pieces are in the cup, then counting to find the actual amount
- determining if the total is an odd or even number
- counting the pieces by twos
- counting the pieces by fives
- determining which color has the most (or fewest) number of pieces
- creating a color or shape pattern

After she completes the tasks, invite the student to munch her manipulatives as a reward for her hard work.

Guess: 62
Actual: 70   even

Red is the color I have the most pieces of.

Purple is the color I have the fewest pieces of.

Fishing For Facts

There's nothing fishy about this learning center for basic-fact practice! Cut a large fish shape from colored bulletin-board paper. Glue each top edge of several construction-paper semicircles to the fish cutout (to resemble scales). Number the top corner of each scale; then program each scale with a math problem. Lift each scale and write the answer to each problem underneath. Place the fish at a center along with paper and pencils. A student numbers a sheet of paper, answers the corresponding problems, then lifts the scales to check her work. Students are sure to be hooked on basic skills!

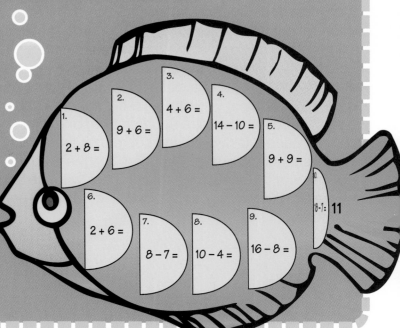

Partner Measurement

Review linear measurement with this hands-on partner activity. Create several task cards similar to the ones shown. Laminate the cards for durability; then place the cards, two rulers, and a supply of modeling clay at a center. A student selects a task card, molds the clay to the desired length, then asks his partner to use a ruler to check his work. Challenge your students to complete five task cards each time they visit the center. No doubt students' measurement skills will really take shape!

Roll the clay to make a rope three inches long.

Mold the clay into a shape that is two inches tall.

Pat the clay into a pancake that is four inches across.

A Day In The Life

Review time-telling skills with this booklet activity. To make a booklet, staple five sheets of blank paper between two construction-paper covers. Place a class supply of booklets, a clock-face stamp, an ink pad, and crayons at a center. A student writes "A Day In The Life Of [student's name]" on the front cover of a booklet and decorates it as desired. Then he stamps a clock face on the next five pages. He chooses five different times during the day and uses a crayon to sequentially program each clock with one of the times. Then, on the bottom of each page, he writes the time and illustrates what he might be doing at that time of the day. Have students share their completed booklets with their classmates. Good "times" will certainly be had by all!

I wake up at 7:00.

All About Me

These simple drawings will reveal many interesting details about your students. Program a sheet of chart paper with directions similar to those shown below. Place the directions, a supply of writing paper, and crayons at a center. A student folds a sheet of paper into fourths, opens it up, and numbers the resulting sections from one to four. She follows the directions on the chart to draw a picture in each section of the paper. Display the completed drawings and the directions on a bulletin board for students to observe. To extend the activity, have students use the information to answer questions about their classmates.

Box #1:
Draw a **star** if you prefer reading.
Draw a **moon** if you prefer math.

Box #2:
Draw a **cat** if you are an only child.
Draw a **dog** if you have brothers and/or sisters.

Box #3:
Draw an **apple** if you are seven years old.
Draw a **banana** if you are eight years old.

Box #4:
Draw an **arrow pointing left** if you have pets.
Draw an **arrow pointing right** if you don't have pets.

Pasta Punctuation

How do you make reviewing contractions more fun? Try adding a little pasta! Place a box of elbow macaroni, glue, a supply of index cards programmed with word pairs that form contractions, and sheets of blank paper at a center. A student folds one sheet of paper into fourths, then unfolds it so that the paper is visually divided into four sections. He selects a programmed index card and copies the words onto one section of his paper. Next he writes the contraction made from the word pair, gluing a piece of macaroni in place of the apostrophe. He repeats this process with the remaining three sections. Now there's an activity where a student really has to use his noodle!

Finger Spelling

Generate plenty of hands-on fun with this finger-spelling idea. Place a plastic shoebox, a can of shaving cream, and a list of the current spelling words at a center. A student sprays a small amount of shaving cream into the shoebox and uses her finger to write a spelling word in the foam. After checking the list to confirm that the spelling is correct, she spreads the foam around to erase the word, then repeats the procedure until all words have been spelled correctly. Cleanup is easy—simply have the student wipe the shoebox with a paper towel, or rinse it out in the classroom sink.

Book-Report Recipe

Set up a book-report writing center featuring this easy-to-use recipe for literature reviews. Copy the recipe shown onto poster board, and decorate it to resemble a recipe card. Laminate it for durability; then place the card, crayons, and supplies of writing and drawing paper at a center. A student follows the directions on the recipe to report on a desired book. Remind students to answer the questions with complete sentences. After a student answers the questions, he illustrates a favorite scene from the story. No doubt this recipe for better book-reporting skills will receive rave student reviews!

Book-Report Recipe

1. Name the title and author of the book.
2. Tell when and where the story takes place.
3. Describe the main character.
4. Write a sentence or two telling what the story is about.
5. Explain why you did or did not like the book.

red   sweet
eat   delicious
APPLES   juicy
crunchy
yummy   tasty

Student-Made Word Banks

This simple vocabulary-building activity will speak for itself! Draw and label a desired picture on a sheet of chart paper. Place the chart paper, dictionaries, and an assortment of colored markers in an easily accessible area. Invite students to write words to describe the picture along the sides of the chart paper. After a few days, display the completed word bank for students to refer to during writing assignments, journal time, or language activities.

IDEA FACTORY

Complement any unit of study with this center that focuses on creative abilities and results in a class book. Decide on a topic for the learning center, either from a unit of study, a holiday theme, or an area of student interest. Place a supply of writing paper, drawing paper, markers, colored pencils, and reference books at a center. Encourage each student to visit the center and complete a page about the designated topic. Students can write an informative paragraph, compose a poem, draw a picture, or relate information about the topic in another creative form. Compile the completed pages into a class book. Invite each student to take the book home overnight to share with his family.

Dinosaurs

Dinosaurs lived a long time ago. Some ate meat. Some ate plants. Dinosaurs are extinct now.

Billy

Vaness

bell   candle   gift   holly   present

WHAT A HANG-UP!

For a fast and easy sequencing center, just hang a clothesline and gather a set of clothespins! Program a set of seasonal shapes with desired vocabulary words or numbers; then laminate the shapes for durability and store them in a clothespin bag. Also make an answer key for self-checking and place it in the bag. A student sequences numbers or alphabetizes words by suspending them on the clothesline in the correct order. Students won't have any hang-ups about sequencing practice with this clever activity!

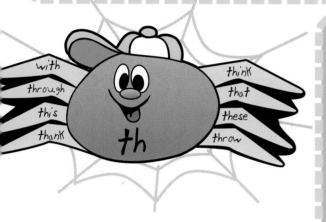

Word-Skill Web

Spin a center of word-skill reinforcement with the help of these super spiders. Duplicate a class supply of the spider pattern on page 121, and place them at a center along with crayons, scissors, and markers. Post a sign showing a desired sound, letter blend, or vowel combination. A student labels a spider pattern with the featured letter(s), then writes a word containing the letter(s) on each of the spider's legs. She then colors and cuts out the spider. Display the completed projects on a bulletin board covered in artificial webbing material.

For a variation, have the student program a spider with a predetermined number. Then have the student write an addition or subtraction problem equal to the number on each of the spider's legs. Your students will create a web of wonderful work!

In The News

This versatile learning center will make headlines in your classroom! Post a list of skill-based tasks (similar to the ones shown) at a center. Also place a supply of discarded newspapers, scissors, glue sticks, and sheets of blank paper at the center. A student chooses a task from the list. Next he searches for words in the newspaper to complete the task. He then cuts out the words and glues them to a sheet of paper. If desired, post a different skill each week to provide review or reinforcement. Students will enjoy the scavenger-hunt approach to skills practice!

- Find ten proper names. Glue them in alphabetical order.
- Find five nouns and five verbs.
- Find five words that contain the *sh* digraph.
- Find ten number words. Glue them in numerical order.
- Find five words that have the long *a* sound.
- Find a headline that contains a compound word.
- Find ten words that end in silent *e*.

Carlos

1. **Atlanta**
2. Canada
3. David
4. **France**
5. *George*
6. Kansas
7. *London*
8. Mars
9. Pacific
10. **Wednesday**

Dictionary Detectives

Are you looking for a way to reinforce dictionary skills? Then turn your students into dictionary detectives! Post a list of spelling words, content-related words, or vocabulary words at a center. Place several dictionaries, pencils, and a supply of writing paper at the center, too. A student looks up each word on the list; then, on provided paper, she writes the guide words for the page where the word was found. The student repeats this process for the additional words. If desired, provide an answer key at the center so that students can check their work after looking up the words. In no time at all, your students will be on the trail of good dictionary skills!

POCKET PALS

Get students hopping with this capitalization review game. Duplicate two copies of the kangaroo pattern on page 122. Color and cut out the patterns; then label one kangaroo's pocket "correct" and the other kangaroo's pocket "incorrect." Glue the kangaroos to the inside of a file folder as shown. Program five cards, each with a correctly written sentence, and five cards with sentences containing capitalization errors. Label the backs of the cards for self-checking. Laminate the cards and the folder for durability. Store the cards in a resealable bag clipped to the folder; then place the folder at a center. A student reads each card and places it on the corresponding kangaroo's pocket. She flips the card to check her work.

Reinforce other skills by creating additional folders and card sets for real/make-believe, correct/incorrect math problems, complete/incomplete sentences, or correct/incorrect punctuation.

Mitten Match

Students will warm up to this compound-word game. Duplicate construction-paper copies of the mitten pattern (page 121) to create several pairs of mittens. Program each left-hand mitten with the first half of a compound word. Write the second half of the word on the right-hand mitten. Create an answer key if desired. Laminate the mittens for durability; then store them in a resealable bag at a center. To play the game, two or more students turn the mittens facedown on a table. Each player takes a turn selecting two mittens and turning them faceup. If the mittens make a compound word, the player keeps them and takes another turn. If the mittens do not make a compound word, the player returns them to their facedown position and it becomes the next player's turn. Play continues in this manner until all mittens have been matched. The player with the most pairs wins.

To vary the game, program each mitten pair with a math problem and its answer, a vocabulary word and its definition, rhyming words, a number word and the corresponding numeral, or a picture and its matching initial consonant.

Pattern

Use with "Word-Skill Web" on page 119.

Pattern

Use with "Mitten Match" on page 120.

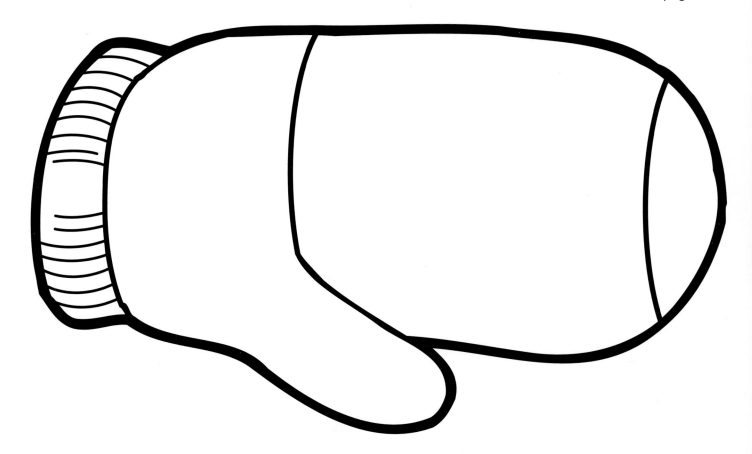

Pattern

Use with "Pocket Pals" on page 120.

GAMES

GAMES

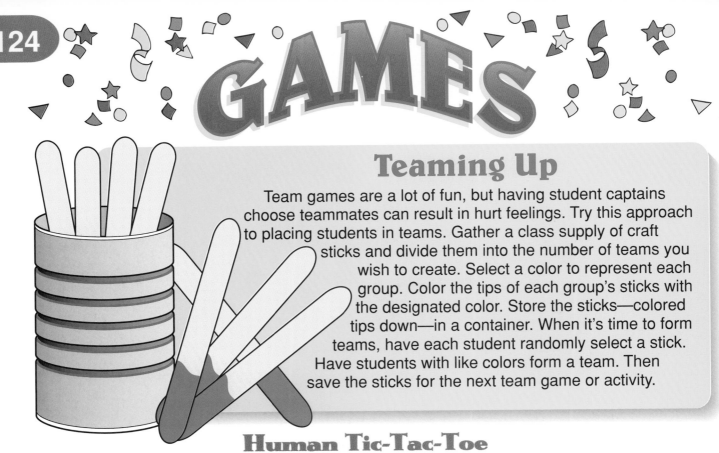

Teaming Up

Team games are a lot of fun, but having student captains choose teammates can result in hurt feelings. Try this approach to placing students in teams. Gather a class supply of craft sticks and divide them into the number of teams you wish to create. Select a color to represent each group. Color the tips of each group's sticks with the designated color. Store the sticks—colored tips down—in a container. When it's time to form teams, have each student randomly select a stick. Have students with like colors form a team. Then save the sticks for the next team game or activity.

Human Tic-Tac-Toe

Put this new twist on a favorite game! Arrange nine chairs to resemble the spaces on a tic-tac-toe grid. Divide the class into two teams—one to represent Xs and one to represent Os. Give each team member a construction-paper sign programmed with his team's symbol. Then flip a coin to see which team will have the first turn. Ask a member of the chosen team to spell a word, solve a math problem, or answer a curriculum-related question. If he answers correctly, the student may sit down in the chair of his choice. Continue the procedure, alternating the questions between the two teams. The first team to place three students in a row wins the round. Play additional rounds until each student has had an opportunity to participate.

Spelling Detectives

Sharpen your students' observation skills with this spelling-review game. Write the weekly spelling words in random order on the chalkboard. Instruct the class to study the words for one minute; then have everyone turn away from the chalkboard. Erase one of the words; then rewrite it, spelling it incorrectly. Ask the class to turn around and study the words again, this time for 30 seconds. At the end of the time period, call on a volunteer to identify the misspelled word. If she answers correctly, award the class one point. Award the class an additional point if the student can give the correct spelling of the word. If she answers incorrectly, identify the word, and give yourself the point. Challenge the class to earn more points than you do in ten rounds of play.

red   fed
bed   sled
bread   hed

"Head" is misspelled.

Birdies In The Nest

Students will love all the movement involved in this high-flying game. Pick six students to be mama or papa birds. Assign each bird a different number from one to six and post that number on his "nest" or desk. (If this is played in the gym, Hula-Hoops® may be used instead of desks.) Have each remaining student (or birdie) roll a die to determine his number in the game. Write the number on a sticky note, and attach it to the birdie's shirt.

When all birdies have been assigned a number, give a signal for them to "fly" to the nest of their choice. (Students select a nest by sitting by a numbered desk or Hula-Hoop®.) Each mama and papa bird then rolls the die twice. The first roll determines which nest she or he will visit. The second roll determines which numbered birdies can be taken from that nest. (A papa bird who rolls a one and a four will visit nest one and take all birdies wearing fours. If he rolls the number of his own nest on the first roll, he may roll again.)

After each parent bird has had a turn, he returns to his own nest with the birdies he took. The bird counts the total number of birdies he brought with him and adds it to the number of birdies already at his nest. The mama or papa with the highest number of birdies is the winner.

Shake, Rattle, And Roll

Prepare for this spelling game by collecting two potato-chip cans. Fill each can with a set of plastic alphabet letters or paper squares programmed with letters. Divide the class into two teams and line up each team single file behind a desk. Have the first player on each team sit at the desk; then hand each player a container of letters and announce a spelling word. Both players roll their cans on their desks to scramble the letters. Then each player shakes the letters out and finds the letters needed to spell the word. (If a letter appears in a word more than once, it will be necessary to provide extra letters during preparation.) The first player to arrange the letters to spell the word stands up. If he spelled the word correctly, he wins a point for his team. If he is incorrect, the other player may try to win the point by correctly spelling the word. At the end of the turn, each player returns to the end of his line, and another round begins. Continue play until all students have had a chance to participate.

Pitching The Bar

Students will enjoy this version of a game played at the first Thanksgiving feast. The original objective of the game was for each man to show his strength by trying to throw a huge log farther than the others. Adapt this game for your students by purchasing a large Styrofoam® noodle (a floating device found in toy departments). Cut the noodle in half to make two logs for your students to throw. Have your students compete outdoors, two at a time, standing behind a designated line to throw the logs. Declare a winner for each throw, or, if desired, mark each attempt with a chalk line and determine a class winner after everyone has had a turn.

ERASER RELAYS

Perk up a rainy-day recess with these ideas for relay races. Divide students into the desired number of teams. Give each team a clean chalkboard eraser to use for the following relay games:

• Balancing Act
The first member of each team walks to a designated point while balancing the eraser on her head. After reaching that point, she may carry the eraser to the next player in line. Play continues until all members of the team have had a turn. The first team to have all its members complete the relay is the winner.

• Chin Pass
The first member of each team places the eraser under his chin. He must pass the eraser to the second player without either player using his hands. The second player passes it to the third player, and play continues down the line. If the eraser drops, the player who was passing it must pick it up, place it back under his chin, and attempt to pass it again. The first team to pass the eraser to the end of the line wins.

• Knees Squeeze
The first player on each team puts the eraser between her knees and walks to a designated point and back. She hands the eraser to the next player in line, and play continues until all players have had a turn. The first team to have all its members complete the relay is the winner.

DON'T WAKE THE BEAR!

Reinforce spelling, math, or curriculum-related skills with the help of a hibernating bear. Choose one child to sit on the floor and be the hibernating bear. Line up a row of five chairs on either side of the bear. Divide the class into two teams, and have each team line up behind a row of chairs.

To play the game, ask the first member of one team to spell a word, solve a math problem, or answer a question. If he answers correctly, he walks to the end of the line. If he is incorrect, he sits in the chair farthest from the bear. Continue asking questions, alternating between the two teams. Each time an incorrect answer is given, that player takes the next available seat in his row. After all five chairs are filled, the next player on the team to give an incorrect response must "wake" the bear by gently tapping him on the head. The bear gives a roar, then trades places with any seated member on that team. After the two students switch, a new game begins.

Super Scoopers

When the weather keeps you indoors for recess, bring out the Super Scoopers! To make a class set of Super Scoopers, ask each student to bring a clean, plastic one-gallon milk jug from home. Cut the top off each jug, leaving the handle attached (see the example). To play the game, give each student a scooper. Place students in groups of two or three. Distribute a crumpled sheet of paper to each group. The students in each group take turns using their scoops to toss and catch the paper. Students will enjoy the exercise on those wet and wintry days.

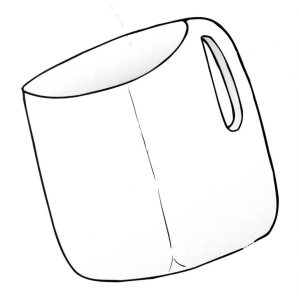

BALLOON CALISTHENICS

Get your students moving with a round of balloon calisthenics. Give each student an inflated balloon to use in a series of motor-skill motions. Try some of these exercises with your class:

- Instruct each student to toss her balloon in the air and clap her hands three times before catching it. Repeat five times.

- Tell each student to keep her balloon in the air by tapping it three times with her right hand, three times with her left hand, and then three times with alternating hands. Repeat twice.

- Place students in pairs facing each other. At your signal have each student toss her balloon to her partner, then catch her partner's balloon. Repeat ten times.

- Instruct each student to bounce her balloon on her bended right knee before catching it. Repeat five times with each knee.

- Have each student keep her balloon in the air by hitting it with her hands clasped in front of her. Challenge students to keep their balloons in the air for 30 seconds.

- Instruct your class to form a circle, with students standing an arm's length apart. (If room is restricted, have students make two smaller circles.) Give a balloon to every other student. At your signal each student passes her balloon to the person on her right. Have students continue passing the balloons for 20 seconds; then have them change directions.

- Have students form two lines, with one student standing directly behind another. Give the first person in each line a balloon. At your signal the student with a balloon passes it over her head to the person behind her. The team that passes its balloon to the end of the line first is the winner.

- Repeat the relay above with an added twist. At your signal the first student passes the balloon over her head to the person behind her. The second person passes the balloon through her legs to the person behind her. The students continue passing the balloon in this over-the-head and through-the-legs pattern. The team that passes the balloon to the end of the line first is the winner.

5-MINUTE FILLERS

5-MINUTE FILLERS

I'm thinking of an animal that lives in the forest. It is covered with fur, and it walks on all four legs.
??? ???

Questions Only!

To fill a few minutes between activities, engage students in this questions-only game. Tell your students that you are thinking of an object related to a current topic of study. Give the students three clues about the object; then let the questioning begin. Each student may ask you one question that can be answered with yes or no. If a student guesses the object during his turn, he may lead a new round of questioning the next time the game is played.

Guess My Number

Your students will be all ears when it comes to playing this listening game. Secretly write a number on a piece of paper. Give each student a chance to guess the number; then say "higher" or "lower" in response to each guess. Encourage students to use their deduction skills to pinpoint the number. Invite the student who guesses the exact number (or comes closest to it) to secretly select the number for the next round of play.

In-Line Assessment

Take advantage of the time your students spend waiting in line with a quick assessment. Give the first student in line a math problem, a spelling word, or another content-related question to answer. Continue down the line. By the time you reach the end, the wait time will be over!

Math Machine

You'll have your students thinking on their feet with this mental-math activity. Next time students are waiting in line, have the first student in line choose a number from one to ten. Announce an operation such as "Add three." The second student in line adds three to the first student's number. Continue down the line, having each student add three to the new total. For an added challenge, have students predict what the last number will be prior to their calculations. What a hardworking math machine!

WORD WIZARDS

This small-group activity is perfect when *you* have a few extra minutes to spare. Divide students into four or five groups. Assign a recorder in each group, and give her a blank sheet of paper. Write a letter combination such as *ad* on the board. Each group brainstorms as *many* words containing the letters as possible while the recorder lists them on the paper. Stop play after five minutes. In turn, call on each recorder to share a word from her list. If another group has that word listed, it is scratched from all lists. If no other group has the word, that team is awarded a point. Comparing continues until all answers have been exhausted. The group with the *most* points is dubbed Word Wizards for the day.

ad

had   pad

bad   sad

glad   add

dad

Books On Review

Read any good books lately? You can initiate an impromptu oral book report using information from a book you are currently reading to your class. Call on student volunteers to name the characters, the setting, and other details relating to the story. Also ask students to respond to open-ended questions about the events in the book. This experience will help students acquire book-reporting skills in a comfortable, conversational setting.

Quick Fix

Have a few minutes? Hold a quick review! Write a list of scrambled spelling or vocabulary words on the chalkboard. Ask student volunteers to write the words correctly on the chalkboard. Then, if time permits, hold a bonus round for volunteers to define the words or name their parts of speech. In just a short time, you will have reinforced several important concepts!

Name That State!

Take your students on a trip across the country with this geographical time filler. Display a large U.S. map, and have your students line up single file beside it. Have the first two students stand in front of the map while you name a state. The first student to point to the state wins the round and remains standing. A new contestant replaces the other player, who returns to the end of the line. It won't take long for your students to become first-class travelers!

Graphing Games

Prepare for quick and easy graphing with this ready-to-go activity. Program a sheet of poster board with an open bar graph. Laminate the graph for durability. When you have a few extra minutes, display the graph and pose a question such as, "How many buttons do you have on today?" Have each student write her answer on a sticky note while you label the graph with a wipe-off marker. Then have each student post her note in the appropriate place on the graph. Use the remaining time to have students interpret the information on the graph. What a timely way to reinforce graphing skills!

0	1	2	3	4	5 or more
0		2			10
0		2		4	7
0	1	2	3	4	8
					5
					5

Magnificent Math

Turn extra minutes in the day into magnificent math moments. On the chalkboard, write the symbols for greater than and less than, followed by four numerals. Ask students to mentally arrange the symbols and numerals to create greater-than and less-than statements. Invite student volunteers to write their statements on the board. After several statements have been written, have the class evaluate them for correctness. Number sense has never been so much fun!

> < 3 6 7 9

36 < 79   73 < 96
93 > 67   39 < 76

Missing Vowels

Reinforce important decoding concepts with this easy time filler. Write several short-vowel words—with the vowels omitted—on the chalkboard. Ask the class to think of vowels that would make each word complete. Then have student volunteers come to the board to complete the words. Students will be amazed at the power vowels have to create different words!

Place-Value Scramble

This simple activity is perfect for a minilesson on place value. Write three numerals on the board. Ask students to arrange the numerals to create the lowest possible number, the highest possible number, a number with the largest numeral in the tens place, and other, similar arrangements. Complete the activity by asking students to assist you in arranging the resulting numbers in sequential order.

Pattern Power

With a few extra minutes, students can play this patterning game that makes *them* the manipulatives. Ask four or five students to come to the front of the room and stand in line according to your directions. Have the rest of the class study the line to determine the pattern you used to organize the students. Try a few simple ABAB patterns (such as blue jeans, tennis shoes, blue jeans, tennis shoes) or ABBA patterns (such as boy, girl, girl, boy). Since appearances change every day, the possibilities are endless!

RHYME TIME

Use the last few minutes at the end of the day for rhyme time. Write a word on the chalkboard and have students brainstorm rhyming words. Record their responses on the board. As the list progresses, point out the different spellings that create similar sounds. As an added challenge, have students use words from the list to compose simple couplets. Students will love the wonderful way that rhymes are used to end the day!

train
chain
pain
cane
plane
stain
rain/rein

Calendar Concepts

Reinforce calendar skills with this timely activity. At the beginning of each month, provide each student with a copy of the calendar pattern on page 134. Help your students to fill in the appropriate dates, as well as information about holidays, student birthdays, and upcoming events. Have each student keep her calendar in her desk. When you have extra time throughout the day, instruct students to take out their calendars. Ask questions to practice calendar-related concepts or to remind students of special happenings. You'll stay on top of a busy school schedule while reinforcing important calendar skills.

Time Flies

Here's an activity that really does make time fly! Keep a large manipulative clock handy. When you have a few extra minutes, position the hands to show the current time. Ask a student volunteer to read the clock. Then ask a question such as, "What time would it be if it were 15 minutes later?" Continue the activity as time allows. Before you know it, it will be time for the next activity!

SUNDAY	MONDAY	TUESDAY	WEDNESDAY	THURSDAY	FRIDAY	SATURDAY

©1998 The Education Center, Inc. • The Mailbox® Superbook • Grade 2 • TEC451

Note To The Teacher: Use with "Calendar Concepts" on page 133.

SUBSTITUTE TEACHER TIPS

SUBSTITUTE-TEACHER TIPS
In A Nutshell

The Substitute Folder

As you settle into your first week at school, putting together a substitute folder should be on your list of things to do. The folder can include a class list, a seating chart, a list of students with special needs, and instructions for dismissal. Your daily schedule and a copy of emergency lesson plans will also be of great help to a substitute. Use the reproducibles on pages 138-140 to provide your substitute with information that will help her day run smoothly.

Plan Ahead

If you know in advance that you will be out for more than a day, leave a small reward or privilege incentive for each day that you will be gone. Before you leave, explain to students that those who complete their work and exhibit good behavior will receive a reward at the end of each day. This motivation will pay off with good reports from your substitute!

If you are planning to be gone for an extended period (three days or more), arrange for your substitute to visit your classroom ahead of time. After introducing the sub to the students, ask her to stay and observe some of your classroom routines. Show her where manuals and basic supplies are kept. Don't forget to include information about taking care of plants and animals while you are away!

A SPECIAL MESSAGE

Plan a treat for your students and your substitute by leaving a special recording in your absence. Tape-record a special message to remind students to be on their best behavior. If desired inform students of the lesson plans for the day and your expectations for completed work. Students will be reminded that they must put forth their best efforts, even when you're gone for the day!

Good morning, class! I won't be here today, but I know you will do your best work!

Starting The Day

Substitute teachers move from age group to age group, and they must adjust their expectations frequently. Help your substitute get to know your students with this simple start-the-day activity. Leave a list of questions, such as those shown, for the substitute to write on the board. Ask her to have each student answer the questions on writing paper. Leave time in the schedule for the students to share their information with the substitute and the class. Your sub will have a much better understanding of your students' interests and ability levels, making for a smoother day.

What's your favorite animal? _____

What's your favorite color? _____

What's your favorite TV show? _____

What's your favorite song? _____

What's your favorite school subject? _____

What do you like to do in your free time? _____

Ending The Day

The last 15 minutes of the day are important ones, especially for young children. Be sure to remind your substitute to utilize those last few minutes by carefully reviewing homework assignments, handing out notes, and reminding students to take home any necessary materials. Parents and students will be much more likely to value the day's work (despite your absence) with these last-minute helps.

"Plen-tea" Of Thanks

A substitute teacher's job can be hectic—she has to deal with unexpected situations, discipline problems, and unfamiliar procedures. You can express your gratitude to your sub by leaving her a little surprise to enjoy at the end of the day. Purchase a supply of flavored tea bags to keep at school. Copy the verse shown on a thank-you note. Tuck a tea bag into the note and leave it with the substitute folder. What a nice way to say thanks for a job well done!

School is over; the day is done.
I hope it was a pleasant one.
Now take a break, and since you're free,
Sit down and have a cup of tea.

Sunshine Farms Herbal Teas

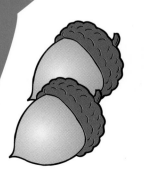

 # Information In A Nutshell

Faculty Information

Principal: _____

Secretary: _____

Custodian: _____

Aide: _____

Helpful Teachers: _____

_____

Procedures For...

Start Of Day: _____

_____

_____

Attendance: _____

_____

_____

Fire Drill: _____

_____

_____

Recess: _____

_____

Lunch: _____

_____

_____

Discipline Policy: _____

_____

_____

Other: _____

_____

_____

Children With Special Needs

Health: _____

_____

_____

_____

_____

Supervision: _____

_____

_____

_____

_____

Learning: _____

_____

_____

_____

_____

Student Pullouts For Special Programs

Name: Class: Day/Time:

_____

_____

_____

_____

Helpful Students: _____

_____

_____

Daily Schedule

Time	Monday	Tuesday	Wednesday	Thursday	Friday

Free-Time Activities: _____

_____

_____

Emergency Lesson Plans

Reading	Language	Math	Science	Social Studies	Other

Note To The Teacher: Use with "The Substitute Folder" on page 136.

LANGUAGE ARTS

GRAMMAR

The ABCs Of Nouns, Verbs, And Adjectives

Your youngsters will love working together on this yearlong parts-of-speech project. Cover a large section of a wall with paper; then tape construction-paper alphabet letters from *A* to *Z* to the paper, leaving space beneath each letter. Add the title "The ABCs Of The Parts Of Speech." Next challenge each youngster to cut pictures of nouns, verbs, and adjectives from discarded magazines. Have him label each picture with its name and part of speech; then mount the pictures under the appropriate letters. Challenge your students to add pictures to the display throughout the year.

Parts-Of-Speech Lotto

This parts-of-speech review game is sure to be a whole "lotto" fun! Provide each child with a blank lotto board. Instruct him to randomly program the 16 squares with four nouns, four pronouns, four verbs, and four adjectives. As students are programming their cards, program an equal number of construction-paper cards with the words *noun, pronoun, verb,* and *adjective,* and place the cards in a container. Also distribute 16 paper markers to each child. To play the game, draw a part of speech from the container. Read the card aloud and have each youngster cover a correct square. The first student to cover four words horizontally, vertically, or diagonally calls out, "Lotto!" To win the game, he must read aloud each word and state its part of speech for verification. If desired, award the winning student with a sticker or another small prize.

MARVELOUS MOBILES!

Have your youngsters make banana-split mobiles to review the parts of speech! Cut three templates from tagboard: an ice-cream scoop, a banana, and a bowl. Place the templates, scissors, glue, and crayons at a center with construction paper prepared as follows: white, brown, and pink squares (for the scoops), yellow strips (for the bananas), and purple strips (for the bowls). To make a mobile, a student traces the templates on the appropriate construction paper and cuts them out. Then he writes an adjective on his white scoop, a noun on his brown scoop, and a verb on his pink scoop. Next he writes a sentence using all three parts of speech on his banana cutout; then he writes his name on his bowl cutout. He then attaches his cutouts to an 18" length of yarn as shown. If desired, invite youngsters to snack on small banana splits as they share their sentences. Display the mobiles around the room for all to enjoy. Now that's a great way to review the parts of speech!

hairy

dog

barked

The hairy dog barked at the cat.

William B.

I Can...

Your youngsters will learn about verbs with this one-of-a-kind activity! Remind students that a verb is a word that shows action. Then have students name examples of verbs. List their ideas on the chalkboard. Pair students; then assign each pair a different verb from the list, keeping each assignment a secret from the other pairs. Have each pair pantomime its verb for the class. Further challenge youngsters by having each student write, then illustrate four verbs on a sheet of divided paper titled "I can..." (see the illustration). If desired, collect the pictures and bind them between two covers; then add the title "What Can You Do?" Place the booklet at a reading center for all to enjoy!

One-Of-A-Kind Word Search!

Challenge your youngsters to learn the parts of speech as they search for words! To begin, share the following information with your students:

- **Nouns** name a person, place, or thing. They can be singular (one) or plural (more than one).
- **Pronouns** are words that are used to take the place of nouns, such as *I, he, she,* and *it.*
- **Verbs** are words that show action, such as *run, skip,* and *hop.*
- **Adjectives** are words used to describe nouns, such as *tall, short, thin,* and *hairy.*

Divide students into four groups. Assign each group a different name: nouns, pronouns, verbs, or adjectives. Then provide each group with a highlighter and a copy of a selected story or passage. Have each group read the story and then highlight examples of its assigned part of speech. Ask groups to share their answers with the rest of the class. If desired, write the students' responses on the chalkboard. As students learn the parts of speech, provide additional sheets for individual youngsters to highlight!

A Picture For Every Verb

Here's an activity that reinforces the concept of verbs! Instruct each youngster to cut a picture from a discarded magazine; then have her glue it to the middle of a sheet of construction paper. Have the student list verbs around her cutout that relate to the picture; then challenge her to write a story that incorporates the verbs on another sheet of paper. Have the youngsters tape their stories to the bottom of their pictures. Display the finished projects on a wall or bulletin board. What a great way to review verbs!

Silly Sentences!

Use this activity to help youngsters understand the importance of nouns and verbs. After reviewing nouns and verbs, write a student-generated list of both parts of speech on the chalkboard (enough to have one noun and one verb per student). Then have each student choose a different noun and verb from the list and write them on separate cards. Collect the cards and place each card into the corresponding container labeled "Nouns" or "Verbs." Each youngster draws one card from each container and writes and illustrates a silly sentence using the words on the cards. Invite student volunteers to share their sentences and illustrations with their classmates. No doubt your youngsters will have a better understanding of nouns and verbs!

Sentences With Spunk!

Invite your youngsters to use adjectives to write these one-of-a-kind sentences! Instruct each student to think of a noun and list adjectives to describe it on a sheet of scrap paper. Then, on another sheet of paper, have her write a sentence that incorporates the noun and adjectives. Challenge students to see who can come up with the longest, most descriptive sentence. To enhance the activity, have youngsters copy and illustrate their sentences on sheets of paper. Mount the completed drawings on a bulletin board titled "Sentences With Spunk!"

The brown, smelly, hairy dog ran quickly down the crowded street.

Guess What?

Play this guessing game to culminate your adjective lesson. Challenge each youngster to think of an object. Instruct students to keep their objects secret. Then have them list adjective clues about their objects on blank cards. Invite a volunteer to read her clues aloud to her classmates. Ask the other students to guess her object based on the clues she gave. Provide time for additional volunteers to share their clues. Now that's an activity every youngster is sure to enjoy!

Describe That!

Challenge your youngsters to create these picture webs as they learn about adjectives! Display an object in a prominent location; then have students use words to describe what they see. List students' responses on the chalkboard. Tell students that the words they shared are adjectives, words used to describe nouns. To make a web, a student cuts a detailed picture from a newspaper or magazine; then she glues it to the middle of a 9" x 12" sheet of construction paper. She draws five lines extending from her picture and writes an adjective to describe her picture at the end of each line. If desired, have her write a sentence for each adjective. Provide time for students to share their work with their classmates.

Adjective Comparisons

Here's a surefire way to review adjectives with your students! Draw a Venn diagram (similar to the one shown) on a sheet of white paper. Duplicate the diagram for each student. Ask each student to choose two different objects and write their names, one on either side of his paper. Next he writes adjectives that describe each object under the appropriate heading. Further challenge students by having them write words that describe both objects in the middle of their diagrams. You can count on your youngsters' understanding of adjectives to grow with each diagram!

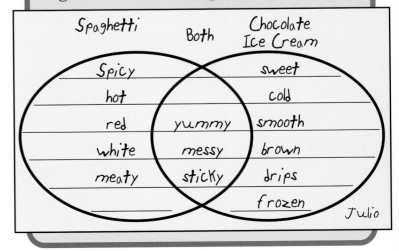

Plural Noun Fun!

Challenge youngsters to sort plural nouns by their endings. Write the names of different nouns (in their singular form) on separate 3" x 5" cards. Also label three berry baskets "-s," "-es," and "-ies." Show students pictures of a kiss, a cow, and a bunny. Have students name the plural form of each noun; then write it on the chalkboard. Discuss the different endings plural nouns may have. Then distribute the singular-noun cards. Ask each student to determine the correct plural ending and place his card into the corresponding basket. As a class, check to be sure each card is in the right basket. Now that's some plural-noun fun!

More Than One?

This idea will aid in your students' understanding of plural nouns. From discarded magazines cut pictures of several nouns (both singular and plural). Mount the pictures on construction paper; then laminate them for durability. After a review of nouns, ask students to sort the pictures into two categories: *one* and *more than one*. With students' help, write the name of each picture on the chalkboard. Lead students to determine that plural nouns name more than one and usually have *-s, -es,* or *-ies* added to the end of them. Then have each student illustrate a different noun in both its singular and plural forms on provided paper. Display the pictures on a bulletin board entitled "More Than One?"

WONDERFUL WALLETS!

These wallets are a great way for students to keep up with plural nouns! To make a wallet, a student folds a 9" x 12" sheet of construction paper lengthwise in half; then she creases the folded paper into thirds. Next she staples her paper along each crease and outside edge to create a wallet like the one shown. She labels the compartments "-s," "-es," and "-ies." To fill her wallet, the student writes a plural noun on a card and places it into the appropriate compartment. Challenge your youngsters to fill their wallets with a variety of nouns throughout the year.

SENTENCE SKILLS

Colorful Sentences

Reinforce basic sentence skills with this colorful idea! Remind students that sentences are complete thoughts with subjects (or noun phrases) and predicates (or verb phrases). Ask students to share sentences; then help them identify each part. Next invite a student volunteer to write the subject part of a sentence on the chalkboard. Then ask another student to finish writing the sentence with a different color of chalk. Challenge students to name the subject and predicate. Have additional youngsters write sentences on the chalkboard until every child has had a turn. Using two different-colored crayons, each student then writes and illustrates a sentence (in a similar manner) on a sheet of construction paper. Provide time for each youngster to share his sentence with his classmates. You can count on students' sentence skills to grow!

The hairy monster hid in my closet. Josh

Picture This!

This activity provides a hands-on way for youngsters to practice writing complete sentences. Cut four pictures from magazines and glue each one to a separate piece of construction paper; then mount the pictures on a wall or bulletin board with the title "Picture This!" Next assign an equal number of students to each picture. Have each youngster write a complete sentence about his assigned picture on a sentence strip. Invite students to share their sentences with their classmates. Collect the strips; then display them under the corresponding pictures. Replace the pictures and sentence strips weekly to keep youngsters on their toes with sentence skills.

SENSIBLE SENTENCES?

Your youngsters are sure to chuckle when they play this silly game that reviews sentence structure. Have each youngster write a complete sentence on a 3" x 24" strip of paper. The student draws a line on her strip between the subject (or noun phrase) and the predicate (or verb phrase); then she cuts the strip apart along the line. Collect the strip parts. Place the subject parts in one box and the predicate parts in another; then label each box accordingly. Invite a youngster to draw a part from each box and read the new sentence aloud to the class. Have students decide whether the sentence is silly or if it makes sense. Then select another student to draw two new parts. Continue the process until every youngster has had a turn. Then return the parts to the appropriate containers and play the game again!

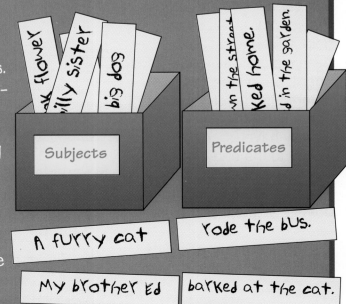

There are red flowers.

The vase is blue.

One flower is yellow.

My mom | went to the store.

Descriptive Sentence Fun!

Here's a creative way for students to practice their sentence-writing skills! Display three different objects for students to view. Divide students into three groups; then assign each group a different object. Instruct each group to write descriptive sentences about its assigned object on separate slips of paper. Collect the slips and place them in an empty container. Invite a student to draw a slip from the container and read it aloud. Challenge the youngsters to decide which object the sentence describes. Then have another child draw a slip from the box. Repeat the activity until each slip has been read aloud. If desired, place another object and blank slips of paper at a center in your classroom. Encourage students to visit the center for additional descriptive writing practice.

Is It A Sentence?

Here's a good sentence review game to play with your students. Remind students that a sentence is a complete thought with both a subject and a predicate. Explain to the youngsters that without a subject *and* a predicate, a group of words is a phrase, not a sentence. Next have each student number a sheet of paper vertically from one to ten. Tell the youngsters that you will be reading aloud ten groups of words. Each student will have to decide whether each one is a sentence or a phrase. Read the first group of words aloud. The student writes *S* if it is a sentence or *P* if it is a phrase. Provide time for youngsters to discuss their answers. Continue in the same manner until each group of words has been read. For an added challenge, have each youngster write an original sentence or phrase on a slip of paper. Then collect the slips and play the game again!

Sentence Shenanigans!

Play this sentence game and let the shenanigans begin! After a review of writing sentences, pair your youngsters. Ask each pair to write a complete sentence on a sentence strip and read it aloud to the class. Then collect the strips. Cut each strip between the subject and predicate. Distribute one of the halves to each student. Challenge each youngster to read his strip and walk around the room to find his match. Have the matched pairs stand next to each other, holding the strips to make a sentence. If time allows, redistribute the strips and play the game again. Let the shenanigans begin!

Awesome Acrostics

These acrostic poems provide a clever way for youngsters to review writing sentences. Review how to write complete sentences with students. Then invite each youngster to create an acrostic poem about herself. To make a poem, a child uses capital letters to write her name vertically down the left side of a sheet of drawing paper. Next she writes a complete sentence about herself that begins with each letter in her name. She then illustrates her poem as desired. Invite each student to share her work with her classmates. Now that's an ingenious way to write sentences!

Every day, I read a book.

My sister's name is Amy.

I like dogs, cats, chocolate, and soccer.

Leslie is my best friend.

Yesterday I went to the park with my dad.

How Does It End?

Introduce your youngsters to ending punctuation with this one-of-a-kind idea! Write an equal number of ending punctuation marks (periods, question marks, and exclamation points) on a class set of blank cards. To begin, tell students that punctuation marks help make the writer's meaning clear. Then explain the three kinds of ending punctuation marks: *periods, question marks,* and *exclamation points.* Invite youngsters to share a sentence for each punctuation mark. Then involve students in this simple game. Distribute one prepared card to each student; then read aloud a sentence to the class. Have each youngster hold her card above her head if her ending punctuation mark is appropriate for that sentence. Engage students in a discussion about the results. Then repeat the activity with additional sentences. How does it end? With fun!

Punctuation Power!

This hands-on game will turn your youngsters on to punctuation practice! Divide students into teams of three. Have each team write a different ending punctuation mark (period, question mark, or exclamation point) on each of three cards. Tell the team members to lay the cards on the floor in front of them. Next assign each team member a different number: 1, 2, or 3. To play the game, read a sentence aloud and announce either number 1, 2, or 3. The numbered team member chooses the correct ending punctuation card and holds it above his head. Give each team a point for a correct answer. Continue for a predetermined amount of time, making sure students have an equal number of turns. The team with the most points wins!

Have A Seat

To help youngsters better understand ending punctuation marks, try this approach. Write one ending punctuation mark (period, question mark, or exclamation point) on each of three sheets of construction paper. Tape one sheet to the back of each of three chairs. Then divide students into two teams. Ask each team to stand in a straight line, facing the chairs. To play the game, read aloud a sentence to the first player on Team 1. He decides which ending punctuation mark the sentence would use and sits in the appropriate chair. Reward Team 1 with a tally mark for a correct answer. Then read another sentence and repeat the activity with a student from Team 2. Play continues down the two lines in this manner until every child has taken a turn. Before you know it, your students will have mastered ending punctuation!

Capitalization Creations

Use this hands-on approach to review capital letters. Remind students that names, places, months, and holidays all need capital letters. Then provide each youngster with a discarded magazine and a sheet of construction paper. The student folds her paper into thirds; then she labels the thirds "Names," "Places," and "Months And Holidays." She cuts words with capital letters from the magazine and glues each one in the appropriate column on her paper. If desired, have youngsters write additional words under each heading. Change the categories throughout the year for extra capitalization practice!

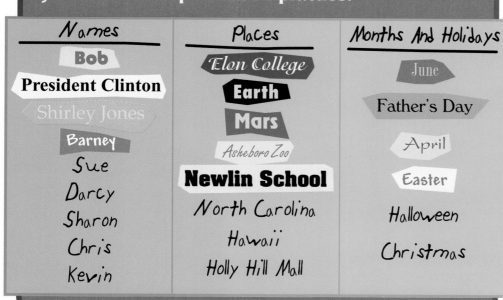

Names	Places	Months And Holidays
Bob	Elon College	June
President Clinton	Earth	Father's Day
Shirley Jones	Mars	April
Barney	Asheboro Zoo	Easter
Sue	Newlin School	Halloween
Darcy	North Carolina	Christmas
Sharon	Hawaii	
Chris	Holly Hill Mall	
Kevin		

A Capital Idea

Introduce youngsters to capitalization with this activity. Cut out one short newspaper or magazine article for each student. Also obtain a class set of highlighter markers. To begin, tell students that they will be investigating what kinds of words need capital letters. Next distribute one article and one highlighter to each student. The youngster highlights the words in his article that begin with capital letters; then he copies the words onto a separate sheet of paper. Next he cuts the words on his list apart and sorts them into three categories: words at the beginning of sentences, names of people, and names of places. Now that's a capital idea!

Captain Capital!

Students will love taking turns playing the role of Captain Capital! After reviewing capitalization with your students, select a youngster to be Captain Capital. The captain selects a category, such as girls' names that start with the letter *S.* Each student then writes as many examples as she can that fit the captain's category during a predetermined time limit. The captain then checks each student's paper with the help of the teacher. Present the youngster with the most words an award similar to the one shown. Then select another child to be the captain. Play a few rounds of the game each day until every youngster has had a turn. Aye, aye, Captain!

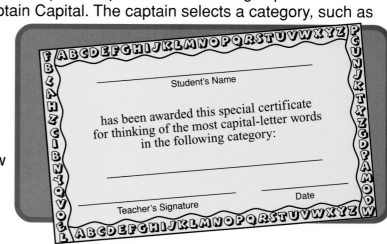

_____
Student's Name

has been awarded this special certificate for thinking of the most capital-letter words in the following category:

_____

_____
Teacher's Signature   Date

WORD SKILLS

SPELLING FOOTBALL

This creative approach to spelling practice will really score with your students! Draw a large football field on the chalkboard, marking off the yard lines as shown. Also tape two brown construction-paper footballs, one labeled "Team A" and the other labeled "Team B," on the 50-yard line. Divide students into two teams and have each team stand in a straight line. Assign a goal line to each team. To begin play, announce a spelling word to the first member of Team A. If he spells the word correctly, he moves the ball ten yards toward his team's goal line. If he misspells the word, the ball remains at the 50-yard line. Then provide the first member of Team B a chance to spell the same word. If he spells it correctly, he moves his team's ball five yards toward his team's goal. Continue in this same manner, alternating turns. The team that reaches its goal line first wins a point. Play resumes with both balls on the 50-yard line. The team with the most points at the end of the designated game time wins! Hut one! Hut two! Hike!

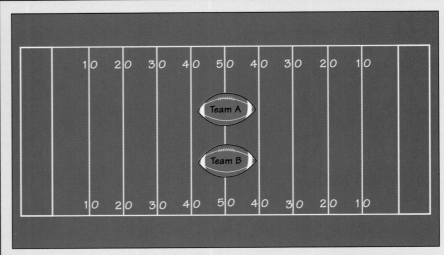

Down The Line

You can count on this fast-paced spelling game being a class favorite! Group students into four teams and have each team sit in a straight line. Give the first person in each row a small chalkboard and a piece of chalk. To begin play, announce a spelling word. The first player in each row writes the first letter of the word on the chalkboard and then passes it to the second player. The second player writes the second letter of the word on the chalkboard, and so on until the entire word has been spelled. The player who writes the final letter of the word stands up. The first team that has a member standing with a correctly spelled word wins a point. Before beginning play again, the first player of each team moves to the back of the line. The team with the most points at the end of game time wins!

Stop And Go

Reinforce several weeks' worth of spelling words with this partner activity. Write at least 30 spelling words on individual index cards. Also program six index cards with stop signs. To play, a student shuffles the cards and places them facedown on the playing surface. To begin, one player (the "caller") draws a card from the deck and announces the word. He listens carefully as his partner spells the word for him. If a correct spelling is given, he draws another card and reads the word aloud. If an incorrect spelling is given, the caller repeats the word and the two partners spell it together. The caller places the spelled words in a discard pile. Play continues in this manner, until the caller draws a "stop" card. The partners then change positions, and the activity is repeated. Since this game has no winners or losers, students are eager to participate in this spelling review!

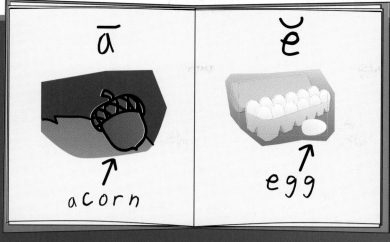

$\bar{a}$

acorn

$\breve{e}$

egg

The Long And The Short Of It

These nifty booklets will encourage students to look for long and short vowels. For each student, staple five 6" x 9" sheets of paper between a folded 9" x 12" sheet of construction paper. To make a booklet, a student writes "Long And Short Vowels" on the front cover. Next she writes each short vowel on the front of a separate page and each long vowel on the back. She then searches through discarded magazines for a picture that contains each vowel. To complete the booklet, she glues each picture to its corresponding page and labels it. Students can use their vowel booklets as a review or as a reference for future vowel activities.

Real-Life Phonics

To reinforce phonetic concepts, try this real-life approach! Ask each student to bring to school a wrapper or an empty box from a food product. Mount the wrappers and boxes on a large sheet of bulletin-board paper. Then use the names of the products to create your phonics lessons. For example, have students brainstorm words with the *ch* sound found in Cheerios® or the *oo* sound found in Kool-Aid®. As students contribute to each discussion, form a list of words from their responses. At the conclusion of each lesson, post each list near its corresponding product. Students are sure to enjoy these nifty alternatives to pencil-and-paper phonics drills.

Phonics Scavenger Hunt

This scavenger-hunt phonics review is sure to receive rave student reviews! After introducing or reviewing several phonics concepts, have students search the classroom or their homes for items that contain the featured sounds. Instruct students to write the words on a sheet of scrap paper. Then have students copy the words from their papers to the corresponding columns on a chart similar to the one shown. For an added challenge, have each student complete a copy of the reproducible on page 167. No doubt students will be on the lookout for phonics everywhere!

bl	cl	pl	fl
blender	clock	plaid	flag
blanket	clothes	plow	float
blue	cleaning supplies	plant	flannel

Alphabetizing Alert

Alphabetizing skills are in the bag with this nifty activity. Program two-inch tagboard squares with different letters of the alphabet, excluding hard-to-find letters such as *q, v, x, y,* and *z.* Then place the resulting cards in a paper lunch sack. Each student, in turn, draws a card. From discarded magazines or newspapers, she cuts three words that begin with her chosen letter and have different second letters. Then the student glues the words in alphabetical order on a 5" x 7" index card. After checking each student's work, enlist students' help in compiling the cards in alphabetical order. If desired, punch the top left corner of the cards and bind them with a metal ring. Then place the cards at a center for students to review.

ABC!

This small-group game proves that three heads are better than one! For each group of three students, label ten index cards with grade-appropriate vocabulary words. Place each set of cards in a resealable plastic bag. To play, give each group of three students a bag. When you say "Go," each group places its cards in alphabetical order as quickly as possible. The first team to complete the activity calls out, "ABC!" To win the round, a group member must read aloud the words on its cards in alphabetical order for verification. If desired, award the winning group with stickers. Repeat the activity daily, making sure that each group gets a new bag of cards.

ABC Classroom

Students will take stock of their classroom with this alphabetical-order activity. Write each letter of the alphabet on chart paper (each letter on a different line). Ask students to name items in the classroom that begin with each letter. Write students' responses beside the corresponding letters. Then have each student select a different letter and write the words listed for that letter in alphabetical order on a sheet of paper. Staple the completed pages in alphabetical order between two construction-paper covers labeled "The ABCs Of Our Classroom." Then place the book in the classroom library for everyone to enjoy.

A apple, alphabet chart, art center
B book, beanbag, bathroom
C closet, computer, chalk, crayons
D desk, door, dictionary
E eraser, egg timer
F fish, friend, flowers, fan
G glue, garbage can
H headphones, handwriting book
I index card, ink pen
J juice box, jar, jackets
K keys, kids
L lights, letters, loud speaker
M math book, map, magnet
N newspaper, number chart
O oval, orange crayon

won't

will not

Contraction Match

This large-group game helps youngsters master contractions lickety-split! For every two students, program an index card with a different contraction; then, for each contraction, label an index card with the words that make up the contraction. Laminate the cards for durability. To play, randomly distribute the game cards. Each student reads the word(s) on his card and searches for the classmate who has the corresponding word(s). When two students discover that their game cards match, they sit down. After each student has found his match, collect and shuffle the cards; then play the game again!

On The Lookout

Encourage students to look for contractions with this activity. Have each student cut ten different contractions from discarded magazines or newspapers. The student then glues the contractions to a sheet of paper. Then, beside each contraction, he writes the two words that make up the contraction. Invite each student to share the contractions he found with his classmates.

Tim

1. she's — she is

2. isn't — is not

3.

can't 4.

Picture-Perfect Compound Words

Puzzling for a different way for students to practice compound words? Then try this center activity. Enlist students' help in making a list of compound words (one for each student) that would be easy to illustrate (see the list on page 163 for ideas). Have each student select a compound word. On the unlined side of an index card, each student draws a picture of each word in the compound word as shown. On the other side, the student writes the compound word. Then the student vertically cuts the card into two puzzle pieces. Collect the puzzle pieces and store them in a resealable plastic bag at a center. A student removes the cards from the bag and matches each compound-word pair. She checks her answers by fitting the pieces together.

sunlight

Synonym Dictionary

Reinforce synonyms with this daily activity. Each morning write a word on a 9" x 12" sheet of drawing paper. Post the paper in a prominent location. Challenge students to brainstorm as many synonyms for the word as possible. Write students' responses under the synonym. Then hole-punch the paper and have a student place it in alphabetical order in a three-ring binder titled "The Synonym Dictionary." Place the dictionary in the writing center for students to use in their writing activities.

run

race
hurry
sprint
dash
speed
flee

Fishing For Antonyms

Two players will be fishing for matching antonyms with this adapted version of Go Fish. Write pairs of antonyms on index cards, one word per card. Laminate the cards for durability; then place the cards in a resealable plastic bag at a center. To begin, one student deals seven cards to himself and seven to the other player; then he places the remaining cards facedown to form a draw pile. Each player places all his matching pairs of antonyms on the table. Player 1 begins by asking Player 2 for an antonym to match one that he is holding. If he receives the match from Player 2, he places the pair on the table and takes another turn. If Player 2 does not have the card Player 1 requested, Player 2 says, "Go fish," and Player 1 draws a card from the pile. If he draws the card he requested, he may lay down the pair and take another turn. If he does not draw a match, he keeps the card and Player 2 takes a turn. Any time a player lays his last card on the table, he takes one card from the draw pile. When the draw pile is gone, the game ends. The player with the most pairs wins the game! The cards can also be programmed for synonyms or homophones.

Helpful Homophone Chart

Help students learn to spell troublesome homophones with this whole-group activity. Make a list of homophones on a sheet of poster board. Have each student select a different word from the list. Then have him illustrate the word on a small square of white paper. Glue each illustration beside its corresponding word. Then post the completed project on a classroom wall. Encourage students to use the list in their writings.

Helpful Homophones

eight — ate
write — right
pair — pear
flower — flour

See the Ready Reference on page 162 for a list of homophones, synonyms, and antonyms.

Suffixes:

-able, -ible, -fy, -ful, -er, -est, -ance, -ence, -ing, -less, -ly, -ment, -ness, -y, -ey, -like, -ion, -sion, -tion

Prefixes:

a-, bi-, de-, extra-, dis-, im-, in-, ir-, non-, pre-, pro-, re-, un-, super-, tele-, over-, mis-

Affix Of The Day

This activity gives each student the opportunity to teach an interesting prefix or suffix to her classmates. Have each student select a prefix or a suffix (see list above for ideas). Then, in a letter sent home, ask parents to assist their children in selecting interesting vocabulary words that incorporate the chosen affixes. Explain that each youngster must be able to say and write her vocabulary word and explain its meaning. As the student presents the word and its definition to the class, copy the student's definition of the word on a sheet of writing paper. Place the paper in a binder behind a prefix or suffix divider. Store the binder at the writing center for students to use as a reference.

Charades, Anyone?

Try an exciting game of charades to help your students understand affixes. Write words with prefixes or suffixes on separate slips of paper and place them in a container. Write the same words on the chalkboard and read them aloud to your students. To begin the game, divide students into two teams. Have one member of Team 1 draw a word from the container and silently act it out. Challenge Team 2 to determine the word from the list on the chalkboard. If Team 2 guesses correctly, erase the word from the board and let a student from Team 2 draw a word and silently act it out for Team 1. If Team 2 guesses incorrectly, invite another student from Team 1 to help his classmate act out the word using words. Play continues with the teams alternating turns until all the words have been mimed. Oh, what fun!

- cheerful
- misspell
- repaint
- unpack
- untie
- jumper
- teacher
- cleaner
- sickness
- quietly
- sadly
- pianist
- artist

PREFIX AND SUFFIX BOOKS

These flip books are guaranteed to help your students uncover many new words! Divide students into small groups and assign each group a different suffix or prefix. Have one student from each group write the assigned affix on either the beginning (if it's the prefix) or the end (if it's the suffix) of a 3" x 9" construction-paper strip. Then have each group brainstorm base words that can combine with the affix. For each group, assign a student to record each base word on a separate 3" x 5" card. After a predetermined amount of time, have each group stack its cards and staple them on the paper strip (as shown) to make words. Ask each group to share its completed flip book with the class; then place the books in the writing center for students to refer to in their writing.

READING

Story Chains

Help your youngsters understand sequencing as they work together to make story chains! Read aloud a favorite children's book. Ask students to brainstorm significant events from the story. List the students' ideas on chart paper. Then divide youngsters into small groups. Have each group member choose an event from the list, write a sentence about it on a 3" x 24" strip of construction paper, and then illustrate it. Ask one student from each group to write the title of the book and the author's name on another strip. Instruct students to sequence their strips and link them together as shown. If time allows, have groups share their chains with their classmates. Encourage youngsters to create additional story chains throughout the year. What a great way to learn about sequencing!

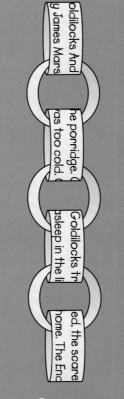

Flip-Book Creations

After reading a story aloud, have students make flip books to learn how to sequence story events. To make a booklet, a student stacks three 8 1/2" x 11" sheets of white paper and holds the pages vertically in front of him. He slides the top sheet up approximately one inch, then repeats with the next sheet. Next he folds the paper thicknesses forward to create six graduated layers. Then he staples the pages close to the fold. Instruct students to write about and illustrate five events from the story in order, beginning with the second page. Have each student write his name and the title of the book on the front cover. No doubt your students will be flipping over sequencing!

One day a fish with many beautiful scales was swimming in the ocean.

Comic-Relief Sequencing

Have youngsters put comic strips in order to reinforce sequencing events. Obtain several comic strips from the Sunday paper. Glue the strips to a sheet of tagboard; then cut the frames apart. For each strip, number the backs of the frames for self-checking. Laminate the frames and store each set in an envelope. Place the envelopes at a learning center in your classroom. A student chooses an envelope and takes out the frames. He sequences the frames and then flips them to check his work. Now that's an idea that will tickle your youngsters' funny bones!

One-Of-A-Kind Pantomimes!

Your youngsters will love acting out the steps of a familiar routine as they learn about sequencing events! Ask each student to think of an everyday activity he participates in, such as brushing his teeth, combing his hair, or getting dressed. Instruct each child to carefully list the steps of his activity in order on a sheet of writing paper. Then have a volunteer pantomime his activity for his classmates. Invite youngsters to guess the student's activity. Repeat the activity with additional volunteers. For added fun, have students cut their sequenced steps into strips and then swap strips with a classmate. Challenge youngsters to put the strips in order and then exchange strips with someone else!

I take out my toothbrush.

I take out the toothpaste.

I brush my teeth.

I put the paste on the brush.

I wet my toothbrush.

Sequencing Seat

Have your youngsters recall the events of a story by playing this sequencing game. To begin, read aloud (or have students independently read) a short passage or story. Invite one youngster to take a seat in a designated chair. Have the student start the game by telling the beginning event of the story; then ask another student to come sit in the chair. The second child then tells the next event from the story; then he asks another student to take his place. Continue to have youngsters tell the events of the story in the same manner until they reach the ending. Throughout the year, play the sequencing game with a variety of story passages and books. Let the game begin!

TV Time!

Invite youngsters to use television tachistoscopes to practice sequencing story events. Duplicate a class supply of the patterns on page 168 onto construction paper. Slit the dotted lines on each television pattern with an X-acto® knife. Then read aloud a story to the class. To make a tachistoscope, a student colors her television pattern and then cuts out the television and the strips. She glues the strips together where indicated. Next she writes the title and the author's name in the first section; then she illustrates the remaining sections with events from the story. To use the tachistoscope, the student inserts the strip into the television as shown and slides the strip to tell the story. For added fun, invite youngsters to program additional strips with their own stories.

Sensational Statements!

This interactive bulletin board is a surefire way to review facts and opinions! To prepare, cover a bulletin board with paper, and add the title "Is It Fact Or Opinion?" Copy either a fact or an opinion onto sentence strips; then staple the strips to the middle of the board. Also label one side of the board "Fact" and the other side "Opinion." Ask youngsters to read the statement on the board and secretly decide whether it is a fact or an opinion. Have each student write his name on a sticky note and post it under the appropriate heading on the board. Reveal the answer and encourage students to discuss the results. Change the statement weekly or monthly to keep youngsters on their toes with facts and opinions!

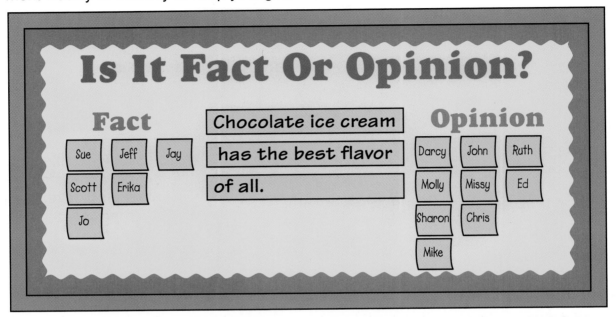

Fact & Opinion Bowl

Reinforce the concepts of fact and opinion with this one-of-a-kind idea! After reviewing the difference between a fact and an opinion, announce a topic, such as pets or toys, to students. Have each student write a fact and her opinion about the topic on separate index cards. Place the cards in a large bowl or container. Have a student draw a card from the bowl and read it aloud to his classmates. Challenge youngsters to decide whether the student has read a fact or an opinion. Select different students to repeat the activity until all the cards have been drawn. Throughout the year, assign new topics to encourage youngsters to think of additional facts and opinions.

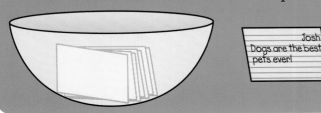

Fact Or Opinion Flash!

Your students will enjoy the excitement of playing a game of "Fact-Or-Opinion Flash!" Instruct students to write "Fact" and "Opinion" on two separate cards and then glue each card to a craft stick. To play the game, announce a statement. Instruct youngsters to decide whether the statement is a fact or an opinion, then flash the appropriate card. As a class, count the number of Fact and Opinion cards displayed. Then tell your students the answer and involve them in a discussion about the results. Extend the lesson by having students write their own facts or opinions. Collect the sentences; then use them to play the game again.

Tabletop Tents

Teach youngsters about cause and effect as they make these tabletop tents. Ask students to stand at their seats if they have a favorite story; then ask them why they are standing. Tell them that the reason they are standing is that they responded to a question. The teacher asked a question, which *caused* them to respond. The *effect* was that the students stood up at their seats. Ask students to brainstorm additional examples of cause and effect. Write the students' responses on the chalkboard; then ask each child to select one from the list. To make a tent, a youngster folds a sheet of construction paper lengthwise into fourths. He glues the first section atop the last section to create a tent like the one shown. Next he writes "cause" on one side of the tent and "effect" on the other side; then he illustrates a picture for each one. Invite youngsters to share their tents with their classmates. Then display the tents on a table to create a cause-and-effect village.

Drawing-Conclusions Trip

Have youngsters take imaginary trips to learn about drawing conclusions. Create an activity sheet similar to the one shown; then duplicate the sheet for every student. Ask each student to think of a special place she would like to take a trip, keeping it a secret. Have her list words and ideas that describe her place on her sheet. Then have student volunteers read aloud their clues to their classmates. Students will enjoy trying to guess the destinations of their classmates' trips!

Drawing-Conclusions Trip

Things To Be Packed	Length Of Travel And Transportation
	Weather/Temperature

Mystery Items

Challenge your youngsters to guess mystery items as they practice drawing conclusions. Select an item and place it in a shoebox. Write a number of clues about the item on separate cards. Each day have a student read a clue aloud to the class. After all the clues have been read, have each student write his guess and his name on a slip of paper. Collect the papers, and reveal the mystery item. Provide time for students to discuss their answers. Spotlight a different mystery item each week to aid in your students' understanding of drawing conclusions!

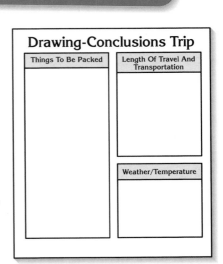

Details, Details, Details!

This idea is sure to help students recall details from a story! To begin, divide your class into groups of five students. In each group, assign each student a different part of the story: characters, setting, beginning, middle, or end. After reading the story aloud, have students recall details about their assigned story parts with their group members; then, as a class, compare the details that were remembered. If desired, further challenge each group to organize its information on a class chart. Without a doubt, this is a great way to learn about details!

Spin Up A Great Story!

Make learning story parts fun by playing this nifty game! To prepare, duplicate four copies of the spinner from page 169 onto construction paper. Cut out each spinner. Then use a brad to attach a large paper clip to the middle of each spinner as shown. Next divide your students into four groups. Read a story aloud, or have each group read one together. Distribute the spinners to the groups. In turn, have each group member rotate the paper clip on the spinner and recall details from the selected story part. Now let's start spinning!

Posters With Character

Invite your youngsters to create these posters with character! After sharing a favorite story, ask students to recall the names of the characters. List students' responses on the chalkboard. Next have each student select a character from the list and draw a picture of the character on a large sheet of construction paper. Tell the student to write the character's name and phrases or words to describe the character around the illustration. Invite youngsters to share their character posters with their classmates. Then display the posters around the room for all to enjoy!

HIGH-FLYING STORIES!

Your students will fly into story mapping with this one-of-a-kind idea! To prepare, duplicate a class supply of the airplane pattern on page 170 onto construction paper. After sharing a story, provide each student with an airplane pattern. Have her write the title and author of the story on the wing of her airplane, then color the plane and cut it out. Next she cuts four cloud shapes from white construction paper and labels them with these headings: "Characters," "Setting," "Problem," and "Solution." Then she writes a description about each one. Next she tapes one end of a 12-inch length of yarn to the tail of her plane. She then tapes each cloud to the yarn behind the plane as shown. Mount the planes on the walls for a classroom that is sure to soar!

Real Or Make-Believe?

Use this idea to help your youngsters distinguish reality from fantasy. To begin, tell students that something is *real* when it can actually happen and that something is *fantasy* (make-believe) when it cannot really happen. Then assign the class a topic of choice. Have each student write four real sentences and one make-believe sentence about the topic on a large index card. Collect the cards and place them in a container. Have a student randomly select a card and read the sentences aloud to his classmates. Challenge students to guess which sentence is make-believe. Then select another student to draw a card. Continue in the same manner until every card has been read aloud. Repeat the activity with various topics throughout the year.

Ryan
1. Cats can purr.
2. Cats can meow.
3. Cats like to talk.
4. Some chase mice.
5. Most cats have four legs and a tail.

Reading Records

Have your students make predictions and organize information from a story. Label three sheets of chart paper with these headings: "Characters," "Story Events," and "New Words." Divide your students into three groups; then give each group a programmed sheet of chart paper. After reading a chosen story aloud, have each group record ideas about its assigned topic on its paper. If desired, have the groups illustrate the information on their sheets. Invite youngsters to share their sheets with their classmates.

Homophones

Homophones are words that sound alike but have different spellings and meanings.

ate—eight	feat—feet	made—maid	soar—sore
be—bee	flour—flower	male—mail	some—sum
bear—bare	forth—fourth	meat—meet	son—sun
beet—beat	great—grate	one—won	stare—stair
blew—blue	groan—grown	pail—pale	steak—stake
bored—board	hair—hare	pair—pear	tail—tale
break—brake	hear—here	pane—pain	there—their
buy—by—bye	hole—whole	piece—peace	through—threw
cell—sell	hour—our	plane—plain	to—too—two
cents—scents—sense	knead—need	red—read	wait—weight
course—coarse	knew—new	road—rode	waste—waist
creak—creek	knight—night	sale—sail	way—weigh
deer—dear	knot—not	sea—see	week—weak
do—dew	know—no	sew—so	would—wood
eye—I	knows—nose	sight—site	write—right

Synonyms

Synonyms are words that have similar meanings.

above—over	end—finish	jog—run	small—little
afraid—scared	false—untrue	jump—leap	soggy—wet
aid—help	fast—quick	keep—save	story—tale
alike—same	find—discover	kind—nice	stroll—walk
angry—mad	fix—repair	late—tardy	throw—toss
auto—car	friend—pal	look—see	
begin—start	glad—happy	loud—noisy	
below—under	go—leave	neat—tidy	
big—large	grin—smile	rip—tear	
chilly—cold	hard—difficult	road—street	
correct—right	home—house	shout—yell	
cry—weep	hot—warm	skinny—thin	

Antonyms

Antonyms are words that have opposite meanings.

above—below	cold—hot	float—sink	noisy—quiet
add—subtract	come—go	forget—remember	old—new
alike—different	cry—laugh	found—lost	over—under
asleep—awake	day—night	frown—smile	peace—war
backward—forward	down—up	give—take	play—work
bad—good	dry—wet	happy—sad	polite—rude
beautiful—ugly	early—late	hard—soft	poor—rich
begin—end	enemy—friend	hot—cold	right—wrong
big—small	false—true	in—out	rough—smooth
buy—sell	fancy—plain	left—right	save—spend
catch—throw	fast—slow	lose—win	short—tall
clean—dirty	fat—thin	mean—nice	sour—sweet
close—open	few—many	more—less	whisper—yell

Compound Words

afternoon	cowgirl	football	mailman	seashore	toothache
airline	cupboard	footprint	mealtime	seesaw	toothbrush
airplane	cupcake	friendship	milkman	shipwreck	treetop
anybody	daybreak	gentleman	milkshake	shoebox	underground
anyone	daydream	gingerbread	moonbeam	sidewalk	underline
anything	daylight	goldfish	moonlight	skateboard	understand
anyway	doghouse	grandfather	motorboat	smokestack	underwear
anywhere	dollhouse	grandmother	motorcycle	snowball	upright
armchair	doorbell	grapefruit	mousetrap	snowflake	wallpaper
artwork	doorknob	grasshopper	necklace	snowman	washcloth
ballpark	doormat	greenhouse	necktie	somebody	watchman
bareback	doorway	groundhog	newspaper	someday	waterfall
barnyard	doughnut	hairbrush	nighttime	someone	watermelon
baseball	downhill	haircut	nobody	something	weekend
basketball	downstairs	halfway	notebook	somewhere	whatever
bathrobe	downtown	handshake	outdoors	spaceship	wheelbarrow
bathroom	driftwood	headache	outline	springtime	whenever
bathtub	driveway	headband	outside	stagecoach	whirlwind
bedroom	drugstore	headfirst	overall	stairway	wildlife
bedspread	drumstick	headlight	overcome	starfish	windmill
bedtime	eardrum	headline	overlook	starlight	windshield
beehive	earring	headrest	overtime	steamroller	wintertime
birdbath	earthquake	headstand	paintbrush	stopwatch	within
birdhouse	eggplant	highchair	pancake	storeroom	without
birthday	eggshell	hillside	patchwork	storybook	woodland
blackboard	evergreen	homemade	peanut	strawberry	worthwhile
blacksmith	everybody	homework	pillowcase	suitcase	yourself
bluebird	everyone	hopscotch	playground	summertime	
boxcar	everything	horseback	pocketbook	sunburn	
breakfast	everywhere	horsefly	policeman	sundown	
broomstick	eyeball	horseshoe	popcorn	sunflower	
butterball	eyebrow	hourglass	postman	sunlight	
buttercup	eyelash	houseboat	quarterback	sunrise	
butterfly	eyelid	household	rainbow	sunset	
campfire	farmland	housewife	raincoat	sunshine	
campground	fingernail	hubcap	raindrop	sweatshirt	
cannot	firecracker	indoor	rattlesnake	sweetheart	
cardboard	firefighter	inside	rowboat	swordfish	
catbird	firefly	into	runway	tablecloth	
catfish	fireman	junkyard	sailboat	tablespoon	
cattail	fireplace	keyboard	salesman	taillight	
chalkboard	firewood	ladybug	sandpaper	teacup	
cobweb	fireworks	landmark	scarecrow	teamwork	
copycat	fishbowl	lifetime	schoolhouse	teapot	
cornbread	fisherman	lighthouse	schoolyard	teaspoon	
corncob	flagpole	lookout	scrapbook	textbook	
cornmeal	flashlight	lunchroom	seahorse	thumbtack	
cowboy	flowerpot	mailbox	seashell	toadstool	

Plurals

- The plural of most nouns is formed by adding *s*.
  apple—apples
  cat—cats

- Nouns ending with *ch, sh, s, x,* or *z* are made plural by adding *es* to the singular noun.
  bench—benches
  dish—dishes
  glass—glasses
  fox—foxes
  buzz—buzzes

- Most nouns ending with *o* preceded with a vowel are made plural by adding *s*.
  zoo—zoos
  stereo—stereos

- Most nouns ending with *o* preceded with a consonant are made plural by adding *es*.
  hero—heroes

- Most nouns that end with a consonant followed by *y* are made plural by changing the *y* to *i* and adding *es*.
  fly—flies

- Most nouns that end with a vowel followed by *y* are made plural by adding *s*.
  key—keys

- Most nouns ending with *f* or *fe* are made plural by adding *s* if the sound of *f* is still heard in the plural.
  chief—chiefs

- If the *v* sound is heard in the plural, change the *f* to *v* and add *es* to form the plural.
  knife—knives
  wolf—wolves

Contractions

A contraction is a shortened form of a single word or word pair. An apostrophe is used to show where a letter or letters have been omitted to create the shortened form.

words with "am"
I am	I'm

words with "are"
they are	they're
we are	we're
you are	you're

words with "has"
he has	he's
it has	it's
she has	she's
what has	what's
where has	where's
who has	who's

words with "is"
he is	he's
it is	it's
she is	she's
that is	that's
there is	there's
what is	what's
where is	where's
who is	who's

words with "have"
I have	I've
they have	they've
you have	you've
we have	we've

words with "not"
are not	aren't
cannot	can't
could not	couldn't
did not	didn't
do not	don't
does not	doesn't
had not	hadn't
have not	haven't
has not	hasn't
is not	isn't
must not	mustn't
should not	shouldn't
was not	wasn't
were not	weren't
will not	won't
would not	wouldn't

words with "us"
let us	let's

words with "will"
he will	he'll
I will	I'll
she will	she'll
they will	they'll
we will	we'll
you will	you'll

words with "would"
he would	he'd
I would	I'd
she would	she'd
they would	they'd
who would	who'd
you would	you'd

Capitalization Rules

The following items should always be capitalized:

- **the first word in a sentence**
  Examples: The girl went to the store.
  When does the movie begin?
  Shut the door, please.

- **proper nouns**
  — holidays, weekdays, months, special days
  — cities, countries, states, counties
  — names, titles, initials
  — streets, boulevards, buildings, parks
  Examples: Florida
            Dr. J. L. Washington
            Main Street

- **the pronoun *I***
  Example: Should I bring a sweater?

- **the greeting and closing of a friendly letter**
  Examples: Dear John,
  Your friend,
  Sincerely,

- **titles of books, magazines, newspapers, poems, and songs**
  Examples: <u>Charlotte's Web</u>
  <u>Ranger Rick</u>®

- **abbreviations**
  Examples: P.T.A.   M.D.   Ph.D.

Punctuation Rules

1. **Use a period...**
   - **at the end of declarative sentences (statements) and imperative sentences (commands).**
     Examples: I like ice cream.
     Bring me a spoon.

   - **after each part of an abbreviation or a person's initials.**
     Examples: Mr. Pierson
     C. A. Weaver

2. **Use a question mark at the end of interrogative sentences (questions).**
   Example: Where is the office?

3. **Use an exclamation point to express strong feeling or emotion.**
   Examples: Stop that!
   Watch out!

4. **Use quotation marks...**
   - **to show a direct quote.**
     Example: Chris said, "I am going to play golf tomorrow."

   - **to show titles of short poems, stories, or songs.**
     Example: "Row, Row, Row Your Boat"

5. **Use an apostrophe...**
   - **to show omission of letters in contractions.**
     Examples: can't
     shouldn't
     didn't

   - **to show possession.**
     Example: Crystal's purse is on the table.

6. **Use a comma...**
   - **to separate items in a date or an address.**
     Examples: February 17, 1960
     Tampa, Florida

   - **after a greeting or closing of a letter.**
     Examples: Dear Mike,
     Sincerely,

   - **to separate words in a series.**
     Example: He found rocks, shells, and feathers.

   - **with nouns of direct address.**
     Example: Robert, where are you going?

7. **Underline the titles of books, plays, magazines, movies, television shows, long poems, and visual works of art.**
   Example: <u>Annie</u>

Vowel Combinations

au	**oi**	**ow**	**oy**	**oa**	**ee**	**oo**
taught	oil	low	boy	boat	see	cook
haul	choice	grow	toy	coat	three	good
because	point	know	joy	road	keep	foot
launch	noise	snow	royal	soap	sleep	book
vault	join	yellow	cowboy	float	green	cookie
caught	hoist	show	enjoy	oak	bee	shook
haunt	coin	tow	oyster	moan	queen	stood
	spoil	throw	convoy	croak	sneeze	took
aw			loyal	toad	sheet	
raw	**ou**	**ea**				**ai**
saw	cloud	eat		**ow**	**oo**	rain
draw	blouse	please	**ay**	town	bloom	wait
law	ground	beach	day	brown	moon	mail
yawn	house	meat	clay	now	food	paint
hawk	about	team	play	how	zoo	snail
jaw	scout	clean	way	cow	school	raise
claw	mountain	bean	say	clown	soon	drain
	bounce	deal	stay	flower	hoop	pain
			away	growl	scoop	stair
			spray		smooth	
			tray			

R-Controlled Vowels

ir	**ar**	**er**	**or**	**ur**
bird	farm	fern	corn	church
girl	car	zipper	horse	nurse
skirt	barn	her	stork	turkey
shirt	shark	germ	torch	turtle
circle	star	hammer	horn	hurt
fir	harp	clerk	storm	burn
third	dart	person	sport	curve

Consonant Digraphs

sh	**ch**	**th**	**wh**	**wr**	**qu**	**kn**
shine	chair	thief	whale	wrap	quack	knee
shark	chain	thimble	white	wreath	quake	kneel
sheep	cheese	thumb	wheel	wrench	quart	knew
sharp	chicken	third	whistle	wrinkle	quick	knife
shoe	check	thick	what	wrong	question	knit
shirt	church	thirteen	which	write	quiet	knock
shell	bench	teeth	wheat	wrote	quit	knot
brush	lunch	bath	whip	wrist		know
dish	inch	wreath	when			
crash	each	mouth	where			
fish	much	math				

On The Lookout

Look through newspapers or magazines for words that contain the sounds shown below.
Cut out each word and paste it in the correct column.

Vol. XXI **In The News** 25 cents		
ai	**ay**	**ea**
ee	**oa**	**oo**
sh	**th**	**wh**

1998 The Education Center, Inc. • *The Mailbox® Superbook* • *Grade 2* • TEC451

Patterns

Use the television and the strips with "TV Time!" on page 157.

Glue here.

1998 The Education Center, Inc. • *The Mailbox® Superbook • Grade 2* • TEC451

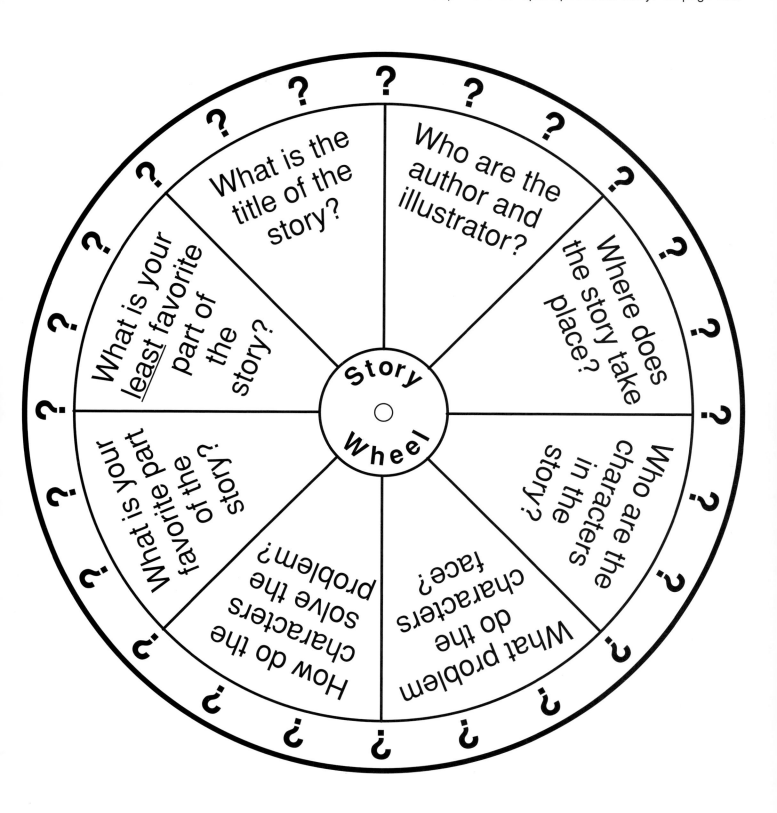

Story Wheel

What is the title of the story?

Who are the author and illustrator?

Where does the story take place?

Who are the characters in the story?

What problem do the characters face?

How do the characters solve the problem?

What is your favorite part of the story?

What is your least favorite part of the story?

Pattern

Use with "High-Flying Stories!" on page 161.

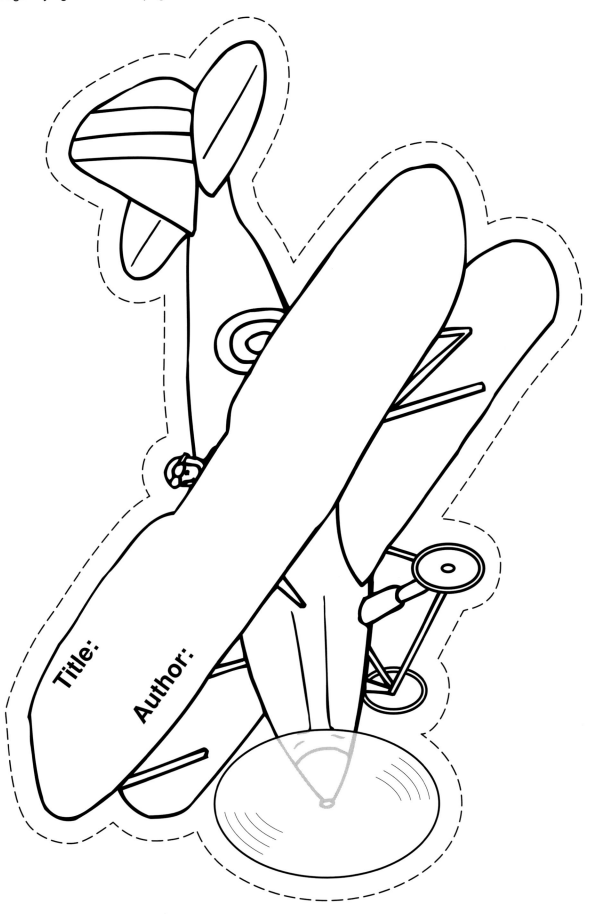

Title:

Author:

WRITING

THE JOY OF JOURNALS

Begin the school year by having your students write, write, write! Include on your school supply list a notebook for each student. Have the students keep the notebooks at their desks to use as journals. Then begin each day by writing a journal assignment on the chalkboard. A typical assignment might be, "Today there is a chance for rain. Do you like rainy days? Write a journal entry explaining your answer." By the time students have completed their assignments, you'll be finished with your morning routine.

I like rainy days because I get to use my umbrella. It is nice to see the rain fall from the sky. Rain helps trees and flowers grow. I like rain.

POSITIVE PONDERINGS

Use the last few minutes of each day as a time for students to reflect on the good things that happened at school. Ask each student to write a sentence or two about positive feedback he received about his work, a nice thing someone said or did for him, or a way he was helpful to another student. If time allows, ask student volunteers to share their entries. You'll end the day in a positive way, and students will be eager to share the good things about their day with their parents.

THE CLASSROOM JOURNAL

Model journal-writing techniques with your class by keeping a big-book account of weekly activities. At the end of each week, ask students to recall the events of the past few days—what they learned, class birthdays, visitors, and other special happenings. List the responses on the chalkboard. After a list has been generated, transfer each event to chart paper in chronological order and in the form of a complete sentence. Use transition words—such as *first, next, then,* and *last*—to help with the flow of ideas. Then have your students read the completed entry aloud with you. This is a good way to model effective writing with the added bonus of having a weekly account of your school year.

This has been an exciting week! First we had a visitor from the fire department. Then we had class pictures taken. On the last day of the week we used fingerpaint.

SECRET-PAL JOURNALS

Set the stage for writing excitement with secret-pal journals! Arrange with another teacher to buddy up her class with your class for this writing activity. Without revealing identities to the students, pair each child in your class with a student in the other classroom. Instruct each student to write a question in his journal, such as "Do you have any pets?" or "What is your favorite book?" Gather your students' journals and trade them with those from the other class. Provide time for each student to answer the question in his secret pal's journal and include a question of his own before you return the journals to their original owners. Continue the secret-pal activity for the remainder of the grading period; then have a pal-revealing celebration in which each set of pals discovers his writing partner's identity. You may decide to let the pals continue writing to each other, or switch to a new set of secret pals for another round of journal-writing fun.

ALL ABOUT ME

If the thought of journal writing is a little overwhelming to your students, begin the writing process by providing topics that are personal and familiar. Twice a week, have your students write about an assigned topic from the list below. The students will feel more comfortable writing about themselves and their own experiences. Keep each child's completed papers in a separate folder. At the end of the semester, help each student compile her journal pages into a booklet. Provide construction-paper covers for the booklet, and have the student add the title "All About Me." These booklets will be a treasured keepsake when displayed at Open House, and they will serve as good journal-writing practice for students.

 Tell about your family.

 Describe your favorite meal.

 List the things in your room.

 Write about a special toy.

 Tell about a friend of yours.

 Describe your favorite place to go.

 Share a story about a vacation or trip.

 Tell about your pet or a pet you would like to have.

 List some of your favorites (color, food, TV show, book).

Who? the dog
What? chased a cat
Where? up a tree
When? yesterday
Why? because it was in
the yard

SUPER SENTENCES

Guide your students into writing super sentences with a simple illustration and the five *W*s. Display a picture large enough for students to view easily. On the chalkboard, write the words *who, what, where, when,* and *why*. Explain that when these words are used to ask questions about the picture, the answers can help in writing a super sentence that tells about the picture. Model the technique using the example shown at the left. Then display a different picture and have each student try his hand at using the five *W*s to write a sentence about it. For additional reinforcement, encourage student volunteers to share their sentences with the class. When students are familiar with the technique, have them use their own drawings as the basis for super sentences. Before long your students will be able to write super sentences for science, social studies, and other writing activities. (Note: A reference of synonyms for commonly used words is provided on page 184. Share the list with your students to further improve their sentence writing.)

STORY DICTATION

Provide individual attention to each student while incorporating reading and writing practice. While your class is working independently on a writing assignment, call one student to the classroom computer and have her dictate a story to you. After you type each sentence, have the student read it back to you. Remind the student that the completed story does not have to be lengthy, but it should contain a beginning, a middle, and an end. Print out the completed story for the student to illustrate. Then call additional students to dictate as time allows, making sure you give each student an opportunity to dictate once during the week. The children will enjoy the one-on-one attention, and you will have the opportunity to individualize a brief reading and writing lesson for each student.

THE AUTHORS' CORNER

Show off student work with a special area in your classroom for displaying student writing. Create a display with a 9" x 12" sheet of colored construction paper for each student in the class. Label the top of each paper with a student's name. As a child completes a final copy of her story, attach it to her sheet of paper on the display. The other students will enjoy reading their classmates' work, and you will have a visual reminder of which students need to finish rough drafts in a more timely manner.

Alicia

Saturday we took a trip to my grandma's house. She lives in the country. Her house is on a farm. She has two horses and six chickens. My grandma let me ride a horse. I helped her feed the chickens. After a day at Grandma's house, we went home. The End

PREWRITING PLAN

Are your students having trouble getting started with story writing? Provide each student with two copies of the prewriting form on page 186. Initially use the form as a whole-group activity. Direct students, as a group, to decide on a topic for a story and write it in the Topic Web on one copy of their forms. Have students brainstorm descriptive and related words for the topic and write them on the blanks around the topic. Next have students think of possible characters and settings for the story, and add that information to the form. Finally have students write topic sentences for the beginning, middle, and end of the story.

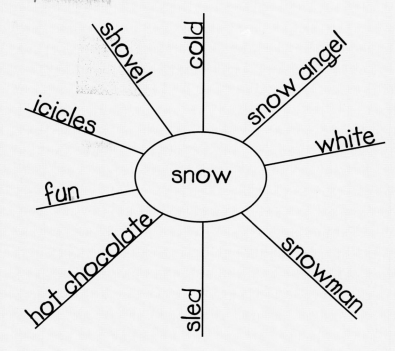

Step 1: Brainstorm

shovel · cold · snow angel · white · snowman · sled · hot chocolate · fun · icicles

snow

As students become accustomed to putting their writing plan on paper, have them complete their second forms individually. Provide writing paper for students to use in transferring the information on their pre-writing forms into story format. Remind students that their planning sheets are for generating ideas, and the final story may differ slightly from the original plan. For a final touch, distribute a sheet of drawing paper to each student so that he can illustrate his story. Invite students to share their completed works with the class, or display them for students to read during free time.

EVERY PICTURE TELLS A STORY

This story-starter activity will inspire students to use their imaginations! Label four brown paper bags, each with one of the following categories: people, places, animals, and objects. Have students cut out pictures from discarded magazines and place them in the corresponding bags. After a class supply of each type of picture has been collected, have each student randomly select a picture from each bag. Next have each student glue his pictures to a sheet of construction paper; then have the student write a story incorporating the pictures into the story line. Display the pictures and completed stories on a bulletin board or in the Authors' Corner described on page 174.

people

places

animals

objects

THE CLUE BOX

Use a favorite class event—show-and-tell—to launch a daily writing activity. All you need to start the activity is a sturdy, easy-to-carry box (a hat box works well) and an object to place inside. (If desired, use an object relating to a current unit of study or a seasonally appropriate item.) Without the students observing you, place the object in the box. Write three clues about the object on an index card, listing the most general clue first. Present the box to your students and read the clues aloud. The first student to identify the object gets to take the box home. Inside the empty box, put a note to the student's parents explaining that their child is to select an object to place in the box and write three clues about it. Provide time during the following day for the student to read her clues to the class. The classmate who identifies the object gets to take the box home that night. Continue the activity until each student has had an opportunity to present the clue box. Students will have so much fun taking the box home that they won't realize they're using deductive-reasoning, public-speaking, and sentence-writing skills!

1. Every time you look at this, you see something different.

2. You have one at home.

3. It reflects light.

AND THEN WHAT HAPPENED?

Provide an opportunity for writing as you encourage students to use prediction skills. Choose a short story to read to the class, but stop before reading the ending. Ask students to imagine what might happen in the conclusion. Distribute a sheet of writing paper to each student, and instruct her to write a logical ending for the story. Have student volunteers share their endings with the class before you read the original ending to the class. Ask students to evaluate the different endings—their favorite may be one written by a classmate instead of the story's original author!

A LITTLE FUNNY BUSINESS

Look to the comics section for a writing activity guaranteed to tickle the funny bone. Cut out a comic strip from the Sunday paper. Use correction fluid to remove the original dialogue from the speech bubbles; then enlarge the comic strip on a copy machine and duplicate a class supply. Distribute a copy to each pair of students. Instruct the partners to create a new dialogue for the comic. Remind students to use context clues as they write text to match the cartoon pictures. Have students meet in small groups to share their completed comic strips. Repeat the activity once a week with a new comic. See you in the funny papers!

Use a picture prompt to introduce the concept of a paragraph—it will reinforce the main idea and allow students to focus on a familiar topic for writing. Select a page from a coloring book that features two characters and a simple background. Duplicate a class supply. Provide time for each student to color his page; then have him think about the objects in his picture. Next distribute a sheet of writing paper to each student, and have him write a paragraph about the picture using the following formula:

- Write one sentence identifying the characters and the setting of the picture.
- Write one sentence about the first character.
- Write one sentence about the second character.
- Write one sentence about the setting.
- Write one sentence telling how the picture makes you feel.

By using this formula, the student has a simple way to develop the topic sentence, supporting details, and summary sentence. Use the completed writing samples to point out each of these elements of a paragraph. Your students will have a clear picture of what a paragraph is all about!

PICTURE THIS!

Use students' artwork to inspire creative writing. Distribute a sheet of drawing paper to each student. Have her fold down a one-inch section across the top of her paper as shown. Instruct the student to draw a picture of a seasonal character—such as a scarecrow, an elf, or a leprechaun—on the paper. Encourage her to add several details and colors to her illustration. Have her decide on a name for her character and write it under the folded section so the name is hidden from view. Next provide each student with a sheet of writing paper, and instruct her to write a paragraph describing and naming the character in her picture. Display the completed drawings and paragraphs on a bulletin board. The class will have fun reading each paragraph and trying to match it to one of the illustrated characters. To check their guesses, the students flip up the folded section on each drawing to reveal the character's name. This descriptive-writing exercise will also promote the use of context clues as students match the paragraphs to the pictures!

LUCKY LOUiE

FISH STORIES

Children love to enhance the ordinary—why not capitalize on this to develop imaginative sentences? Begin by discussing the concept of exaggeration; then explain that some exaggerated tales are called fish stories because of the way fishermen may enhance tales about the size of fish they catch. Next have your students complete some of the sentences below with an exaggerated idea. Then provide each student with a copy of the fish pattern on page 187. Instruct the student to copy on her pattern a sentence starter from the list below and then complete the sentence with an exaggerated idea. Finally have students color and cut out their fish patterns. Staple the fish stories onto a bulletin board covered with blue bulletin-board paper. Now who told the biggest fish story in the class?

- It was thundering so loudly that...
- The quarterback threw the ball so far that...
- The kangaroo jumped so high that...
- The bird flew so fast that...
- It was so cold that...
- The stars were so bright that...
- The sun was so hot that...
- It rained so hard that...
- The opera singer hit a note so high that...
- I was so tired that...

The kangaroo jumped so high that it bumped its head on the moon.

I was so tired that I fell asleep on the roller coaster.

It rained so hard that the Sahara Desert turned into the Sahara Ocean.

INFORMATIVE WRITING

Introduce your students to informative writing with this class project that enhances any unit of study. Announce a general topic for writing, such as rain forests or weather. On the chalkboard, write a student-generated list of words that relate to the topic. Have each student select a word from the list and use complete sentences to tell three things about it. If desired, have him add an illustration to his page. Enlist students' help in arranging the completed papers in alphabetical order according to their topic words. Add a construction-paper cover and bind the pages into a booklet. The result will be a classroom dictionary of words about your unit of study. Your students will be so proud of their reference writing!

wind

Wind is moving air. It can be gentle. It can also be dangerous.

rain

Rain falls from the clouds. It makes puddles. Plants need rain.

Ice cream is good to eat. **There are lots of flavors.** You can add different toppings. I like vanilla with chocolate sprinkles on top.

ROUND-ROBIN WRITING

Do your students ever claim that they can't think of anything to write about? Try round-robin writing to help keep the ideas flowing. Distribute a sheet of writing paper to each student and instruct her to write a topic sentence on the page. (You can provide topic sentences for students to copy, or if appropriate, have them develop sentences on their own.) Have each student then pass her paper to the classmate sitting to her right. Each student adds a related sentence to the new paper before passing it again to the right. Continue having students pass the papers, adding new sentences until five or six sentences are written on each page. Provide time for each student to read the paper she ends up with. Students will enjoy hearing the completed paragraphs developed from their original topic sentences in this open exchange of ideas!

Positively POETIC

Poetry provides an opportunity for students to use creative expression and to enhance their oral and written vocabulary. Although children are most familiar with rhyming poetry, there are many other types of poetic styles that are easier for young writers to compose. Have each student try her hand at writing several of the different types of poems described on pages 180 and 181. If desired, distribute colored copies of the writing paper on page 188 for students to write their poems on. (Note: A reference of additional types of poems and writing devices can be found on page 185.)

ACROSTIC POEMS

Build vocabulary and reinforce description words with acrostic poetry. Announce a topic, such as dinosaurs, rainbows, or firefighters. Have each student write the topic on his paper vertically. Instruct him to use each letter in the word for the initial letter of an adjective or a phrase that describes the topic.

D angerous
I nteresting
N o longer alive
O utrageous lizards
S o big!
A ll kinds
U nusual animals
R oar!
S earched for food

THE FIVE *WS*

A simple and fun poem for children to write is the Five *W*s verse. Each line of this poem answers one of the five *W*s of questioning: *who, what, where, when,* and *why.* Brainstorm a list of topics with your class; then model the poem as follows:

Who is the subject?
What does he do?
Where does he do it?
When does he do it?
Why does he do it?

The puppy
Chases his tail
In the yard
Every morning
Because he's silly!

SHAPE POEMS

Even the most reluctant poets will enjoy writing shape poetry! In a shape poem, words are written around the outline of a picture of the subject. The words may define, describe, or analyze the subject. Duplicate copies of a simple shape, or provide a stencil for each student to trace on her paper. Then encourage your young poets to list words about the subject around its outline.

DIAMANTE POEMS

Reinforce the parts of speech with this seven-line diamond-shaped poem. The student selects a topic, then completes the poem with related information in this format:

Line 1: topic (noun)
Line 2: two adjectives
Line 3: three action words
Line 4: a four-word phrase
Line 5: three action words
Line 6: two adjectives
Line 7: rename the topic

Ants
Black, red
Running, building, digging
Always in a hurry
Moving, lifting, crawling
Tiny, busy
Ants

SYLLABLE CINQUAINS

Can your students write a poem syllable by syllable? In a syllable cinquain, the student creates a five-line poem using a determined number of syllables in each line. Model the format of a syllable cinquain as follows:

Line 1: Title	2 syllables	Sunshine
Line 2: Description of title	4 syllables	Rays of bright light
Line 3: Action about the title	6 syllables	Making the earth so warm
Line 4: Feeling about the title	8 syllables	Sunny days make me feel happy
Line 5: Synonym for the title	2 syllables	Golden

SENSORY POEMS

Students combine the five senses with similes and metaphors to create this expressive type of poetry. Have your students brainstorm a list of possible topics while you record their responses on the board. Instruct each student to select a topic and complete the following sentences to create a "sense-sational" verse.

Topic

A (topic) looks as _____ as _____.
A (topic) sounds as _____ as _____.
A (topic) smells as _____ as _____.
A (topic) tastes as _____ as _____.
A (topic) feels as _____ as _____.
A (topic) is _____.

Lemon
A lemon looks as yellow as a football.
A lemon sounds as quiet as a mouse.
A lemon smells as fresh as clean sheets.
A lemon taste as sour as a pickle.
A lemon feels as nervous as a rock.
A lemon is a mystery.

BOOKMAKING BONANZA

Bookmaking is the perfect way for students to put their writing skills to use! Books can be completed during a single lesson, or can be extended as a weeklong project. Gather a variety of writing papers and materials; then let your students' creativity take hold as they produce examples of the following types of books.

ALPHABET BOOKS

These simple booklets are perfect for a small-group project. Place four to six students in a group, and assign each child several different letters of the alphabet, so that all 26 letters are assigned in each group. Provide each group with pencils, markers, and copies of the reproducible on page 189. Instruct each student to complete a page for each of his assigned letters. The page should include the assigned letter, a drawing that begins with the letter, and a sentence telling about the drawing. Assist each group in arranging the completed pages in alphabetical order. Have each group design construction-paper covers for its book, then staple the compiled papers between the covers. If desired, have your students share their completed books with children in a younger grade.

COUNTING BOOKS

One, two, buckle my shoe…three, four, make counting books galore! Reinforce number patterns with these fun-to-make booklets. Begin the project by designating a number pattern for students to use in creating their counting booklets. Next have each student select a topic for counting, such as circus performers, ocean animals, or bakery treats. Instruct each student to create the first page for her booklet by writing the first number of the pattern at the top of the page and drawing pictures in the corresponding amount. Also have her write a sentence about the pictures at the bottom of the page. Continue the procedure for each number in the pattern. Have each student arrange her finished pages in sequential order and staple them between tagboard covers. Provide time for students to illustrate their covers with drawings that relate to their counting themes. Seven, eight, counting books are great!

RIDDLE BOOKS

What do you get when you cross a writing project with a guessing game? Riddle books! To make these unique books, each student will need six sheets of construction paper stapled together, five letter-size envelopes, five small index cards, glue, and crayons or markers. Instruct each student to decorate his first sheet of paper as the cover for his riddle book. Then, on each following page, have the student write a riddle at the top of the paper and glue an envelope to the bottom of the page as shown. Instruct him to write the answer to the riddle on an index card and place it in the unsealed envelope. Student volunteers will love reading their riddles to the class and having their friends guess the answers before removing the cards to show the correct responses.

Why does a hummingbird hum?

He doesn't know the words.

MEMORY BOOKS

Create a lasting keepsake of each child's second-grade year with these individual memory books. Each time a special event occurs at school, have each student complete a copy of the reproducible on page 190. The student records the date, describes the event, and creates a sentence and illustration to help him remember the event. Collect the completed papers and store them in folders labeled with the students' names. At the end of the year, distribute the folders to the students. Provide materials for each student to decorate his folder to use as a booklet cover. Help each student sequence his pages in chronological order and staple them inside the cover. What a nice keepsake of field trips, guest speakers, special programs, and other favorite events of second grade!

Synonyms For Commonly Used Words

Bad—despicable, disagreeable, evil, harmful, horrible, nasty, rotten, spoiled, unpleasant, wicked, wrong

Beautiful—attractive, elegant, glorious, gorgeous, lovely, magnificent, pretty, splendid, stunning

Big—colossal, enormous, gigantic, great, huge, large, mammoth, tall, tremendous

Cold—chilly, cool, frosty, icy, wintry

Come—approach, arrive, reach

Funny—amusing, comical, humorous, silly

Get—collect, earn, fetch, find, gather

Good—excellent, fine, friendly, kind, marvelous, splendid, well-behaved, wonderful

Happy—cheerful, delighted, glad, joyful, pleased, satisfied

Interesting—challenging, entertaining, exciting, fascinating, intriguing, spellbinding

Like—appreciate, enjoy, relish, savor

Little—dinky, puny, shrimp, slight, small, tiny

Look—discover, examine, gaze, glance, glimpse, notice, observe, peek, see, spy, study, view, watch

Make—build, construct, create, design, develop, invent, produce

Run—dash, flee, hurry, race, rush, sprint

Say—advise, announce, command, declare, discuss, explain, instruct, mumble, mutter, notify, order, roar, sigh, speak, state, tell, vow, whine, whisper, yell

Scared—afraid, alarmed, disturbed, frightened, terrified, troubled, worried

Take—catch, choose, grasp, hold, select, steal

Think—believe, consider, judge

Unhappy—discouraged, gloomy, heartbroken, miserable, sad, sorrowful

General Glossary Of Writing Terminology

Acrostic Poem—a poem in which each letter of the title is used as the initial letter in a line of poetry

Alliteration—the repetition of beginning consonants (Summer slips by silently.)

Alphabet Poem—each line of the poem begins with a letter of the alphabet in sequential order

Cinquain—a five-line verse with a specific number of syllables or words in each line; a syllable cinquain has a syllable pattern of 2–4–6–8–2; a word cinquain has a word pattern of 1–2–3–4–1

Clerihew—a four-line verse about a person; verse consists of two rhyming couplets; the first line of the first couplet ends with the person's name

Concrete Poem—a poem in which the shape or design of the words helps convey meaning in the poem

Couplet—a two-line verse that usually rhymes and expresses one thought

Dialogue—a conversation between two or more characters

Edit—to make changes to improve a work; to make ready for publication

Essay—a short personal composition in which the writer states her views

Free Verse—poetry that does not include a specific rhyme or rhythm

Haiku—a three-line Japanese poem about nature; poem has a syllable pattern of 5–7–5

Hyperbole—an extreme exaggeration (It was hot enough to melt the tires on my car.)

Imagery—figures of speech or vivid description to create a mental image

Limerick—a funny five-line verse; rhyme pattern is AABBA

Metaphor—a comparison without using like or as (She is a lovely rose.)

Narrative—a short story or description

Onomatopoeia—words that sound like the action being described (The grease hissed in the skillet.)

Personification—using human qualities to describe an object (Raindrops danced across the windowpane.)

Plot—a series of events that make up a literary work

Prewrite—to get ready for writing by selecting a topic, collecting or generating information about the topic, and planning what to include in the writing

Proofread—to carefully check a written work for errors

Quatrain—a four-line stanza; common rhyming patterns are AABB or ABAB

Report—an account of facts and information

Revise—to make improvements to a rough draft

Rough Draft—a first written form of a literary work

Simile—a comparison of two things using either like or as (She is as lovely as a rose.)

Tanka—a Japanese five-line verse; poem has a syllable pattern of 5–7–5–7–7

Name _____

Prewriting Plan

Topic Web

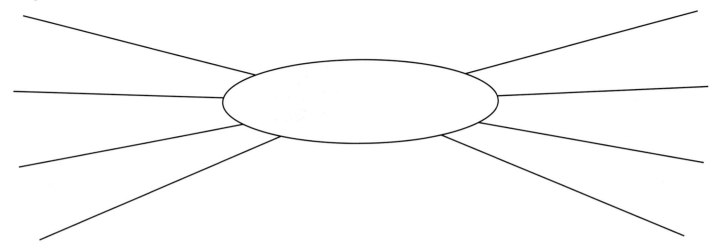

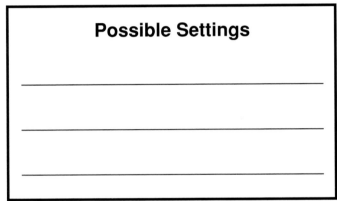

Possible Characters

_____

_____

_____

Possible Settings

_____

_____

_____

 **Topic Sentence For The Beginning Of The Story:**

_____

_____

 **Topic Sentence For The Middle Of The Story:**

_____

_____

 **Topic Sentence For The End Of The Story:**

_____

_____

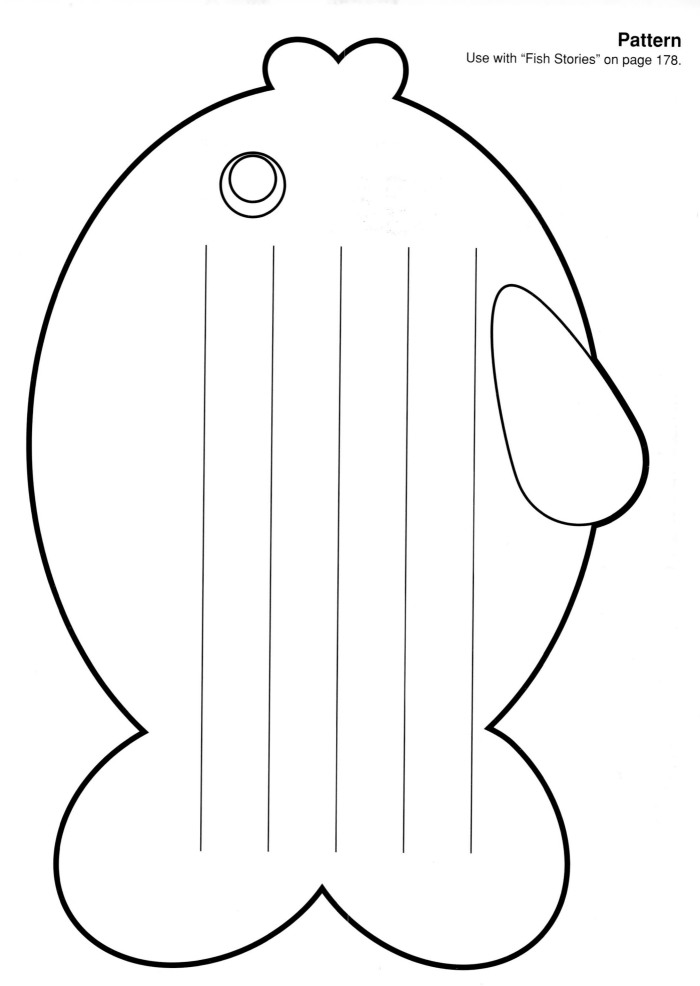

Name ________________________________ *Open reproducible*

____
(title)

____
____
____
____
____
____
____
____
____
____
____
____
____
____
____
____
____
____
____
____
____
____

 Note To The Teacher: Use with the poetry ideas on pages 180 and 181.

A B C D E F G H I J K L M N O P

Q R S T U V W X Y Z (right side, top block)

Z Y X W V U T S R Q (left side, top block)

_____
(letter)

is for

[picture box]

(picture)

_____

_____

(sentence)

P O N M L K J I H G F E D C B A (bottom, top block)

A B C D E F G H I J K L M N O P

Q R S T U V W X Y Z (right side, bottom block)

Z Y X W V U T S R Q (left side, bottom block)

_____
(letter)

is for

[picture box]

(picture)

_____

_____

(sentence)

P O N M L K J I H G F E D C B A (bottom, bottom block)

Note To The Teacher: Use with "Alphabet Books" on page 182.

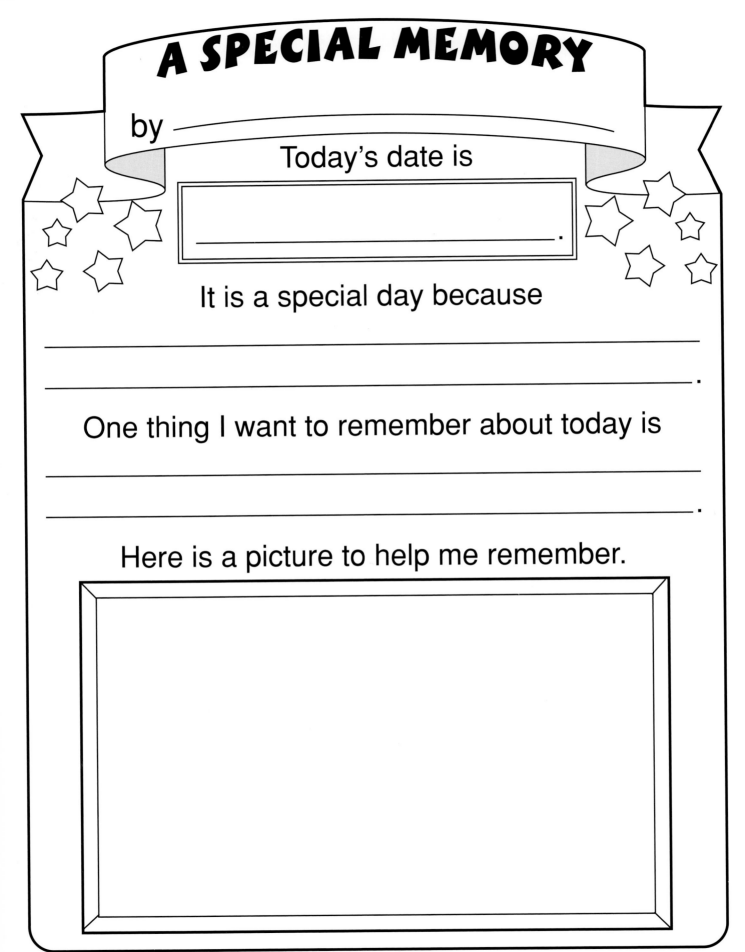

A SPECIAL MEMORY

by _____

Today's date is

[   ] .

It is a special day because

_____
_____ .

One thing I want to remember about today is

_____
_____ .

Here is a picture to help me remember.

Note To The Teacher: Use with "Memory Books" on page 183.

LITERATURE

Book-Report Bonanza

Are your students ready to present book reports? Story maps, story wheels, and story outlines serve their purpose, but sometimes a new twist can turn book reporting into a more exciting activity. Try the following ideas for unique and fun ways for students to share their favorite literature.

Can It!

A story container will soon become a favorite way of book sharing in your classroom. To make a story container, each student needs a clean, empty soup can with the label removed. Supply the student with a label-size piece of construction paper, a supply of craft sticks, construction-paper scraps, tape, and crayons or markers. Have her decorate the construction-paper label with the title, the author, and an illustration from a chosen book. Then have her tape the completed label around the can. Next have the student use the construction-paper scraps and craft sticks to create a stick puppet for each important character in the story. To tell about her book, the student shows her decorated container and tells about each character puppet. After the presentation she stores the puppets in the container and displays it in the classroom for a "soup-er" exhibit.

COAT-HANGER CHARACTERS

Transform wire coat hangers into clever character displays. To make a character, a student bends a coat hanger into a desired shape and stretches a knee-high stocking over the hanger, pulling it toward the hook of the hanger. At the base of the hook, he secures the stocking with a piece of yarn. Next he cuts craft materials—such as yarn, felt, and fabric—to create facial features to resemble a character from a chosen book; then he glues the features to the stocking. For a final touch, he completes a copy of the bow pattern (page 205) with information about the book's main character. He cuts out the bow and glues it to his project as a hair bow or bow tie. When the glue is dry, have students present their completed projects to the class; then suspend the characters by their hooks.

REPORTS ON FILE

These nifty file-folder book reports will entice your youngsters to read one another's favorite books. To make a file-folder report, a student writes the title of his chosen book on the tab of a colored file folder. Next he completes a copy of the report form on page 206 with information about his book. At the bottom of his paper, he writes a question about the story on the lines provided. Then he draws a scene from the story on a sheet of drawing paper. Finally he staples his completed form to the left side of the folder and his illustration to the right side. Store the folders in a file box for students to review during free time.

It's In The Bag

Students will enjoy giving book reports when they assume the roles of their favorite characters. Have each student use markers, construction paper, and yarn to decorate a paper lunch bag to resemble a character from a favorite story. To report on her book, the student slips the puppet onto her hand and speaks about the story from the character's point of view. After the students have given their presentations, staple the puppets to a bulletin board. To complete the display, post a label near each puppet identifying the character and the story it's from.

Handy-Dandy Reports

Give literature a hand with these cute book reports! Have each student write the title and author of her book on a tagboard copy of the hand pattern on page 207. Next, on separate two-inch squares of white paper, have her illustrate two different characters, an item in the setting, and two objects that were important in the story. Have her cut out the pictures and the hand pattern. Then have her glue one picture to each finger of the hand cutout. Display the completed projects on a bulletin board titled "Give A Big Hand To These Books!"

If You Give A Mouse A Cookie
(Title)
By Laura Joffe Numeroff
(Author)
Name Sarah

A DOZEN OTHER WAYS TO SHARE A BOOK

Book reports and literature sharing can be accomplished in a variety of ways.
Copy the following activities onto poster board and post the chart in a prominent location.
Then encourage students to share their favorite books using activities from the chart.
Fun—and a better understanding of literature—will be had by all!

1 Use a marker to visually divide a sheet of construction paper into puzzle-shaped pieces. Draw or write an event from or facts about the story on each section. Cut the puzzle pieces apart and store them in a resealable plastic bag.

2 Make a poster or an advertisement about a book. Use words and illustrations that will persuade others to read the book.

3 Create a collage of important events from the book. Use magazine pictures, your own drawings, and small objects that relate to the story.

4 Cover a shoebox and its lid with white paper. Use markers or crayons to decorate the shoebox with the book's title and author, and illustrations from the story. Then fill the shoebox with items or pictures of items that were important in the story or significant to the characters.

5 Draw pictures from the beginning, middle, and ending of the book. Explain what is happening in each picture.

6 Construct a diorama showing an important scene from the book.

7 Ceate a character mobile from a wire coat hanger, string, and construction paper.

8 Design a book jacket with an illustration that summarizes the story. Include a brief description of the plot on the inside of the jacket.

9 Tape-record yourself reading aloud your favorite passage of the story.

10 Make a list of important words used in the story.

11 Find another book by the same author and compare the two stories.

12 Pretend you are one of the characters from the book. Write a letter to a friend telling him what happened to you in the story.

Dear Adam,
The other day my classmates teased me because I haven't lost a tooth yet. I tried to loosen it by eating corn and peanut brittle but it didn't work. My mom took me to the dentist and he told me just to wait. The next day Francine knocked my tooth out at recess.

From,
Arthur

Activities For Any Story

Capitalize on your students' love of literature to reinforce language-art skills. Whether you read a story to your class or have the students read it themselves, these high-interest story activities will extend any story with a variety of skill reinforcements.

The Hat
By Jan Brett

woolen
prickles
embarrassing
cackle
gander
brambles
ridiculous
magnificent

Prereading Word Search

Pique your students' interest in new vocabulary with this prereading strategy. Before the class begins reading a new story, provide several minutes of prereading time in which students scan the story for interesting or unfamiliar words. After the allotted time, ask students to report their findings. List their responses on a sheet of chart paper labeled with the title and author of the story. Discuss the meaning and pronunciation of each word on the list before having the students read the story. The children will be more familiar with the story's vocabulary, which will increase their comprehension of the reading material. After reading the story, post the word list in your classroom as a handy reference for students to use with other reading and writing assignments.

WORD SCAVENGER HUNT

Don't stop the learning when you reach the end of a story! Promote additional skills practice with the help of clear bingo chips. Instruct your students to turn back to a designated page of the story. Have them search for compound words, contractions, proper nouns, phonetic blends, or other desired skill words. Instruct each student to cover each word he finds on the page with a bingo chip. You can quickly assess each student's understanding by glancing at his book and checking the words he has covered. Students will love the challenge of looking for the designated words, and you will have provided a simple but effective review!

I can't see the dog. I'm going to look for him.

Totem Tales

This small-group project creates a striking display while reinforcing the elements of a story. In advance gather a class supply of empty, square tissue boxes. Divide your class into groups of five students, and assign each group a different story that has recently been read aloud. Then, in each group, assign each member one of the following topics: title and author, characters, setting, problem, and solution. Have each student decorate a 5 1/4" x 17 1/2" sheet of white paper with information and pictures related to his assigned topic. Assist the student in gluing his completed paper to a tissue box. Have each group stack its finished boxes in a totem-pole arrangement. Secure the boxes with clear tape or hot glue. If desired add a large, self-adhesive bow to the top of each totem pole. Display the totem tales near your classroom library for a decorative reminder of the story elements.

The Berenstain Bears Don't Pollute (Anymore)

By Stan And Jan Berenstain

Characters:

Brother and Sister Bear
Mama Bear, Papa Bear,
Professor Actual Factual

Setting:

Bear Country

Problem:

Pollution and waste of natural resources are damaging Bear Country

Solution:

The bears form The Earthsavers Club.

STORY WHEELS

Put a spin on sequencing skills with story wheels. To begin, ask students to name the beginning, middle, and ending events from a given story. List their responses (in the order they occurred in the story) on the chalkboard. Then have each student illustrate the events on a story wheel. To make a story wheel, a student uses a pencil and a ruler to divide each of two paper plates into four sections. She writes the title and author of the story in the top right quadrant of one plate. Then she rotates the plate one-quarter turn clockwise, labels the top right quadrant "Beginning," and draws a picture of a corresponding event there. In a similar manner, she labels the next quadrant "Middle" and illustrates the problem of the story. Then she labels the final quadrant "Ending" and illustrates the ending of the story. To make a wheel cover, she draws a large dot in the center of the second plate where the four lines intersect. Next she carefully cuts away one section of the plate, leaving the dot intact. Then she erases the pencil marks remaining on the plate and personalizes it as desired. Then, using a brad, she attaches the wheel cover atop the wheel.

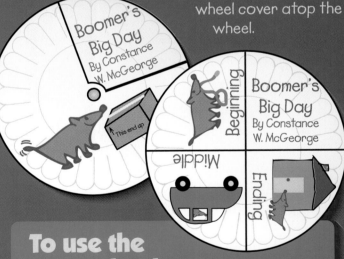

To use the story wheel, the student turns her wheels so that the second event is showing. She tells what happened before and after the second event. To check her answers, she turns the wheel forward or backward to reveal the other events. Continue having students turn their wheels to a determined event and having them tell what happened before and after the event shown. Your students will be on a roll with sequencing!

STORY FOUR-SQUARE

Review sequencing skills with a game of Story Four-Square. After reading aloud a chosen story, have each student fold a sheet of drawing paper into fourths and open it. Starting in the upper left section, have her label the top of each section with one of the following words: *first, next, then, finally.* Instruct the student to retell the story in sequence by drawing a picture and writing a brief sentence in each square. Students who have trouble expressing themselves verbally will have the drawing as a visual prompt to help them organize their thoughts. The retelling of the story will come in four easy, sequenced steps!

First — Little Red Riding Hood sets off for her grandmother's house.

Next — She goes through the woods.

Then — A wolf is in Grandma's bed.

Finally — The hunter kills the wolf, and Grandma and Little Red Riding Hood are OK.

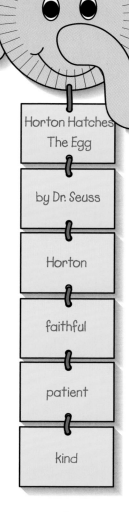

Character Mobiles

Decorate your classroom with a classy cast of characters! Ask each student to select a character from independent or class reading and then use construction paper, markers, and yarn to decorate a paper plate to resemble the character's face. Next have him write the title, author, and character's name on separate 3" x 5" cards. On three additional cards, instruct him to write three different traits about his character. After the student has hole-punched his paper plate and cards, help him use yarn lengths to connect the cutouts as pictured. Suspend the completed mobiles from the ceiling for a dazzling display.

Horton Hatches The Egg
by Dr. Seuss
Horton
faithful
patient
kind

Reading Olympics

Are you ready for some all-star readers? If so, hold a Reading Olympics in your classroom! Determine an appropriate time limit for the contest; it can be a weeklong event, or it can last for an entire grading period. To prepare for the event, establish a number of pages or an amount of time for home reading that each student must complete to qualify for a bronze, silver, or gold medal. Document each student's progress by sending home a copy of the recording sheet on page 208. Remind students that a parent or other adult must initial each entry on the sheet.

At the end of the time period, collect the recording sheets and total the page numbers or minutes of reading time. Then make a medal for each deserving student. To make a medal, spray-paint a cardboard circle bronze, silver, or gold. After it dries use paint pens to decorate the medal. When the decorations are dry, use a permanent marker to write the student's name and achievement on the award. Next punch a hole in the medal, thread a length of ribbon through the hole, and tie the ribbon's ends. Present the medals at a special Olympic Medal Ceremony to which parents have been invited. Your students will feel like reading champions—but the real reward will be the time they spent at home with their books!

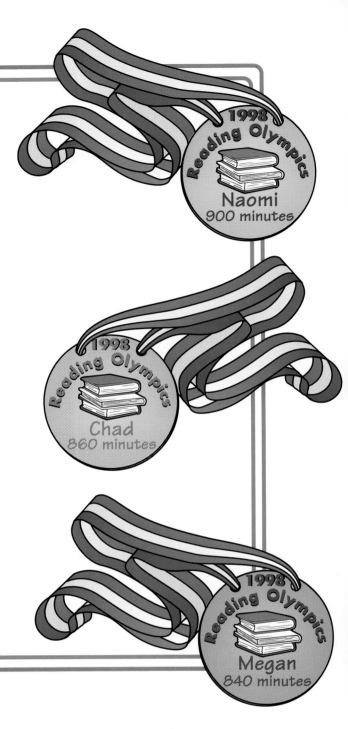

1998 Reading Olympics
Naomi
900 minutes

1998 Reading Olympics
Chad
860 minutes

1998 Reading Olympics
Megan
840 minutes

MAKE FRIENDS WITH A BOOK

Help your students select the best in literature with the references on pages 199–204. You'll find Caldecott books, short-story books, beginning chapter books, a selection of stories to read aloud to your students, and a list of favorite authors. Your class is sure to find several favorites among these teacher-recommended titles. Happy reading!

Caldecott Award And Honor Books, 1993–1997

1997 Medal Winner: *Golem* written and illustrated by David Wisniewski (Houghton Mifflin Company, 1996)

Honor Books:

Hush! A Thai Lullaby written by Minfong Ho and illustrated by Holly Meade (Orchard Books, 1996)

The Graphic Alphabet written by David Pelletier (Orchard Books, 1996)

The Paperboy written and illustrated by Dav Pilkey (Orchard Books, 1996)

Starry Messenger written and illustrated by Peter Sis (Frances Foster Books, 1996)

1996 Medal Winner: *Officer Buckle And Gloria* written and illustrated by Peggy Rathmann (G. P. Putnam's Sons, 1995)

Honor Books:

Alphabet City written and illustrated by Stephen T. Johnson (Viking Penguin, 1995)

Zin! Zin! Zin! A Violin written by Lloyd Moss and illustrated by Marjorie Priceman (Simon & Schuster Books For Young Readers, 1995)

The Faithful Friend written by Robert D. San Souci and illustrated by Brian Pinkney (Simon & Schuster Books For Young Readers, 1995)

Tops & Bottoms written and illustrated by Janet Stevens (Harcourt Brace & Company, 1995)

1995 Medal Winner: *Smoky Night* written by Eve Bunting and illustrated by David Diaz (Harcourt Brace & Company, 1994)

Honor Books:

John Henry written by Julius Lester and illustrated by Jerry Pinkney (Dial Books For Young Readers, 1994)

Swamp Angel written by Anne Isaacs and illustrated by Paul O. Zelinsky (Dutton Children's Books, 1994)

Time Flies written and illustrated by Eric Rohmann (Crown Books For Young Readers, 1994)

1994 Medal Winner: *Grandfather's Journey* written and illustrated by Allen Say (Houghton Mifflin Company, 1993)

Honor Books:

Peppe The Lamplighter written by Elisa Bartone and illustrated by Ted Lewin (Lothrop, Lee & Shepard Books; 1993)

In The Small, Small Pond written and illustrated by Denise Fleming (Henry Holt And Company, Inc.; 1993)

Raven: A Trickster Tale From The Pacific Northwest written and illustrated by Gerald McDermott (Harcourt Brace & Company, 1993)

Owen written and illustrated by Kevin Henkes (Greenwillow Books, 1993)

Yo! Yes? edited by Richard Jackson and illustrated by Chris Raschka (Orchard Books, 1993)

1993 Medal Winner: *Mirette On The High Wire* written and illustrated by Emily Arnold McCully (G. P. Putnam's Sons, 1992)

Honor Books:

The Stinky Cheese Man And Other Fairly Stupid Tales written by Jon Scieszka and illustrated by Lane Smith (Viking Children's Books, 1992)

Seven Blind Mice written and illustrated by Ed Young (Philomel Books, 1992)

Working Cotton written by Shirley Anne Williams and illustrated by Carole Byard (Harcourt Brace & Company, 1992)

Suggested Second-Grade Reading

Short Stories

- *Alexander And The Terrible, Horrible, No-Good, Very Bad Day*
by Judith Viorst
(Aladdin Paperbacks, 1987)
    From having to buy shoes that he doesn't like, to having lima beans for dinner, everything is going wrong with Alexander today. Anyone who's ever had a bad day will enjoy this story!

- *Amazing Grace*
by Mary Hoffman
(Dial Books For Young Readers, 1991)
    When she decides that she really wants the lead part in the class play, Grace finds that determination and hard work really do pay off.

- *Amelia Bedelia*
by Peggy Parish
(HarperCollins Children's Books, 1992)
    As Mrs. Rogers' new maid, Amelia seems eager to please. And she would be a good worker—if only she didn't get all her instructions mixed up!

- *Arthur's Tooth*
by Marc Brown
(Little, Brown And Company; 1993)
    Who knows better than second graders the trials and tribulations of losing teeth? Your students will enjoy this and other stories about the unassuming Arthur.

- **The Berenstain Bears series**
by Stan and Jan Berenstain
(Random House Books For Young Readers)
    Follow the adventures of Papa, Mama, Brother, and Sister Bear. Each story tells about a situation that most students can relate to, and reinforces a lesson of value as the Bears solve each problem as a family.

- *Blueberries For Sal*
by Robert McCloskey
(Puffin Books, 1976)
    While looking for blueberries, both Sal and Little Bear become separated from their mothers. Fortunately, they are rescued—but they almost end up with the wrong mothers!

- *Clifford The Big Red Dog*
by Norman Bridwell
(Scholastic Inc., 1985)
    After reading about this big red dog, your beginning readers will be panting for an oversize pooch of their own! Be sure to introduce your students to the many other books in this series.

- **Curious George series**
by H. A. Rey
(Houghton Mifflin Company)
    What happens when a man with a yellow hat brings a curious little monkey home? Just about everything that you can imagine! Your students will enjoy the many books about George in this easy-reader series.

- **Dance At Grandpa's**
  by Laura Ingalls Wilder
  (HarperCollins Children's Books, 1994)
  For all those who love the Little House books, this adapted story will bring the magic of Laura and her family to younger readers. Look for other adapted stories in the My First Little House Books series.

- **Ira Sleeps Over**
  by Bernard Waber
  (Live Oak Media, 1984)
  Ira gets to spend the night at Reggie's house—what fun! But will Ira be able to make it through the night without his teddy bear?

- **Lilly's Purple Plastic Purse**
  by Kevin Henkes
  (Greenwillow Books, 1996)
  Lilly loves school, her desk, and the chocolate milk in the cafeteria; but she does *not* love what happens when she takes her brand-new purple purse to school.

- **Miss Nelson Is Missing!**
  by Harry Allard and James Marshall
  (Houghton Mifflin Company, 1985)
  Miss Nelson's students learn more than they ever wanted to know when a very stern substitute teacher takes over their class.

- **Nate The Great**
  by Marjorie Weinman Sharmat
  (Bantam Doubleday Dell Books For Young Readers, 1977)
  Never fear—Nate is on the case! In this book (as well as the many others in this series), Nate follows a string of clues to solve some very interesting mysteries.

- **Ruby The Copycat**
  by Peggy Rathmann
  (Scholastic Inc., 1991)
  Students will enjoy this story of a little girl who tries to imitate those she admires and a teacher who handles the situation in a kind and effective manner.

- **Stellaluna**
  by Janell Cannon
  (Scholastic Inc., 1993)
  Beautiful illustrations accompany this story of friendship between a homeless bat and three baby birds.

- **Today Was A Terrible Day**
  by Patricia Reilly Giff
  (Viking Children's Books, 1984)
  Ronald Morgan is having a terrible day—he forgot his homework, he ate Jimmy's lunch by mistake, and he knocked the teacher's best plant off the windowsill. It's a good thing Ronald has a very understanding teacher!

Suggested Second-Grade Reading

Beginning Chapter Books

- **Frog And Toad Are Friends**
by Arnold Lobel
(HarperCollins Children's Books, 1979)
    The charming adventures of Frog and Toad are sure to delight young readers with their simple story lines and familiar vocabulary. Students will be eager to look for other books in this series, too.

- **George And Martha**
by James Marshall
(Houghton Mifflin Company, 1974)
    These two silly hippos are good and loyal friends. Students will love the humor that fills each chapter of this easy reader.

- **The Golly Sisters Ride Again**
by Betsy Byars
(HarperCollins Children's Books, 1994)
    The lovable Golly sisters sing and dance their way through a visit to a talking rock, a chase to get a goat out of the audience, a tussle over who will be the princess in their next production, and many other zany adventures!

- **Gus And Grandpa**
by Claudia Mills
(Farrar, Straus, & Giroux, Inc.; 1997)
    Three simple chapters make this book about a boy and his grandfather a good choice for students ready to progress to chapter books. With topics such as dogs, cars, and birthday parties, this book is sure to hold students' interest!

- **Henry And Mudge**
by Cynthia Rylant
(Simon & Schuster Books For Young Readers, 1992)
    This chapter book for beginners follows the adventures of a boy named Henry and his large but lovable dog, Mudge. Look for the many other books in this series that help students make the transition from storybooks to chapter books.

- **Mouse Soup**
by Arnold Lobel
(HarperCollins Children's Books, 1983)
    A very clever mouse reveals a recipe for a delicious soup—and cooks up a plan so that he won't be included in the ingredients!

- **The One In The Middle Is The Green Kangaroo**
by Judy Blume
(Bantam Doubleday Dell Books For Young Readers, 1991)
    What could be better than being in the school play? Getting to play the part of the green kangaroo, of course!

- **Secondhand Star**
by Maryann MacDonald
(Hyperion Books For Children, 1997)
    For a second grader, Francis has a lot to deal with—she has a new teacher, a large family, a new friend, and now tryouts for the class play are coming up!

- **Young Cam Jansen And The Lost Tooth**
by David A. Adler
(Viking Penguin, 1997)
    Young Cam uses her photographic memory to solve a high-interest case. Just like the *Cam Jansen* books, this beginner series will intrigue young readers as they try to solve the mysteries.

Read-Aloud Favorites

- ***Charlie And The Chocolate Factory***
  by Roald Dahl
  (Buccaneer Books, 1992)
    This mouthwatering tale of a poor boy with a sweet tooth for chocolate will leave your listeners begging for more!

- ***Charlotte's Web***
  by E. B. White
  (HarperCollins Children's Books, 1952)
    This tender story of friendship between a savvy spider and an innocent pig will warm the hearts of your second-grade listeners.

- ***Freckle Juice***
  by Judy Blume
  (Bantam Doubleday Dell Books For Young Readers, 1979)
    Andrew really wants to have a face full of freckles—but will sampling a secret recipe do the trick?

- ***I Was Born About 10,000 Years Ago***
  by Steven Kellogg
  (Morrow Junior Books, 1996)
    This whopper of a tale outdoes the term *exaggeration!* Young listeners will enjoy each outrageous claim made by the narrator of this boastful book.

- ***Justin And The Best Biscuits In The World***
  by Mildred Pitts Walter
  (Lothrop, Lee & Shepard Books; 1986)
    Justin is growing up in a household of women. But when he goes to live on his grandpa's ranch, he learns there's more to "women's work" than he imagined!

- ***Matthew And Tilly***
  by Rebecca C. Jones
  (Puffin Books, 1991)
    This tale of a broken friendship and how it was mended will remind your students of how important a friendship can be.

- ***Ramona Quimby, Age Eight***
  by Beverly Cleary
  (Morrow Junior Books, 1981)
    Ramona has a spunky spirit, and she uses it to deal with all the situations that can befall any eight-year-old girl.

- ***Winnie The Pooh***
  A. A. Milne
  (Puffin Books, 1992)
    Who can resist the tales of this silly old bear and his friends from the Hundred Acre Woods?

Favorite Authors

★ Jan Brett
Annie And The Wild Animals
Armadillo Rodeo
Berlioz The Bear
Mitten, The

★ Marc Brown
Arthur Babysits
Arthur Goes To Camp
Arthur's Chicken Pox
Arthur's Eyes
Arthur's First Sleepover
Arthur's New Puppy
Arthur's Tooth

★ Eric Carle
Papa, Please Get The Moon For Me
Rooster's Off To See The World
Tiny Seed, The
Very Busy Spider, The
Very Hungry Caterpillar, The
Very Lonely Firefly, The
Very Quiet Cricket, The

★ Tomie dePaola
Art Lesson, The
Legend Of The Bluebonnet
Little Grunt And The Big Egg
Quilt Story, The
Strega Nona

★ Kevin Henkes
Chester's Way
Chrysanthemum
Jessica
Julius, The Baby Of The World
Lilly's Purple Plastic Purse
Shelia Rae, The Brave
Weekend With Wendell, A

★ Leo Lionni
Alexander And The Wind-Up Mouse
Frederick
Inch By Inch
Little Blue And Little Yellow
Swimmy

★ Robert Munsch
Alligator Baby
Fifty Below Zero
I Have To Go!
Love You Forever
Thomas' Snowsuit

★ Bill Peet
Big Bad Bruce
Cock-A-Doodle Dudley
Cyrus The Unsinkable Sea Serpent
Jethro And Joel Were A Troll
Pamela Camel
Spooky Tail Of Prewitt Peacock, The
Wump World, The

★ Maurice Sendak
Alligators All Around
Chicken Soup With Rice
Where The Wild Things Are

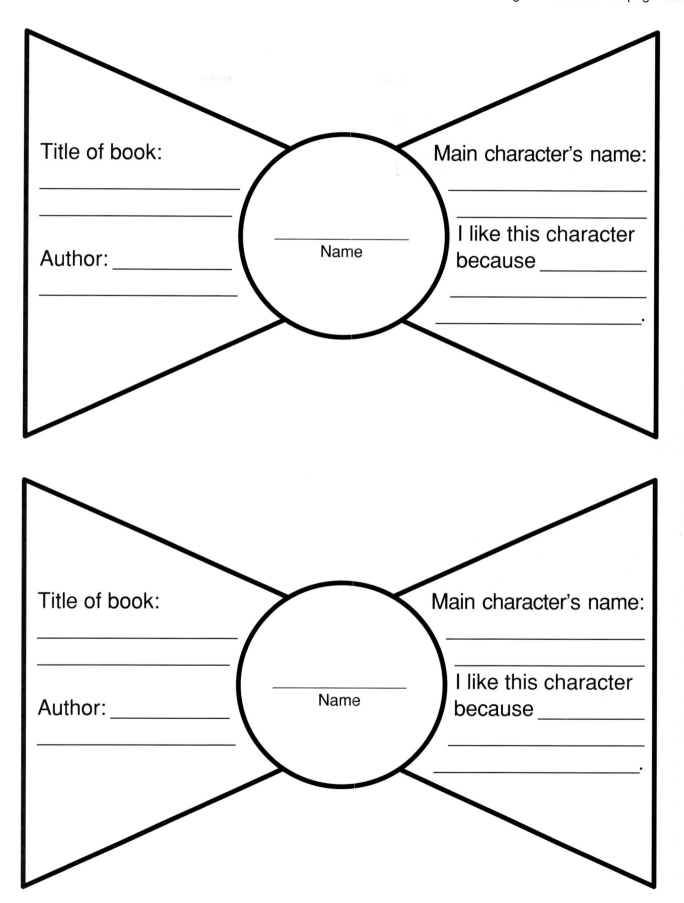

Title of book:
_____
_____
Author: _____
_____

Name

Main character's name:
_____
_____
I like this character
because _____
_____
_____.

Title of book:
_____
_____
Author: _____
_____

Name

Main character's name:
_____
_____
I like this character
because _____
_____
_____.

Name _____ *Book report*

Report On File

Title: _____

Author: _____

Illustrator: _____

My favorite character: _____

_____

My favorite part of the story: _____

_____

_____

_____

Read the story to find the answer to this question:

_____

_____

_____

_____

_____

Note To The Teacher: Use with "Reports On File" on page 193.

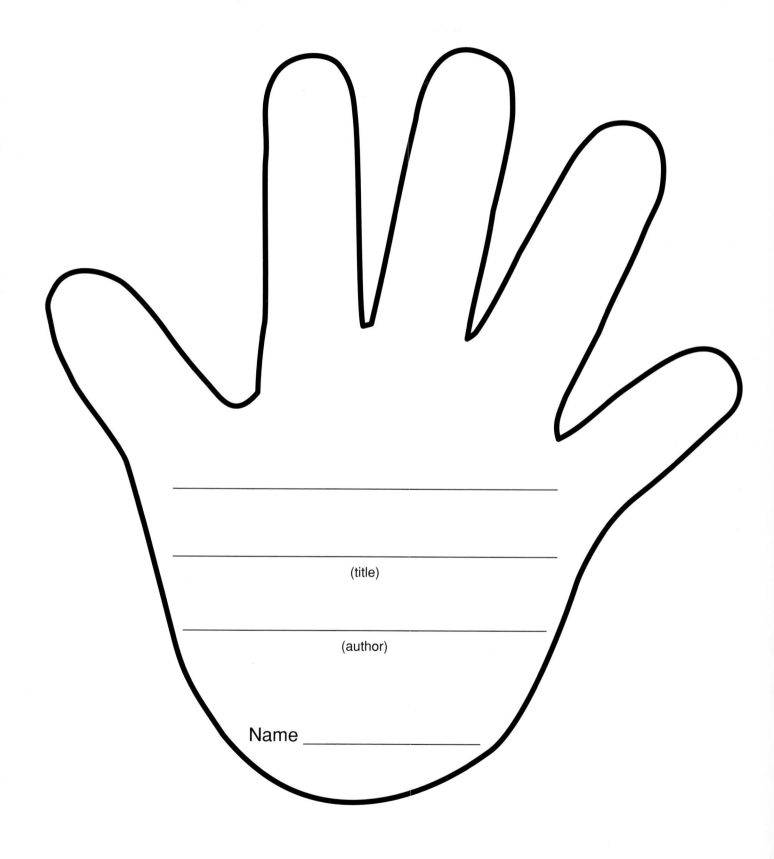

_____

_____
(title)

_____
(author)

Name _____

Name _____

Reading Olympics Recording Sheet

Date	Title Of Book	Number Of Pages Read	Time Spent Reading	Monitor's Initials

Note To The Teacher: Use with "Reading Olympics" on page 198.

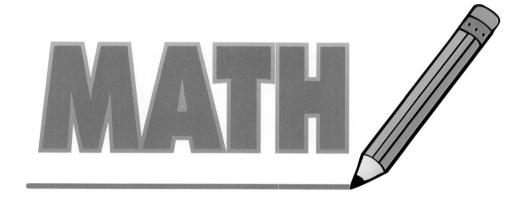

NUMBER CONCEPTS

Number-Line Concepts

Use a number line to review and reinforce basic math concepts. Make an interactive number line on your classroom floor with a strip of masking tape. (Or if weather permits, draw a number line in chalk on the sidewalk outdoors.) Program the line with the numerals 1 to 20. Then program a set of task cards with addition or subtraction problems. On the back of each card, draw a number line with a diagram that shows how the problem should be solved (see example). Have each student, in turn, take a task card and demonstrate how to solve the problem by stepping it through on the number line.

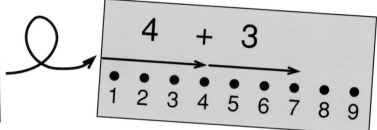

DAILY COUNT

A daily counting activity will help reinforce number concepts with your students. Display a hundreds chart where all students can easily see it, or provide each student with a copy of the chart on page 225. Each day, ask a student volunteer to use a pointer to touch each number on the chart as the class counts out loud. Vary the counting activity each day with instructions such as the following:

▷ Count by fives to 50.

▷ Count by tens to 100.

▷ Say the even numbers to 20.

▷ Say the odd numbers from 21 to 33.

▷ Count from 45 to 65.

▷ Count backward from 90 to 80.

DAILY NUMBER DRILL

Incorporate an ongoing number-concept review as part of a daily routine. Program slips of paper each with a number from 1 to 20 and place them in a cup. At the start of each math lesson, randomly draw a number from the cup. Have your students answer the following questions about the number:

1. Is the number odd or even?

2. What number is one less?

3. What number is one more?

4. What are two numbers that can be added together to total the number?

5. If the number were doubled, what would the sum be?

COMPUTATIONS

Rollin' With Addition

Get your students racing toward addition success as they aim for the finish line of this fast-moving game. To prepare for the game, make a simple racetrack on a piece of bulletin-board paper with lanes marked in increments of 1 to 50 (see illustration). Duplicate the car patterns on page 226, and give one to each student to color, cut out, and personalize. If desired, laminate the cutouts for durability. Get a pair of dice, and you're ready to begin.

Select the appropriate number of students to place their car cutouts at the starting line in the available lanes. (The remaining students can gather around the racetrack as the audience.) To play, each student, in turn, rolls the dice. He adds the two numbers shown and moves his car that number of increments toward the finish line. Play continues until a player reaches the finish line by exact count. Then have a new set of students take their places at the starting line. Are your students ready for an added challenge? Have each student roll three dice during his turn. On your mark, get set, go!

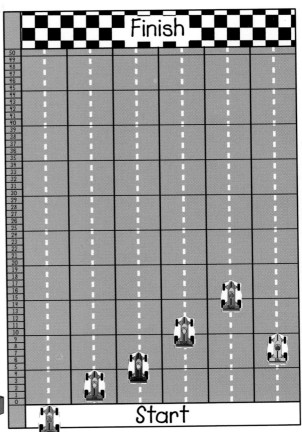

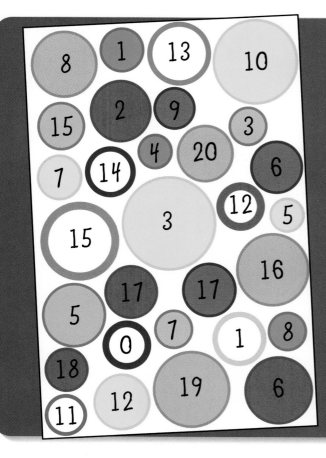

TWISTER ADDITION

Put a new twist on an old game to practice addition facts to 20. Draw approximately 30 colored circles on a length of bulletin-board paper. Program each circle with a number from 0 to 20, duplicating the numbers as necessary. To play this small-group game, ask five students to take off their shoes (so the paper won't tear) and take a place on the edge of the game mat. Have the other students sit around the mat to watch the first round of play. Call out an "answer" from 1 to 20. Each player then looks for a pair of numbers that add up to the answer and places a hand or foot on each number. Ask each student to announce the number sentence he created; then have the players untwist themselves, and invite another group of students to take a turn at play. Your students will bend over backward to practice addition facts!

ADDITION
In The Cards

"Reinvent" some of the card-game classics with addition-reinforcing games. Students should be familiar with the rules of Go Fish and War. Modify the games as described below to provide a fun alternative to written addition practice.

Quick Draw

Students can use an ordinary deck of playing cards for this addition version of the game of War. To simplify the game, remove the face cards and let the ace have a value of one. Pair students and supply each pair with a prepared deck of cards. Instruct the partners to divide the cards equally into two piles and to place one pile facedown in front of each player. On the count of three, each player turns over her top card. The first player to correctly add the two numbers together takes the cards and adds them to the bottom of her pile. Play continues until one partner acquires all the cards. If time is a factor, have students count their cards at the end of the time period. The partner with the most cards in her pile wins the game. Which student in your class will be quickest on the draw?

"13!"

Addition Go Fishin'

Program sets of 20 cards for student pairs to use in this version of Go Fish. On each card, write an addition problem with a sum from 1 to 20. Make sure that the cards will pair up with sums for students to match; for example, a card labeled "5 + 5" would make a match with a card labeled "6 + 4." Pair students; then instruct one student to randomly deal seven cards to each player and place the remaining cards facedown in a pile. Each player places all his matching pairs of sums faceup on the playing area in front of him. Player 1 begins by asking Player 2 for a sum to match one that he is holding. If he receives the match from Player 2, he places the pair on the table and takes another turn. If Player 2 does not have the card Player 1 requested, Player 2 says, "Go fish," and Player 1 draws a card from the pile. If he draws the card he requested, he may lay down the pair and take another turn. If he does not draw a match, he keeps the card and Player 2 takes a turn. Any time a player lays his last card on the table, he takes one card from the draw pile. When the draw pile is gone, the game ends. The player with the most pairs wins! Your students will be hooked on this addition-practice game!

MUSICAL MATH

Kids love to play Musical Chairs, so channel their enthusiasm into a version for a subtraction-practice activity. To prepare for the game, create a class supply of subtraction problems of the desired skill level on separate half-sheets of colored construction paper. Write the problem on one side of the paper and the answer on the other side; then laminate for durability. Next have students move their chairs to create a circle and place a problem on each chair. To begin, play some tape-recorded music and have students march around the circle of chairs. When the music stops, each student grabs the math problem on the chair in front of him and says the answer out loud. To check his answer, he looks on the back of the card. Continue in this manner for a desired amount of time. Since there is a chair for each student, no one sits out or misses a turn, and everyone gets plenty of practice!

15 – 4 =

Subtract-Around-The-Room

This fast-paced game will have students on the move as they practice subtraction facts. Have students sit in a circle on the floor. Select one student to start the game by having him stand behind the student seated to his left. Display a flash card for both students to see. If the standing student is first to call out the correct answer, he moves behind the next student to his left. If he is incorrect or does not call out the answer first, he takes the place of the seated student, who then stands behind the student to his left. The game continues until one student moves around the circle and travels back to his original spot. Students will be eager to brush up on their facts in an effort to be the first to travel all the way around the circle!

Subtraction Action

Your students will be on a roll with this mental-math game! To prepare, write a number between 6 and 20 on the chalkboard. Have your students sit in a circle on the floor and hand a die to the first student. Instruct her to roll the die, then subtract the resulting roll from the number on the board. She announces the difference before passing the die to the next player. The students continue to roll and subtract from the designated number until each student has had a turn. If time allows, write a different number on the board for students to subtract from. Everyone gets a chance to participate as the facts keep rolling along!

20

20 minus 4 is 16!

PLACE VALUE

A DAILY DOSE OF PLACE VALUE

Give your students a daily dose of place value with a readily available source: the date! Each day, have a selected student use manipulatives to demonstrate the date in tens and ones. Have the following materials handy in your calendar center for students to use with the daily demonstration:

- craft sticks, both individuals and in bundles of ten

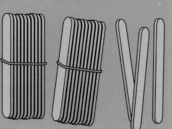

- pennies and dimes

- Unifix® cubes, both individuals and in stacks of ten

- dried beans, both individuals and in re-sealable bags of ten

- handprint cutouts, both individually with the fingers extended, and in pairs stapled together (see example)

- beads, both individuals and in strings of ten

Domino Place Value

Use a set of dominoes to reinforce place value with your students. Distribute a domino to each student. Instruct the student to count the dots on the right side of her domino as ones and on the left side of her domino as tens. Ask each student to identify the two-digit number her domino represents; then ask students to compare to see who has the largest and smallest numbers. Collect the dominoes, redistribute them, and repeat the procedure. For an added challenge, have the students line up in numerical order according to the value of their dominoes. Your students will love these domino digits!

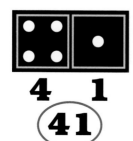

4 1
(41)

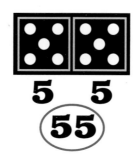

5 5
(55)

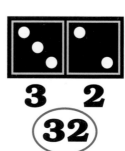

3 2
(32)

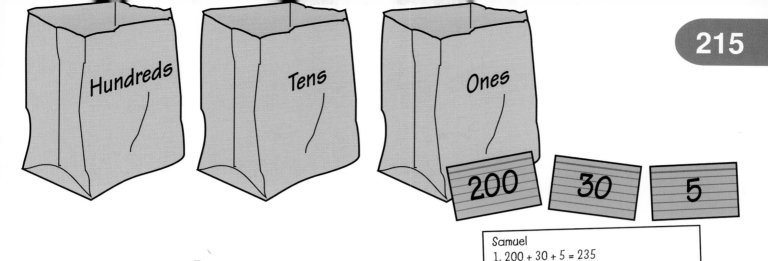

It's In The Bag!

Expanded notation is in the bag with this simple but effective activity. To prepare, gather three paper lunch bags, a supply of index cards, and a marker. Label each of the bags with one of the following values: ones, tens, and hundreds. Program a set of nine index cards for each bag. The hundreds bag will need cards programmed with the numbers 100 to 900, the tens bag will need cards programmed with the numbers 10 to 90, and the ones bag will need cards programmed with the numbers 1 to 9. Place each set of cards in the corresponding bag. Have a student volunteer randomly remove one card from each bag. Next have him write the resulting three-digit number on the board. Ask the other students to determine the numerals that were written on the three cards. After the student confirms the correct answer, have him replace the cards and call on another student to take his place. Continue until all students have had a turn.

For a variation of the activity, have two student volunteers remove one card apiece from each bag. Have each student write his resulting three-digit number on the board. Ask the class to determine which number has a greater numeral in the ones place, tens place, and hundreds place. Next ask the volunteers to determine which three-digit number has the greater value. After confirming the correct answers, ask two more students to repeat the activity. What an easy activity to have on hand for place-value practice!

PLACE VALUE IN THE NEWS

Make headlines with this newsworthy place-value project. Write a list of numbers on the chalkboard for students to find in discarded newspapers. For example, have students look for a number with a 3 in the ones place, a number with a 6 in the tens place, or a number with a 4 in the hundreds place. Instruct each student to cut out the numbers he finds and glue them to a sheet of paper. After the students have completed the activity, have them compare their results. Now those are some numbers that are really in the news!

NONSTANDARD MEASUREMENTS

To introduce the concept of measurement, have each student choose a nonstandard unit of measurement from objects available in the classroom. Instruct him to predict the width of his desk in terms of the size of the object. How many chalkboard erasers would fit across his desk? How many crayons? Demonstrate how to measure with each object by placing it flush against one side of the desk, making an erasable mark where the end of the object rests, and then moving the object so that it is flush with the mark. Continue moving the object until it has spanned the width of the desktop. Have him count the number of times the object was placed on his desk; then have him compare the results with his predictions. Ask each student to share his results. Did everyone get the same answer? Ask students to surmise whether this is a good way for people to take measurements. Then try the activity at the right to reinforce the need for standard units of measurement.

Get In Step With Measurement

How accurate can we be, using nonstandard units of measurement? Have your students find out as they get in step for this activity. Have each student line up with her back against one classroom wall. Tell her to walk across the room heel to toe, using her footsteps as a unit of measurement as she walks the length of the classroom. Remind each student to count silently as she measures. When all students have completed the activity, compare their results. Ask students to determine why there are so many different answers; then discuss the need for a standard unit of measurement. Distribute a copy of the reproducible on page 227 to each student, and have her practice measuring and drawing line segments with the ruler cutout included on the page. If desired, laminate each student's ruler and save it for use with additional measurement activities. When it comes to measurement, your students will be right in step!

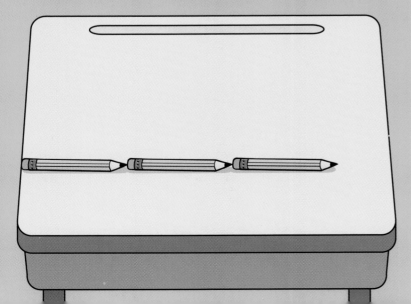

MEASUREMENT MASTERPIECES

Use measurement and addition to inspire works of art in your classroom. To prepare for this art project, cut a supply of construction-paper strips into a variety of lengths ranging from one to eight inches. (Make sure each piece can be measured in increments of inches.) Instruct each student to select several construction-paper strips and measure each one with a ruler, writing the length on the strip. Next have him add the lengths of his pieces. After he determines the total length, have the student glue his pieces onto his construction paper to make a picture or design. To complete the project, the student names his masterpiece with a title that incorporates the total length of his pieces. Display the finished projects on a bulletin board titled "Measurement Masterpieces."

Measurement Task Cards

This learning-center activity will improve both estimation and measurement skills. Program task cards with directions for estimating the lengths of a desired number of manipulatives, such as dried beans, toothpicks, cotton balls, and paper clips. Place the task cards, the manipulatives, and a ruler at a center. A student reads a task card and selects the specified number of manipulatives. Then he lines up the manipulatives end to end and estimates their length. To check his answer, he measures the length with the ruler. Add new manipulatives and task cards to the center periodically to promote practice of these important skills.

Estimate and then measure 8 Unifix® cubes.

Estimate and then measure 15 marshmallows.

Estimate and then measure 20 noodles.

ON THE LOOKOUT FOR LENGTHS

Send students on a classroom scavenger hunt by challenging them to find objects of specific lengths. Place students in small groups and assign each group a different length from 1 to 12 inches. Supply each student with a ruler; then send him off in search of objects of his designated length. After a specified time period, have each student group meet and discuss its findings. Then provide materials for each group to create a poster illustrating the objects it found. Display the posters in the hallway or on a bulletin board with the title "Look How Our Room Measures Up!"

Three Inches

USE YOUR NOODLE!

Begin a study of graphing with this activity that will have each student really using his noodle! Fill a class supply of resealable plastic bags with an assortment of dried pasta pieces. Distribute a bag and a copy of the bar graph on page 228 to each student. Have each student sort his noodles by shape and then glue a different shape under each column at the base of the graph. Next have him record his results by coloring the appropriate number of squares in each column. Mount the completed graphs on a bulletin board; then have your students glue dried macaroni pieces to a precut border. Staple the border to the board and add the title "Now That's What We Call Using Our Noodles!"

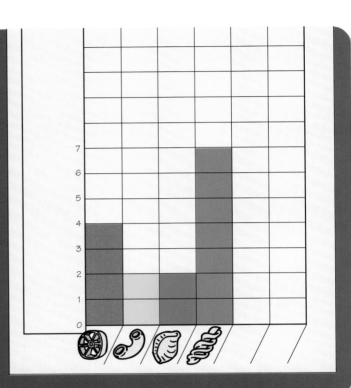

Spin-A-Graph

Put a spin on graphing with this interactive bar-graph project. To prepare, make a spinner by visually dividing a paper plate into four sections, coloring each section a different color. Use a brad-type paper fastener to attach a tagboard arrow to the center of the plate. Distribute a copy of the bar graph on page 228 to each student. Instruct each student to label the columns of his bar graph to correspond with the colors used on the spinner. Next have a student volunteer come to the front of the room and spin the spinner. Announce the result of the spin and have each student color a square in the corresponding column on his graph. Repeat the activity until all students have had a chance to spin the spinner. Then discuss the results of the completed graph by asking questions such as the following:

- Which category has the most items?
- Which category has the fewest items?
- How many items are in the first category?
- How many items are in the second and third categories combined?
- How many more items are in the highest category than in the lowest category?
- How many items are in the highest and lowest categories combined?
- Rank the categories in order from highest to lowest.
- How many items are represented on the graph all together?

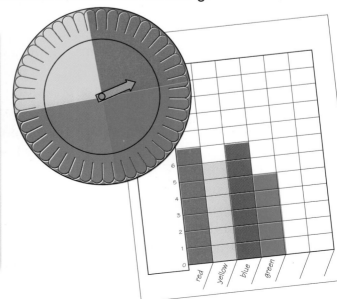

Personal Pictographs

Capitalize on student interest to create pictographs. Take inventory of student information from a topic such as the different pets owned by students, the types of supplies in their desks, or the names of their favorite sports. Write the resulting information on the chalkboard. Distribute a copy of the pictograph form on page 229 to each student. Decide on pictures or symbols to represent the objects that were counted. Show students how to program the graph with these symbols and a title that tells about the topic. Then have them record the results using the information on the chalkboard as a reference. If desired, extend the lesson by asking the questions from the list on page 218 about the results.

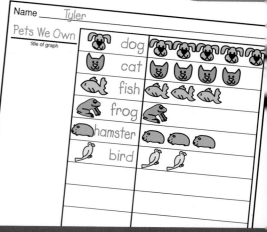

GRAPHS-IN-A-JAR

This unique approach to graphing will also reinforce measurement skills. Select several identical clear, empty jars. Pose a question to the class such as, "What is your favorite school subject?" Label each jar with a corresponding category. Have each student input his data by measuring a designated amount of water and pouring it into the correct jar. After each child has added his data, have the class observe the water level in each jar to determine which categories have the most and least water. Enlist students' help in arranging the jars from least amount of water to greatest amount. Then encourage students to make statements about the results, such as, "More people prefer math than prefer spelling" and, "The same number of people enjoy reading and science."

Hieroglyphic Graphs

A hieroglyphic graph, or "glyph," is a form of picture writing that conveys information. To create a glyph, you collect data for a predetermined topic and create a legend to represent each component of information. Have your class create the clown glyph outlined at the right with information about themselves.

CLOWN GLYPH

red nose—I am a girl.
blue nose—I am a boy.

yellow hat—I am an only child.
green hat—I have at least one brother or sister.

dots on hat—I have always lived in this state.
stripes on hat—I have lived outside this state.

freckles—I own a pet.
no freckles—I do not own a pet.

curly hair—I ride the bus.
straight hair—I do not ride the bus.

GEOMETRY

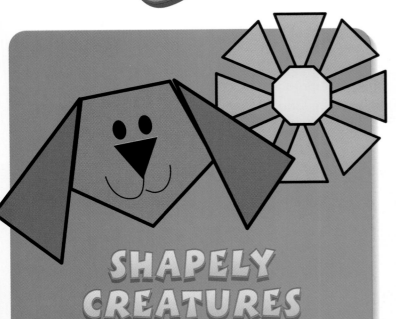

SHAPELY CREATURES

Put your students' imaginations to work as they review the basic shapes. Provide each student with a copy of the shape patterns on page 230. Review the name and attributes of each shape; then direct students to color and cut out the pieces. Next have each student glue the shapes onto a sheet of construction paper to create a picture or design. If desired, extend the lesson by having each student write a story about her completed project incorporating the shapes into the story. Before long your students will be in great shape for geometry!

SHAPE SCAVENGER HUNT

Take students on a scavenger hunt in search of shapes. Review with your class the names and attributes of several shapes; then lead your class on a walk around the school grounds in search of objects that feature these different shapes. Record the objects your students observe on separate cards. After you return to the classroom, post the cards on a bulletin board. Next enlist students' help in creating shape categories for the objects on the list. Write each category on a strip of paper and post it on the board. Finally have student volunteers move the cards under the appropriate categories. If desired, extend the lesson by distributing a copy of the bar graph on page 228 to each student and having him graph the results of the scavenger hunt.

circles	squares	rectangles
doorknob	windowpane	door
intercom	sidewalk square	bulletin board
ball	floor tile	electrical outlet

Congruent Matchup

Reinforce the concept of congruent figures with this partner game. Program sets of 20 index cards on which ten pairs of congruent figures are made. Instruct the partners to arrange the cards facedown on a desk. Each student takes a turn selecting two cards and turning them faceup. If the figures are congruent, the student keeps the cards and takes another turn. If the figures are not congruent, the student replaces the cards to their facedown position, and his partner takes a turn. Play continues until all pairs have been matched. The winner is the student with the most pairs at the end of the game.

Small-Group Organizing Tip

Reinforce congruent figures by using them as a means of dividing students into small groups. Create a set of construction-paper congruent figures for the number of students you want in each group. Place the figures in a bag; then have each student draw one. Have all students holding congruent figures work together for the group activity.

Shaping Up With Symmetry

To introduce the concept of symmetrical figures, have students use tempera paint to create symmetrical shapes of their own. To begin, have each student fold a sheet of construction paper in half and reopen it. Then pour a small amount of tempera paint onto one half of the folded paper. Tell her to gently refold the paper and press down on the top half of the paper, spreading the paint between the two sheets. Have students unfold their papers and examine the resulting symmetrical figures, taking note of how the right and left sides of the figures are mirror images of each other. Set the projects aside to dry; then bind the pages into a class book and place it in the classroom library.

To vary the activity, have each student fold a sheet of construction paper in half and then cut an abstract shape from the paper, leaving the fold intact. Have students unfold the shapes and observe their symmetrical halves.

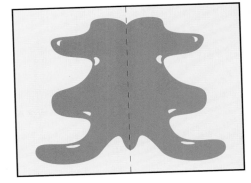

SOLID-FIGURE SHOW-AND-TELL

Enhance a study of solid shapes by presenting students with a homework challenge. Can they find items at home with each of these solid shapes: a pyramid, a cone, a cylinder, a cube, a rectangular prism, and a sphere? After students bring the shapes to school, provide time for students to share the objects. Next divide students into small groups, and have each group place its objects on a separate table. Then have the group sort the objects according to their shapes. After each group finishes sorting, have students rotate clockwise to other tables to observe the work of other groups. Now that's a fun show-and-tell!

CELEBRATE WITH SHAPES

Hold a special snack celebration during your study of shapes. Send a note home prior to the event asking parents to supply snack foods that come in the following shapes: circles, squares, rectangles, triangles, and any other shapes you have studied. The day of the event, arrange the snacks on a large table. Have students form a line near the table; then distribute a plate and a napkin to each student. A student fills his plate with foods from the table, identifying the shape of each treat before he puts it on his plate. What a tasty way to reinforce shape recognition!

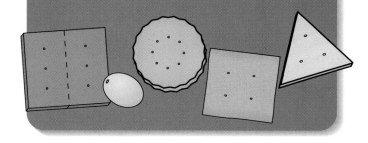

Time

Rockin' Around The Clock

For a rockin' review of time-telling skills, put the practice to music! Find an upbeat recording, such as "Rock Around The Clock" by Bill Haley And The Comets. Distribute a manipulative clock face to each student. (Or make a class set of clocks with the patterns provided on page 226.) To begin, play the music for 15 to 20 seconds; then turn it off and announce a time for students to display on their clocks for your approval. A quick glance can assess students' efforts. Repeat the activity as time allows. Collect the clocks and keep them for students to use during the next rockin' review.

What Time Is It?

Have students practice their time-telling skills throughout the day with this simple activity. At the beginning of the day, have each student number a piece of paper from 1 to 10. At ten various hour and half-hour times throughout the day, ask, "What time is it?" Instruct students to stop what they are doing and write the time on their papers. (Be sure to record the times yourself.) Also have each student write a sentence telling what she was doing at that time. After the tenth time check, announce the list of times that should be listed on students' papers. How's that for a "time-ly" activity?

HICKORY DICKORY DOCK

Practice time-telling skills in a really big way with this giant clock activity. In advance use a permanent marker to program a clock face that includes numbers and minute markings on a solid-color, round tablecloth. To practice time-telling skills, place the tablecloth in an open area, and have your students sit around the lower half of the clock face. Call on a student volunteer to lie on the tablecloth so that his head is near the 12 and his feet are near the 6. Announce a time for the student to demonstrate by using his arms as the hands for the clock. Ask the other students to confirm the answer; then invite additional students, in turn, to take the student's place. After each student's turn, lead the class in this chant:

Hickory dickory dock,
We're learning about the clock.
[Student's name]'s setting the time,
And he's/she's doing just fine!
Hickory dickory dock.

Money Bags

Begin your money unit by sending home a note to parents asking for a bag of coins for their child. Inform parents that each student will need a personalized, resealable plastic bag containing 4 quarters, 10 dimes, 10 nickels, and 20 pennies. Also mention in the note that the money will be sent home after it is no longer needed at school. Have students use the coins for manipulatives when practicing with money amounts. Collect the bags and store them for safekeeping when not in use. Students will feel very familiar in handling these manipulatives and will take extra care to store them properly in their bags for later use!

Coin Collecting

Your students will flip over this learning-center game that provides practice in coin recognition and determining values to one dollar. Place a spinner programmed with the words *penny, nickel, dime,* and *quarter* (as shown) and a supply of coin manipulatives for two to four players at a center. (Or have each student use his personal set of coins as described in "Money Bags.") To play the game, each player, in turn, spins the spinner, names the coin the spinner landed on, identifies the value of the coin, and then selects the coin from the coin manipulatives or his money bag. If he has correctly identified the coin and its value, he keeps the coin. If he is incorrect, he returns the coin to its original place. Play continues until one player collects enough coins to total one dollar. To coin a phrase, your students will be in the money!

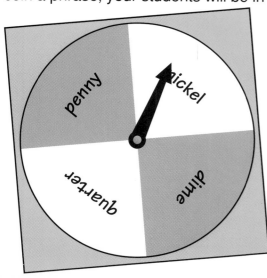

30¢

SPARE CHANGE

Students will be amazed at how a variety of different answers can all be correct with this activity! Provide each student with a set of coin cutouts (or see the "Money Bags" idea above). Write a coin amount on the chalkboard and instruct students to count out coins to total that amount. Ask a student volunteer to name the coins she used to reach the amount. Record her response on the chalkboard. Ask another student to name the coins he selected, and record his response as well. Continue calling on students and listing their responses until the answers start to become repetitious. Point out the many coin combinations used to equal the same amount. Then erase the original total and write a new coin amount for students to count.

Math-Related Literature

Addition:
One Green Island
By Charlotte Hard
Candlewick Press, 1995

Sea Sums
By Joy N. Hulme
Hyperion Books For Children, 1996

Fractions:
Fraction Action
By Loreen Leedy
Holiday House, Inc.; 1994

Give Me Half!
By Stuart J. Murphy
HarperCollins Children's Books, 1996

Geometry:
Grandfather Tang's Story
By Ann Tompert
Crown Books For Young Readers, 1990

The Greedy Triangle
By Marilyn Burns
Scholastic Inc., 1995

Measurement:
Who Sank The Boat?
By Pamela Allen
The Putnam Publishing Group, 1990

Money:
Alexander, Who Used To Be Rich Last Sunday
By Judith Viorst
Simon & Schuster Books For Young Readers, 1987

Pigs Will Be Pigs
By Amy Axelrod
Simon & Schuster Books For Young Readers, 1994

Time:
Get Up And Go!
By Stuart J. Murphy
HarperCollins Children's Books, 1996

Nine O'Clock Lullaby
By Marilyn Singer
HarperCollins Children's Books, 1991

Pigs On A Blanket
By Amy Axelrod
Simon & Schuster Children's Books, 1996

1	2	3	4	5	6	7	8	9	10
11	12	13	14	15	16	17	18	19	20
21	22	23	24	25	26	27	28	29	30
31	32	33	34	35	36	37	38	39	40
41	42	43	44	45	46	47	48	49	50
51	52	53	54	55	56	57	58	59	60
61	62	63	64	65	66	67	68	69	70
71	72	73	74	75	76	77	78	79	80
81	82	83	84	85	86	87	88	89	90
91	92	93	94	95	96	97	98	99	100

Patterns

Use with "Rollin' With Addition" on page 211.

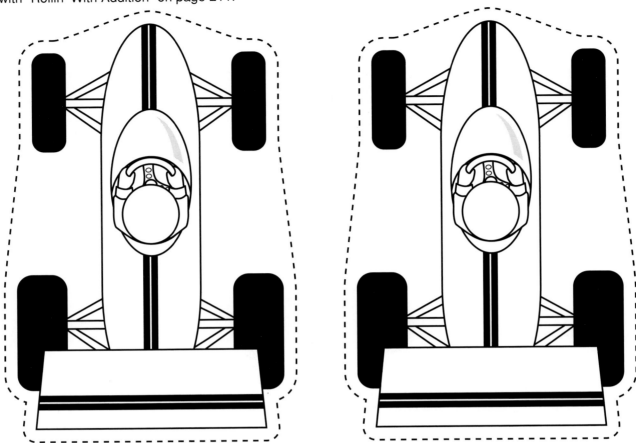

Pattern

Use with "Rockin' Around The Clock" on page 222.

Ready, Set, Measure!

Use the ruler to measure each line segment.
Then, under each segment, draw a line one inch longer than the segment.

1. 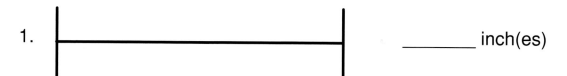 _____ inch(es)

2. 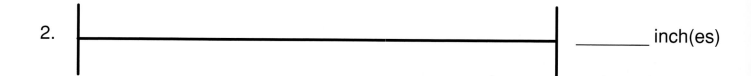 _____ inch(es)

3.  _____ inch(es)

4.  _____ inch(es)

5. 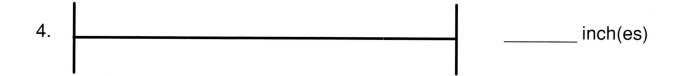 _____ inch(es)

Bonus Box: Use the ruler to draw two lines on the back of this paper. Ask a classmate to measure the lines.

1	2	3	4	5	6

7	8	9	10	11	12

Note To The Teacher: Use with "Get In Step With Measurement" on page 216.

Name _____

_____
(title of graph)

228   **Note To The Teacher:** Use with "Use Your Noodle!" and "Spin-A-Graph" on page 218.

Name _____ *Open pictograph*

_____
(title of graph)

KEY

=

Note To The Teacher: Use with "Personal Pictographs" on page 219.

Patterns

Use with "Shapely Creatures" on page 220.

Triangles

Square

Parallelogram

Rectangle

Rhombus

Trapezoid

Hexagon

Octagon

Pentagon

©1998 The Education Center, Inc. • *The Mailbox® Superbook* • *Grade 2* • TEC451

SOCIAL STUDIES

On The Move With Maps

Introduce your students to one of the most fundamental and important tools of geography—maps!

A Rose Is A Rose

Start your study of maps with one of the basics of map reading—the *compass rose*. Explain to your students that most maps have a symbol to show where the directions of north, south, east, and west are located. This symbol is called a compass rose. Use a classroom map to show your students what a compass rose looks like; then have each student create a model of a compass rose from a small paper plate. Make sure that students label the four directional words in the appropriate places. To show how the compass rose works, point to the north wall of the classroom. Have each student place his completed compass rose on the floor so that it is pointing to the north. Next have him sketch a map of the classroom, making sure to include a compass rose to indicate the positions. Your study of maps will be headed in the right direction!

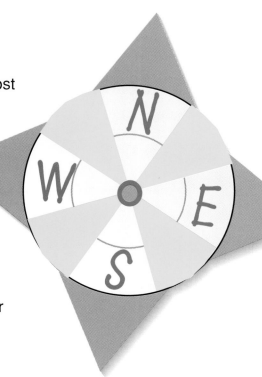

Super Symbols

Another important aspect of map reading is learning to interpret a *map key*. A map key explains what the pictures, or *symbols*, on a map represent. Tell your students to refer to the classroom maps they made in the activity "A Rose Is A Rose." Ask students what symbols they used to represent the desks. Most likely they used squares or rectangles. Draw a large box on the chalkboard and write the words "Map Key" at the top of it. Then draw a square in the box and label it "desk." Explain that the square can be a symbol for a desk. Ask students what other symbols were included on their maps. What did they use to represent the door? A trash can? A table? Draw examples of their responses on your map key. Then have each student create a map key for his own classroom map. If time allows, have student volunteers show their maps and completed keys to the class.

Map Key

desk
table
trash can
door

Using A Map Scale

Learning to use a map scale is fun with this big idea. Purchase an inexpensive shower-curtain liner or a plastic tablecloth, and draw a simple city map on it. (Be sure to include a map key and compass rose to reinforce prior learning!) Include familiar items such as houses, a library, a park, a school, a river, and a simple street layout. When designing your map, keep in mind a scale distance such as one foot equals one mile. Spread the completed map on the floor and invite students to sit around it. Show students how to calculate the distance between objects on the map by placing a ruler at one point and marking off its length to another point. Tell them that each 12-inch increment equals one mile; then have them calculate the scale distance between the two points. Have students take turns determining the distances between other points on the map. Your class will be scaling its way to success!

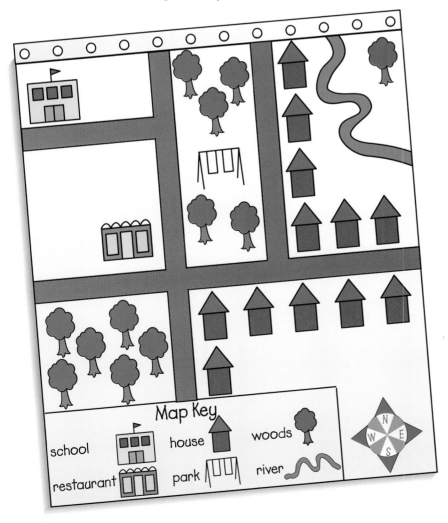

A Bird's-Eye View

Help students understand the concept of maps drawn from a bird's-eye view. Discuss with your students how the school grounds would look to a bird flying above them. What would the school building look like? The playground? The cars in the parking lot? Reinforce that a bird would see only the top of each item. Distribute a piece of drawing paper to each student. Instruct students to sit by objects in the classroom that they can look at from above. Encourage students to each choose an object that they usually don't see from this angle, such as a hat, a chair, a plant, or the pencil sharpener. Then have them draw the items from a bird's-eye view. Provide time for students to show their drawings to the class. For further practice with the concept, have each student complete a copy of the reproducible on page 248. Your class will be looking at things from a whole new perspective!

Chair

Maps That Tell A Story

Use map-skill practice to reinforce story elements. Share your favorite version of a well-known story with your class. After reading the story aloud, ask your students to describe the setting of the book. Then pair students and have each student pair draw a picture of the setting on a large sheet of construction paper. Remind student pairs to include a compass rose and map key on their projects, too! Provide time for each pair to share its completed map with the class.

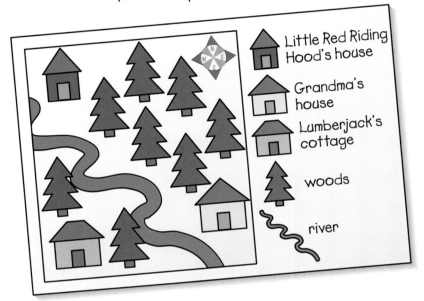

Great Grids

This simple grid activity will provide a daily dose of cardinal-direction reinforcement. Prepare a poster-board grid with two-inch squares as shown. Also create a two-inch copy of your school mascot or another popular character. Laminate the grid and character for durability; then mount the grid on a small bulletin board. Pin the cutout to a square on the grid. Each morning select a student to move the cutout around the grid according to your oral directions. Give instructions such as, "Move the character one square south and two squares east." Ask the class to listen and watch carefully to help monitor the student's work. Increase the difficulty of the instructions as students become more familiar with the cardinal directions.

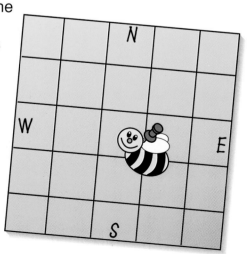

Giant Grid Game

Get your whole class in on the action with this game that reviews cardinal directions. Create a large grid by using a permanent marker to divide a plastic tablecloth into nine-inch squares. Draw a compass rose in the center square. To play the game, spread the grid on the floor. Have as many students as possible each stand on a square on the grid. Ask the remainder of the students to sit around the edge of the grid and monitor the actions of the players. Announce a directional move for the students to follow, such as, "Move three squares north." If a student is unable to move that many squares in that direction, she must leave the grid and take a place with the seated students. Play continues until only one student remains; then invite the seated students to each take a place on the grid for the second round of play.

All Around School

Begin this three-dimensional mapmaking activity with a mini field trip around your school. First provide each student with a drawing tablet and a pencil; then lead students on a walk around the campus. Have each child sketch the area, reminding her to make note of the street names, the buildings, and other important features. Back in the classroom, place students in small groups to compare their drawings. Then have the students draw the surrounding streets on a sheet of poster board. Have students use construction-paper scraps to decorate small boxes to resemble the school building(s) and other campus features. Then have students place the boxes in their appropriate locations on the poster board. Encourage groups to use art materials such as felt, yarn, and markers to create details around the school. After the projects are complete, display them in the library or another prominent school location.

Maps In Literature

Share these map-related books with your students:

As The Crow Flies: A First Book Of Maps
by Gail Hartman
(Aladdin Paperbacks, 1993)

This Is The Way We Go To School
by Edith Baer
(Scholastic Inc., 1992)

Your Best Friend, Kate
by Pat Brisson
(Bradbury Press, 1989)

Around The World With Queenee The Bee
by Victoria Malyurek
(Victoria's Publishing Company, 1996)

Maps And Globes
by Jack Knowlton
(HarperCollins Children's Books, 1985)

A Bird's-Eye View: A First Book Of Maps
by Harriet Wittels and Joan Greisman
(Scholastic Inc., 1995)

Getting Into Globes

Almost every classroom features a globe, an important reference in geography and map studies. Explain to your students that a globe is simply a model of the earth, showing where the continents and oceans are located. Hold up a globe next to a world map. Inform your students that both references show the same areas. Then try the following demonstration to help students understand how a round surface such as the earth can be shown on a flat map.

Place an orange in the palm of your hand for students to observe. Tell them that the orange is similar in shape to the earth. Carefully use a knife to slice the orange in half, not quite cutting through the peel on one side. Separate the two halves, making sure that the uncut section of peel holds the two pieces together. Explain that the map shows the earth with its two halves side by side, like the orange you are holding. Place the halves back together again to let students observe the round model; then open them back up for students to see both sides at once. What a tasty demonstration!

Welcome To Our Community!

Celebrate the unique aspects of your community with a look at the people, places, and events that make it special.

A Look At The Past

How did your community begin? Most communities began near water. Long ago, boats were a main form of travel, and communities near water were easy to reach. When the railroads appeared later, communities sprang up around them, too. Display a large U.S. map. Have your students observe the areas in which there are clusters of cities. Lead your class in a discussion of what may have caused different communities to form. Point out that the colonists settled along the East Coast close to where their ships landed, the gold rush in California attracted people to the West Coast, and the abundance of oil in Texas drew people south. Ask your students to think of resources in their area that may have caused their community to grow. Then have each child draw a picture of something that is important to the community today. If desired, bind the completed pictures between two construction-paper covers and place the booklet in the classroom library for all to enjoy.

Illustrate Your Community

What is a community? It's a place where people live, work, and play. Many of the jobs and recreational events in a community depend on the resources found in the area. Ask your students to think about the many types of workers, people, and things to do in your community. Divide your students into three groups. Provide each group with crayons and a sheet of poster board. Ask the first group to list the different types of jobs, the second to list the types of homes and families, and the third to list the forms of entertainment in the community. Provide time for each group to share its completed poster with the class. Then display the projects on a bulletin board titled "Welcome To Our Community!"

Community-Helper Pantomime

People depend on many helpers to keep their community happy and healthy. Point out to your students that a community relies on an assortment of workers. A community needs workers to help keep it safe, to keep people healthy, to provide transportation, and to help maintain communications. A community also needs people who provide sources of food, clothing, and shelter. Have your students list the types of workers who provide these things in your community while you record their responses on the board. Then have each student secretly select a helper to pantomime in front of the class. Can the children correctly identify all the important workers?

A Community Of Many Groups

Once your students understand that they are part of a community, have them take a look at the other groups to which they belong. Define *group* as a number of people who have something in common. Groups meet together to have fun, to learn, or to get a job done. Ask students to think about things they do, places they go, or people they meet with to focus on a special interest. List students' responses on the chalkboard. Possible responses might include Boy or Girl Scouts, 4-H Clubs, youth groups, sports teams, dance classes, and second grade. Remind students that they are also part of larger groups, such as American citizens, state residents, and community members. Then have each student create a mobile showing all the different groups to which he belongs. To make a mobile, a student illustrates each group he belongs to on a separate card. If desired, also provide each student with a small construction-paper outline of your state and the United States. He then hole-punches the top of each card and map and ties them to a coat hanger with a length of yarn. Suspend the completed projects around the classroom for a display that highlights the importance and fun of belonging to different groups.

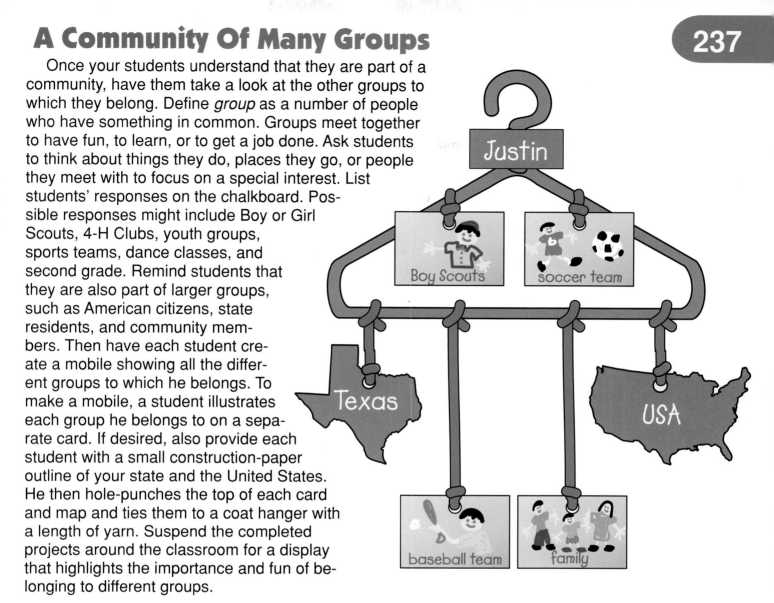

Rules And Laws In The Community

Reinforce the need for maintaining order in the community with a discussion of rules and laws. Explain to students that a rule is a good guideline created for the protection and respect of people and property, such as not running in the halls or raising your hand before speaking in class. A law is a command that everyone must obey to ensure safety and fairness, such as driving the speed limit and not smoking in certain public places. To make sure your students have an understanding of these two concepts, distribute a copy of the reproducible on page 249 to each child. Instruct her to write and illustrate a rule and a law that are enforced in your community. Then compile the completed pages into a classroom booklet titled "We Follow Rules And Laws."

Signs Of A Safe Community

Encourage your students to be safety-savvy with a review of signs and symbols found in the community. Explain to students that signs are important ways to maintain order and safety. Often a sign will have a symbol to help convey a law or to provide information. Ask students to name situations where safety is a concern, such as when crossing the street, playing outdoors, or driving through a construction zone. Next have your students think of times when a sign provides valuable information, such as showing the way to an airport, indicating a bus stop, or marking a no-smoking area. Reinforce the significance of signs and symbols by having each student make a poster of this important community information. Distribute a copy of the signs on page 250. Discuss the correct color for each sign; then have each student color, cut out, and glue her signs to a sheet of white construction paper. To make sure each student understands the meaning of each sign, have her write a sentence under each one telling the safety or information message the sign conveys. Have your students take their completed posters home to share with their families and friends, encouraging community safety for all.

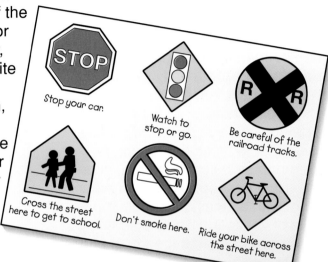

Caring For The Community

Help each student to be a caring member of his community with a lesson on responsible citizenship. Remind your students that a community provides people with places to live, work, and play. It is up to each member of the community to keep it clean, well cared for, and safe. Invite your class to participate in skits showing responsible community behavior in the following situations:

 Two children are walking down the street. One child offers the other a stick of gum, and they must dispose of the wrappers.

 A child notices a woman having difficulty opening the door to the library because her arms are full of books.

 A group of children wants to play jump rope and one child insists that there is more room to play in the middle of the street.

 While walking home from school, a child finds a wallet on the sidewalk.

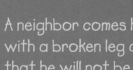 A neighbor comes home from the hospital with a broken leg and expresses concern that he will not be able to walk his dog.

 The neighborhood park is becoming run-down and covered with litter.

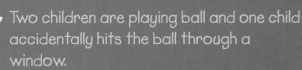 Two children are playing ball and one child accidentally hits the ball through a window.

Communities Of The Past

What were communities like long ago? Ask your class to think about the places in your community now. Where do your students go to get items such as clothes, food, and toys? What do their parents do when the car breaks down, the roof leaks, or the TV is broken? Tell your students to close their eyes and imagine the community before their grandparents were born. Where would people get their clothes, food, and toys? Did they need the same types of repairs that we do today? Share a book, such as *When I Was Young In The Mountains* by Cynthia Rylant (Dutton Children's Books, 1982) or *The Quilt Story* by Tony Johnston (G. P. Putnam's Sons, 1985). After reading one of the stories aloud, have your students make comparisons of how life is different today from what it was for the characters in the story. Challenge students to name something that has changed in the community before the time their grandparents were growing up. Then have each student draw a picture showing how the community might have looked long ago. Provide time for students to share their drawings with the class.

Communities Of The Future

Invite students to catch a glimpse of a future community with an activity that sparks the imagination. After discussing communities of the past, challenge your class to think of changes the future might bring. What will the needs of the community be like? How will people travel? What will they do for entertainment? What type of clothing will they wear? Have each child share her thoughts on the subject by creating an advertisement for a futuristic newspaper. To make an ad, a student decides on a product or service that might be offered in a community of tomorrow. Then she draws an ad for it on a sheet of construction paper. Post the completed ads on a bulletin-board display titled "Coming Soon In A Community Of The Future!"

Underwater cell phones! Don't miss a call while you're swimming.

Communities in Literature

Tour these community-related books with your students:

City Green
by DyAnne DiSalvo-Ryan
(Morrow Junior Books, 1994)

One Afternoon
by Yumi Heo
(Orchard Books, 1994)

Night On A Neighborhood Street
by Eloise Greenfield
(Puffin Books, 1996)

Roxaboxen
by Alice McLerran
(Lothrop, Lee & Shepard Books, 1991)

The Troubled Village
by Simon Henwood
(Farrar, Straus & Giroux, Inc., 1991)

The World Of Work

Wants and needs, goods and services,
buying and saving—it's all part of the working world!

Learning About Wants And Needs

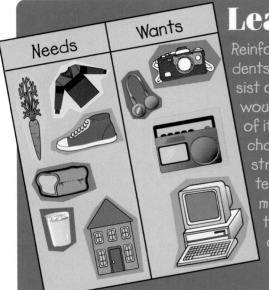

Reinforce needs and wants with this small-group activity. Remind students that *needs* are things necessary for people to live. Our needs consist of food, water, clothing, and shelter. *Wants* are things that people would like to have but can live without. Have your class brainstorm a list of items that belong in each category. List students' responses on the chalkboard. Then have your students work in small groups to demonstrate their understanding of wants and needs. Have each group cut ten pictures of wants and ten pictures of needs from discarded magazines. After a determined length of time, have each group, in turn, present their pictures before gluing them in the corresponding column of a sheet of bulletin-board paper (labeled as shown). Display the resulting class poster in a prominent place during your study of the world of work.

The Spin On Goods And Services

Now that your students understand the wants and needs of consumers, show them how these demands are met. Tell your students that there are workers in the community who provide goods and services for consumers. *Goods* are things that workers grow or make. *Services* are things that workers do to help people. Both goods and services help take care of our wants and needs. Reinforce this concept by having students create goods-and-services spinners. To make a spinner, a student illustrates three occupations that provide goods and three occupations that provide services on a tagboard copy of the wheel pattern on page 251. Then help her use a brad to attach a tagboard arrow (page 251) to the center of the illustrated wheel. Pair students and have them exchange spinners. One student in each pair spins the arrow and identifies the occupation as one that provides a good or a service. After verifying the answer, her partner then repeats the process on her spinner. Student pairs continue in this manner until each picture on both spinners has been identified. Your class will have the spin on consumer concepts!

Making Money

How do people pay for goods and services? Most students will know the answer—with money! Tell students that when people enter the world of work, they are paid for the jobs they do. The money they make is called *income*. Ask students whether they have ever earned money. Provide time for them to tell what they did to earn the money. Also encourage them to tell whether they spent the money right away or saved it for a special purchase. Explain that when you decide how much money it is wise to spend, and how much money you should save for other things, you are making a *budget*. Ask your students to decide on a typical weekly allowance for a second grader. Have them name ways that they could spend their allowances during the week. Suggest that each student think of a moderate long-range goal to save for. Have him determine how much money he should save each week in order to purchase the item in a timely manner. Then help the student calculate how long it would take to save for the item with his budget plan. Your class will soon see that an important part of income is learning to budget wisely.

Tom
$5.00 allowance per week
I spend my allowance on ice cream at school, movies, and toys.
I want to buy a baseball hat. ($10.00)
If I save $2.00 every week, I can buy my hat in 5 weeks.

Considering Careers

"Guess what I'm going to be when I grow up?" Ballet dancers, football players, famous singers—students often claim they already know what their career choice will be! Help them become more aware of career choices by asking them to consider the questions below. Read aloud the questions and have each student record her answers on a piece of scrap paper. Then have each student write a paragraph telling what career choice might be a good one for her based on her answers. If time allows, provide materials so students can draw pictures of themselves in their future careers.

- Do you like to help people?
- Do you like to create things?
- Do you like making things grow?
- Do you like working with animals?
- Would you like to work with others or by yourself?
- Would you like to work during the day or at night?
- Would you like to wear a uniform to work?
- Would you like a job that involves travel?

Welcome, Workers!

During your study of the world of work, invite guest speakers to visit your classroom to discuss their careers. After each speaker concludes his presentation, ask your class to determine whether the worker supplies wants, needs, or both. Also ask students if the worker provides goods or services for the community. Be sure to take a picture of each guest speaker and use the photos in a display that celebrates the working world.

Taking Care Of Planet Earth

Instill a sense of responsibility for taking care of our planet with these earth-friendly activities.

Dreams For A Healthy Planet

Introduce your unit on environmental responsibility with *Just A Dream* by Chris Van Allsburg (Houghton Mifflin Company, 1990). In this story, a young boy who does not practice waste management has a dream about the future of our planet. He dreams of overflowing landfills, vanishing natural resources, and polluted air. After reading the story aloud, brainstorm with your students various solutions for these real-life problems. Follow up your discussion by having your students write short stories about dreams for a happier future for the earth. If possible, have the students read their stories at an assembly to encourage a schoolwide cleanup campaign.

What A Bright Idea!

Turn your students on to conservation with this bright idea! Encourage energy conservation by having each student design a switch-plate cover with a reminder to use our energy sources wisely. Make a light-switch pattern with the same dimensions as a school switch-plate cover. Duplicate tagboard copies of the pattern and distribute one to each student. Have her write a slogan on her pattern, then decorate it with crayons or markers. Tape the patterns atop switch plates around the school. What earth-friendly reminders!

Save The Whales!

When it comes to taking care of our planet, don't overlook the endangered species! Raise your students' awareness of threatened wildlife with these sandwich boards that convey important messages about animals in need. To begin, have each student select an animal to research. Encourage him to find at least two interesting facts about the species and make note of the information on index cards. Assist each student in proofreading the facts for spelling, punctuation, and capitalization. Then supply the student with a sheet of poster board that has been cut in half. Instruct him to illustrate one half of the poster board with a picture of the endangered species and write the researched information on the other half. Punch two holes at the top of each board and connect them with lengths of yarn as shown. Invite your students to parade around the school wearing their sandwich boards. What a way to call attention to the plight of our endangered friends!

Reinforce The Three "Rs"

Inform students that when it comes to conservation, the three "Rs" are *reduce, reuse,* and *recycle.* Explain these very important concepts for taking care of the earth.

Reduced items are those that should be used only in small amounts because they are hard to dispose of. Styrofoam® and aerosol cans are not biodegradable and cause problems in landfills.

Reused items are not discarded after one use; they are used again for the same or a different function. Grocery sacks are often reused as wastebasket liners or as overnight bags, or they can be taken back to the grocery store and used again there.

Recycled items pass through a cycle that reprocesses the materials instead of throwing them away. Aluminum cans are often recycled. After being reprocessed the aluminum can be used again.

Reinforce these concepts with a classroom project. Set up three boxes in your classroom and label one box for each of the three Rs. Encourage students to bring in examples of items to put in each box. Invite students to take objects from the *Reuse* box if they can put them to good use. Arrange for the items in the *Recycle* box to be taken to a recycling center. Then have your students find the best way to discard the items in the *Reduce* box, and remind them to be careful of purchasing those items again in the future.

Pollution Solutions

For a simple review of your conservation unit, have your students create this earth-wise display. Distribute an index card to each student and have her write an idea for taking care of the earth. Challenge students to write a proactive statement rather than one beginning with the word *Don't.* While students are completing their cards, staple a large reduce, reuse, and recycle symbol to a bulletin board. Collect the cards and mount them inside the symbol. Complete the display by adding the title "We Have Solutions To Pollutions."

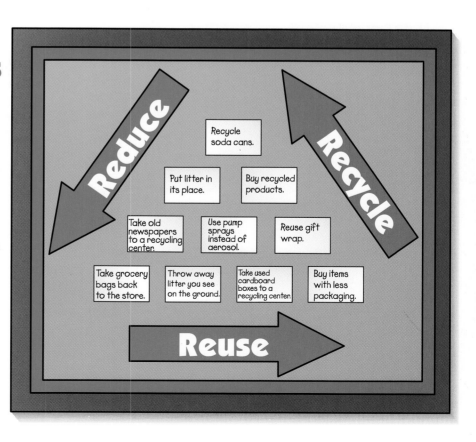

People In Touch And On The Go

Communication and transportation—
they help people share information, products, and experiences with others.

What's Going On?

Begin your study of communication by displaying an envelope, a newspaper, and a radio. Ask your students to determine what the three items have in common. Allow time for responses, and then confirm that the items help people communicate: we can share information by writing a letter, reading a newspaper, and listening to the radio. Place students in small groups and have them brainstorm other items that help us share news and ideas with others, such as telephones, televisions, computers, telegrams, magazines, books, and billboards. After a desired amount of time, have each group present its ideas. List students' responses on the chalkboard. Then have each student refer to the list and draw a picture of each form of communication she uses at home. Provide time for the students to share their drawings. Happy communications!

What's The Big Idea?

Get your students' attention without saying a word—then capitalize on the moment to review some important forms of communication. Stand in the front of the room and glance at your watch; then fold your arms in front of you and tap your foot. Point to any students who continue to talk, and hold your finger to your lips while shaking your head. When everyone is quiet, ask students to identify ways you communicated without using words. Most students will be familiar with signs of impatience, such as glancing at the time and folding your arms. Even more will know the sign for "Please be quiet." Explain that we do not always have to use words to share an idea. People can communicate with gestures, music, art, and sign language. Try some of these activities so students can practice interpreting "wordless" communication:

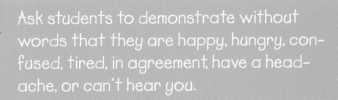

Ask students to demonstrate without words that they are happy, hungry, confused, tired, in agreement, have a headache, or can't hear you.

Play recorded music for your class. Include a march, a soothing classical piece, a bouncy tune, a blues piece, and a waltz. Ask students to describe the way each selection makes them feel.

Show students several works of art in a variety of styles. Gather pictures that feature bright colors, darker tones, people in different attitudes and settings, and still-life subjects. Ask the children to respond to each picture.

Getting From Here To There

People are always on the move—just ask students to name all the different places they have been to already today. They started out at home, came to school, entered the classroom, went to the cafeteria, and perhaps played on the playground or in the gym. A typical day is filled with lots of coming and going! Most of the movement around school is done by walking, but students don't all arrive at school the same way. Make a graph of the different forms of transportation students use to get to school in the mornings. Create a bar graph on a sheet of chart paper, and label the categories with the words *feet, car, bus, bike,* and *other.* Have each student personalize a self-stick note. Then have each student, in turn, place his note in the appropriate column on the graph. Discuss the results with the students. Which is the most common way of morning transportation for your second graders?

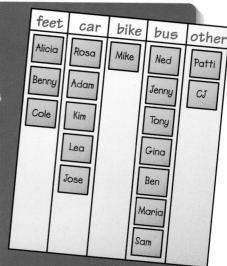

feet	car	bike	bus	other
Alicia	Rosa	Mike	Ned	Patti
Benny	Adam		Jenny	CJ
Cole	Kim		Tony	
	Lea		Gina	
	Jose		Ben	
			Maria	
			Sam	

Away We Go!

After looking at the different types of transportation, have students identify the many places different kinds of transportation can be found. Use the bulletin-board display described in "Wings, Wheels, And Rudders" to generate a list of places where transportation takes place. Cars travel on highways, trains move on tracks, ships sail into ports, and planes take off from airports. What other special transportation places can your students name? Have each student select a form of transportation and illustrate it, showing where it is typically found. Also have him write a sentence telling why we depend on this form of transportation. Compile the completed pages into a class booklet titled "Away We Go!"

We need airplanes to help us get places faster.

Ships take us across the oceans.

Wings, Wheels, And Rudders

This student-created bulletin board reinforces the different types of transportation. Visually divide a bulletin board into three sections. Use bulletin-board paper to cover the top section light blue, the middle section brown, and the bottom section dark blue. Label the sections "air," "land," and "water" respectively. From discarded magazines, have students cut out examples of transportation for each category. Encourage students to draw examples of items to add to the display as well. For an added challenge, have students include transportation from long ago, such as covered wagons, steamboats, and sailing ships. Mount the pictures in their corresponding categories; then have students identify forms of transportation that help provide us with services, entertainment, research, product delivery, construction, and ways for people to move from place to place.

Hats Off To American History

Take a look into the past for a better understanding and appreciation of our American heritage.

Set The Stage For History

This sizable visual aid will help students see the big picture of American history. Make an overhead transparency of the map on page 252; then project and trace it to create a bulletin-board display. As you introduce each settlement described below, have your students locate and label it on the map. (Remind students that the states, as shown, did not exist at this point in history.) Then have them help you decide on an important fact about each settlement to write on a separate card and staple to the display. Use colored yarn to match the information to the appropriate location on the map.

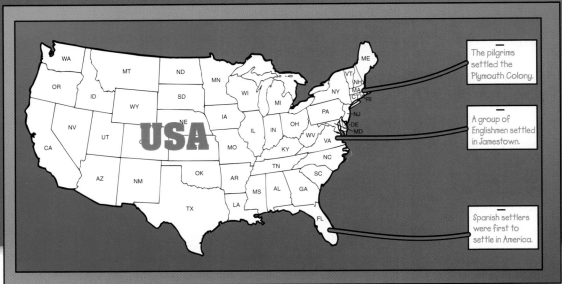

Who's On First?

At first the Native Americans were the only people in our country, but eventually other people decided to build *settlements,* or small communities, here. Spanish settlers were the first new people to settle in America. They settled in Florida and named their settlement St. Augustine. The Spanish came to America looking for gold but failed to find any. Their fort in St. Augustine still stands today, more than 300 years later.

From Merry Old England

Another early group to form a settlement in America was the English. A group of men crossed the Atlantic Ocean on a voyage that took four long months. They landed in Virginia and built a settlement near a large river. In honor of their king, they named their settlement Jamestown. The English, led by John Smith, began to settle the wilderness around Jamestown. You can visit the site of this first English settlement today.

Keep On Coming!

As time passed, more and more people from England decided to set sail for America. One of the most well-known groups, the Pilgrims, sailed from England on the *Mayflower* and settled the Plymouth Colony in what is now Massachusetts. Strong religious beliefs and the desire for freedom of worship brought them to our land. After a difficult first year, the Pilgrims gave thanks for their new settlement with a celebration attended by the Native Americans who helped them survive many hardships.

A Peek Into The Past

What were things like for these new settlers? How did they get food, clothing, and shelter in a new land? Have your students find answers to these questions by sharing the books *Sarah Morton's Day* by Kate Waters (Scholastic Inc., 1989) and *Samuel Eaton's Day* by Kate Waters (Scholastic Inc., 1993). After reading each story, display a poster-board chart labeled with the headings "Today" and "Long Ago." Ask students to think of differences in lifestyles between modern times and those pictured in the stories. List students' responses on the chart. Then post the chart in a prominent position in your classroom, and encourage students to add additional information to it during your study of America in the past.

Today	Long Ago
We travel in cars. We buy clothes in stores. We order pizza.	They rode horses. They made their clothes. They cooked all their meals.

History In Literature

Take a step back in time with the following books about our history and the changes in our past. As specific places are mentioned in the stories, have students locate and label them on the map display described on page 246.

Can't You Make Them Behave, King George?
by Jean Fritz
(G. P. Putnam's Sons, 1982)

The First Thanksgiving Feast
by Joan Anderson
(Houghton Mifflin Company, 1989)

Who's That Stepping On Plymouth Rock?
by Jean Fritz
(G. P. Putnam's Sons, 1975)

Heron Street
by Ann Turner
(HarperCollins Children's Books, 1989)

If You Grew Up With George Washington
by Ruth B. Gross
(Scholastic Inc., 1993)

If You Sailed On The Mayflower
by Ann McGovern
(Scholastic Inc., 1991)

Growing And Changing

Show how a community can evolve as more people settle the land. Cut a length of white bulletin-board paper and tape it to the wall where your students can easily reach it. Draw a thin, blue river running across the paper. Explain to your students that before settlers arrive, the land remains undeveloped, as seen in your illustration. With the coming of people, many changes take place. To demonstrate, have each child add to the drawing one picture that represents a change made by settlers. Offer suggestions such as a row of crops, a cow, a sheep, a fence, a bridge, a road, or a building. After each student has added to the picture, point out how the scene changed from an empty piece of land to a settlement. Then have the students think of a name for the settlement and dictate an imaginary history about it. Transcribe the account and post it next to the mural of the class-created community.

From A Bird's-Eye View

Look at things from a bird's-eye view!
Cut on the dotted lines.
Match and glue.

1.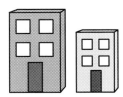

2.

3.

4.

5.

6.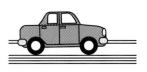

7.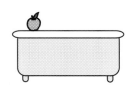

Bonus Box: On another sheet of paper, draw a picture of your bedroom from a bird's-eye view.

Note To The Teacher: Use with "A Bird's-Eye View" on page 233.

Rules And Laws

A community has rules and laws.
Rules and laws protect people.
Write one rule and one law in your community.
Draw a picture to go with each sentence.

Rule: _____

_____

_____

_____

_____

_____

Law: _____

_____

_____

_____

_____

_____

Note To The Teacher: Use with "Rules And Laws In The Community" on page 237.

Patterns

Use with "Signs Of A Safe Community" on page 238.

Stop Sign

Traffic Light

Bike Crossing

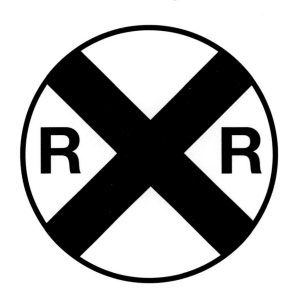

Railroad Crossing

No Smoking

School Crossing

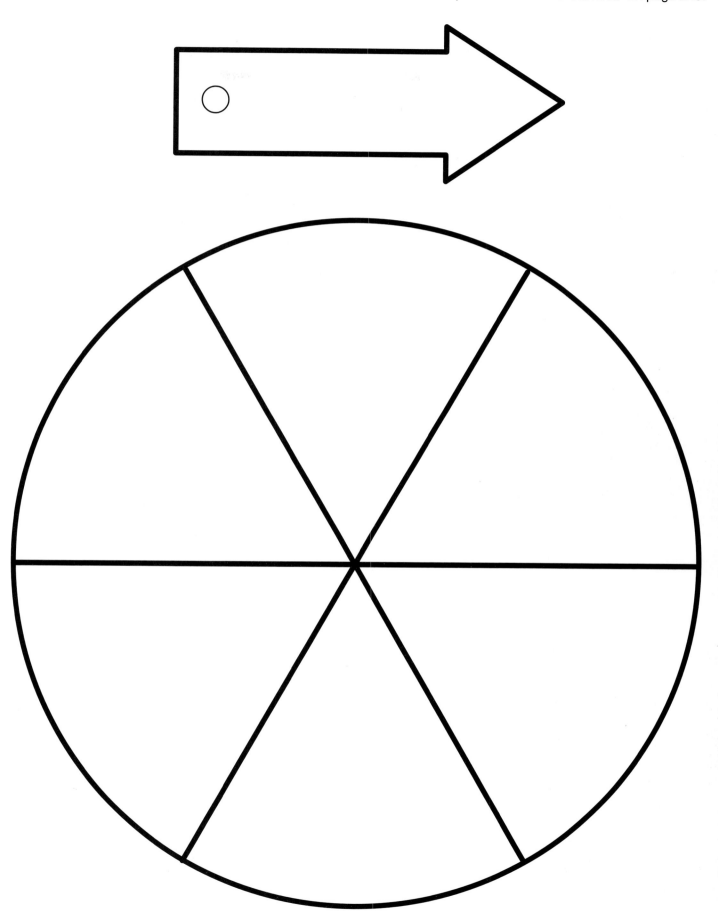

Pattern

Use with "Set The Stage For History" on page 246.

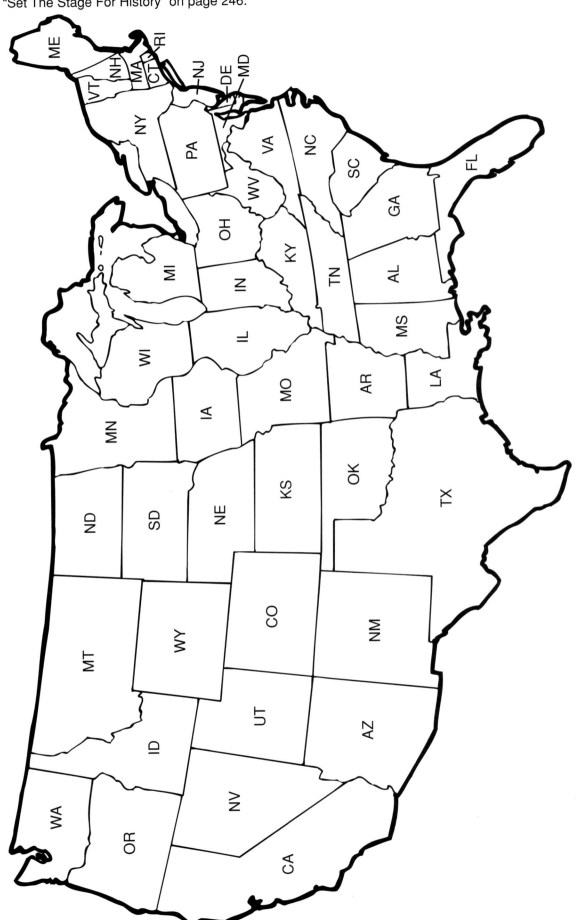

©1998 The Education Center, Inc. • *The Mailbox® Superbook • Grade 2* • TEC451

SCIENCE

It's Alive!

People, plants, and animals—they grow, they change, they're living things!

WHAT'S IN THE BAG?

Introduce the needs of living things by piquing your students' curiosity! Create a mystery bag by filling a paper lunch sack with items that represent the needs of living things: an uninflated balloon, a bottle of water, a sock, a piece of wood or a brick, and an apple. One by one, pull the objects out of the mystery bag. (Inflate the balloon to represent air after pulling it out of the bag.) Ask students to guess what these items signify. After a few responses, explain to your students that these objects represent the needs of living things—air, water, food, and some type of shelter. People also need clothing to help keep them warm. Nonliving things don't have these needs. For a fun follow-up, have each student name examples of needs as you record them on a chart similar to the one shown. Keep the chart on display during your study. Do your students understand the needs of living things? The answer is in the bag!

air	water	food	shelter	clothing
in a balloon	rain	apple	tent	hat
in a bag	snow	orange	house	coat
	pond	bread	apartment	pants
	lake		condo	shirt
	stream			socks

Mystery Bag

Student Study

Incorporate into your study of living things the liveliest things around—your students! Emphasize that living things grow and change by having your students keep records of the differences that occur in themselves during the school year. Duplicate copies of the recording sheet on page 268 and distribute one to each student. On the top row, have each student write the date, draw a self-portrait, write his favorite things, and sign his name in the corresponding columns. Then measure each student's height and have him record his height in the remaining column. Collect the papers and store them in a secure location. Then, at three additional times during the year, distribute the same recording sheets and have students repeat the previous recording process. If desired, keep the completed papers in your students' portfolios to document the growth and progress they have experienced in second grade. Your students will be amazed at the changes that occur in only a year's time!

People, Pets, And Plants

Most students have had experience with pets, either at home or in the classroom. Capitalize on students' knowledge of these animals to look at the different needs of living things. Have your students brainstorm a list of things that pets need in order to stay healthy. Responses might include pet food, water, a shelter or cage, chew toys, exercise, and vaccinations. Write students' responses on the chalkboard. Then repeat the activity having students brainstorm a list for people. Use the information from the lists to make a Venn diagram on the chalkboard. Ask students to help you determine where each item on the lists should be placed. To reinforce the concept of living things and their distinct needs, repeat the activity comparing pets and plants. For an added challenge, create a three-way Venn, and have students assist you in plotting the information for people, pets, and plants. Then provide time for students to discuss how they help take care of these living things at home.

Classification Relay

Use teamwork to help students classify living and nonliving things. Post a length of bulletin-board paper on a wall, visually divide the paper into two halves, and label one half "Living Things" and the other half "Nonliving Things." From discarded magazines and newspapers, have each student cut out a separate picture of a living thing and a nonliving thing. Collect the pictures and put an equal number in two large, brown paper bags. Divide the class into two teams. Line up each team behind a bag of pictures. At your signal, the first player on each team randomly draws a picture from the bag, walks to the chart, and tapes it to the correct side. He walks back to his team and gently tags the next player, who repeats the procedure. The game continues until all players have had a turn. After the activity, review the chart with your students. Keep the chart on display and encourage students to bring more pictures from home to add to it.

Needs Change Through Time

Take a look into the past to see how our needs have changed through time. Highlight three different periods of time: cave times, Colonial times, and modern times. Discuss the different ways people in each period satisfied their needs. Then enlist students' help in making a chart to compare the needs of the different groups. To make a chart, write headings on a large piece of bulletin-board paper as shown. Pair students and have each pair illustrate a different category on a sheet of drawing paper. Next have each pair glue its picture in its corresponding place on the chart. Use the completed chart as a springboard for a discussion of the importance of taking care of natural resources so that our needs will continue to be met in the future!

	Cave Times	Colonial Times	Modern Times
Air			
Water			
Food			
Shelter			
Clothes			

A BOOKLET YOU CAN COUNT ON

Reinforce the types of living and nonliving things with this delightful bookmaking project. Review the characteristics of living things with your students. Distribute ten half-sheets of drawing paper to each student. To make a booklet, a student uses a red crayon to sequentially number the center of each page. Next she draws living things on the pages with even numbers and nonliving things on the pages with odd numbers. (The number of items on each page should correspond with the page number.) Then, to demonstrate her understanding of living and nonliving, she writes a statement about the pictures on each page. Assist each student in stapling her completed pages between two construction-paper covers. Encourage her to take her book home to share with family and friends.

Is That You, Mom?

For a funny look at living and nonliving things, share with your students *Are You My Mother?* by P. D. Eastman (Random House, Inc.; 1998). When a baby bird finds himself separated from his mother, he asks a variety of living and nonliving objects if they might be the missing parent. As the baby bird encounters each new creature in the story, ask your students to classify it as a living or nonliving object. After the story, have your students discuss the needs of the baby bird and how they could or could not be met by each of the different characters in the book.

Sidewalk Survey

Take your students on a sidewalk field trip to survey the different living and nonliving things on your school grounds. Distribute paper, a writing surface such as a clipboard, and a pencil to each child; then head outdoors to a convenient location for scoping out the surroundings. Challenge each student to record ten living objects and ten nonliving objects. Back in the classroom, have students work in small groups to compare their findings. Your class will be amazed at all the different objects that can be found on school grounds!

Science Games Galore

For a fun-and-games way to reinforce the difference between living and nonliving things, try the following variations of familiar children's games.

ALPHABET ANTICS

This round-robin game will give everyone plenty of opportunities to participate. Have your students sit in a circle. Tell them that they are going to think of a different living thing for every letter of the alphabet. Select a student to start the game by naming a living thing that starts with the letter A. Continue clockwise, having the next student name an object that starts with the letter B. If a student can't think of an object for his letter, he may pass his turn. After reaching the letter Z, begin the game again using nonliving things as the category.

alligator

bear

cat

dog

I SPY

Play I Spy in the traditional manner, except have students begin the game by identifying the object that they have selected as living or nonliving. For a wider variety of living objects to choose from, take the students outdoors or by a large window to play the game.

CHARADES

Have each student silently think of a living thing to act out in front of the class. After his pantomime, he calls on students to identify his living thing. The student who guesses correctly takes the stage for the next round of play. After all students have had a chance to participate, challenge one child to think of a nonliving thing to act out. Then discuss which type of object is easier to demonstrate and the reasons why.

TOUCH TAG

This outdoor extension is similar to the game Freeze Tag. One student is selected to be It and tries to tag the other players. Once tagged, a player is frozen to his spot until another player tags him, giving him the opportunity to get back in the game by running to you and naming a living (or nonliving) thing. After a designated amount of time, select another student to take the role of It. Play continues for a desired amount of time or until every child has been frozen and has correctly identified a living or nonliving thing.

Learning About LIFE CYCLES

From egg to chicken or seed to flower, show your students the circle of life!

Which Came First?

This activity is "eggs-actly" what you need for an introduction to animals that come from eggs. Begin your study by sharing *An Extraordinary Egg* by Leo Lionni (Alfred A. Knopf Books For Young Readers, 1994). In this story, three curious frogs find a beautiful white egg. Although they have never seen a chicken before, they assume that one will hatch from the egg. Imagine their surprise when the creature that hatches has scales instead of feathers! After reading the story aloud, give each student a plastic egg filled with a small plastic or paper chicken, frog, alligator, or turtle. Ask each child to think about what might be inside his egg; then have him record his guess on a copy of page 269. Next have him crack open the egg to see what is waiting inside and record the animal's name in the corresponding box on the reproducible. Then have him write guesses for the next three statements before setting his paper aside. To complete the activity, help students research facts about each animal's life cycle; then have students use the information to complete their reproducibles.

HOME MOVIE Featuring LIFE CYCLES

These individual tachistoscopes provide students with reinforcement of the life cycles of any species. To begin, read aloud one of the books on page 259 to share information with your students about a specific life cycle. Ask students to recall what they've learned. List their ideas on the chalkboard. Then have each student use the information to create a tachistoscope. To make a television tachistoscope, a student labels and illustrates each stage of the animal's life cycle on a separate index card. She tapes her cards together in sequence to create one strip; then she tapes a blank card on each end of the strip. Next she opens a business envelope, holds it upside down, and cuts out a 3" x 4 1/2" section from the envelope front as shown. She trims the ends of the envelope, seals the remaining flaps on the back, and then colors the envelope (still upside down) to resemble a television set. She then inserts the strip into the television. To use her tachistoscope, the student moves the strip to view the stages of the animal's life cycle.

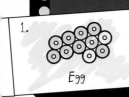

1. Egg

2. Tadpole

tadpole grows hind legs.

4. The tadpole grows front legs

5. The tadpole's tail gets smaller.

6. Frog

SEEDS AND THEIR CYCLES

Students may be surprised to learn that plants go through growing cycles, too. To demonstrate how plants grow, soak a class supply (and a few extra) of lima beans in water overnight. The following day, give each student a bean to examine. Instruct her to gently remove the outer covering of her seed, then separate the seed into two parts. Have her look carefully to examine the beginnings of the tiny plant located between the two parts of the seed. Explain that in a plant's life cycle, the seed starts to grow when it has air, water, and warmth. The seed coat (the part the students removed from their seeds) splits open, and the tiny seed begins to sprout—that's the baby plant inside the seed that students observed. A small root begins to push itself down into the soil. Then the baby plant pushes up through the soil so it can continue to get the air and light it needs to grow.

Your students can get an "underground" look at new plants emerging by placing layers of wet paper towels around the insides of clear, plastic cups. Distribute a dry lima bean or pinto bean to each student, and instruct her to place it between the paper towels and the cup. Have her store the cup away from direct sunlight and observe the changes every day. (If the paper towel becomes dry, have her add a little water to the cup for the towel to absorb.) Within a few days, a root and tiny plant will begin to grow. If desired, have the students carefully remove the plant from the cup, throw away the paper towel, and fill the cup with soil. Help each student gently place the new plant in her soil. Move the cups to a sunny location and watch your classroom garden grow!

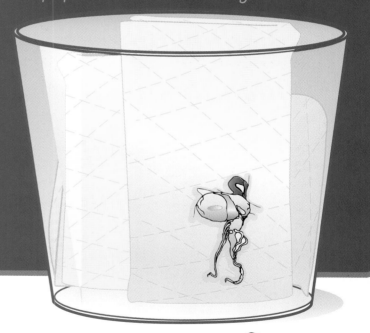

Life Cycles In Literature

Include these books in your study of life cycles.

This Is The Seed • by Alan Trussell-Cullen • (GoodYearBooks, 1996)

What Happens When Flowers Grow? • by Daphne Butler • (Raintree Steck-Vaughn Publishers, 1995)

How A Seed Grows • by Helene J. Jordan • (HarperCollins Children's Books, 1992)

Animals And Their Young • by Anita Ganeri • (Joshua Morris Publishing, Inc.; 1995)

The Foal's Seasons • by Linda Hartley • (Garrett Educational Corporation, 1996)

Creepy, Crawly Baby Bugs • by Sandra Markle • (Walker Publishing Company, Inc.; 1996)

From Tadpole To Frog • by Wendy Pfeffer • (HarperCollins Children's Books, 1994)

CLASSIFICATION QUEST

Sorting, grouping, comparing, and contrasting—
these high-interest activities will provide students with
plenty of hands-on classification practice.

SAME AND DIFFERENT

Build self-esteem and cooperative spirit in your classroom with this activity that reinforces the unique qualities of each student. Provide each child with a copy of the reproducible on page 270. Instruct each student to complete the first column with information about himself. Then, in the next two columns, have him write the name of someone who has the same answer and the name of someone who has a different answer. Provide time for students to complete their papers; then reinforce the different groups to which students can belong by calling out special seating corners. Number each corner of your room with a number from one to four. Designate a corner for each possible answer for the categories on the reproducible. For example, have blue eyes sit in corner one, brown eyes in corner two, green eyes in corner three, and hazel eyes in corner four. After each student has had time to see the others in his group, announce another category, such as only children in corner one, one sibling in corner two, two siblings in corner three, and more than two siblings in corner four. Continue in the same manner with the other categories on the reproducible. Students will soon see that they have many things in common with many of their classmates!

Critter Classification

Capitalize on students' interests by having them bring in favorite things to classify. Ask each child to bring a small stuffed animal to school. Place the stuffed animals on a table and tell students that they will be looking for ways to group the toys. Ask for some grouping ideas, such as color, size, tail or no tail, or wearing a bow or not wearing a bow. Enlist students' help in putting the animals into different groups. For a challenge, ask students to think of a way to group the animals into three different categories, such as standing, sitting, or lying down. After the activity, invite each student to place his animal on his desk for the rest of the day.

Lots Of Leaves

Use the greenery around you to provide practice with classifying objects. Ask each student to gather five different leaves from around his home. Place all the leaves on a table for students to observe. (Make sure all leaves are safe for students to handle.) As students look at the different types of foliage, point out that some leaves have smooth edges; some have rounded, lobed edges; and some have sharp, toothed edges. Then place students into small groups and have each group sort a collection of leaves in a desired way. Circulate around the classroom and have each group report its sorting method to you. To complete the activity, have each group draw its sorting method on a sheet of drawing paper. Provide time for each group to share its drawing with the class.

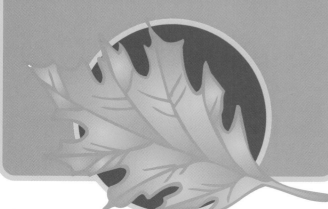

Arranging The Animals

Introduce your second graders to the different animal classifications with this activity and assessment. Distribute a copy of the reproducible on page 271 to each student. Review the characteristics of each animal category on the sheet. Then, to assess your class's understanding, have each student complete the page by writing the names of two animals under each heading on her paper. Conclude the lesson by asking each student to draw her favorite animal on the back of the paper and identify the category to which it belongs.

School-Supply Sorting

There's no shortage of things to sort when you use objects in the classroom for classification practice. Announce a topic from the list shown and give students three minutes to look around the classroom for items that could be included in the category. After the designated time, have students name their findings as you record their responses on the chalkboard. You'll be amazed at the different objects your classroom contains!

- *things to write with*
- *things to write on*
- *things to attach two or more items together*
- *things that make noise*
- *things made of glass*
- *things made of wood*
- *things made of paper*
- *things with numbers on them*
- *things that are living*
- *things to measure with*

Wonderful Weather & Sensational Seasons

Rain, snow, sleet, or hail—students will enjoy exploring the world of weather and seasons!

How's The Weather?

Introduce your unit on weather with a journey through an imaginative forecast! To begin, have your students brainstorm a list of weather words while you record their responses on the chalkboard. After a list has been generated, ask each student to choose one type of weather and then close his eyes and think of the sights, sounds, smells, and types of clothing that are associated with his choice. Then turn off the lights and have each child, in turn, describe his chosen weather. The other students may close their eyes, put their heads on their desks, and imagine the type of weather that is being described. After everyone has had a chance to participate, your students will feel as though they have changed from raincoats to bathing suits to mittens and parkas!

Wild Weather!

When it comes to weather, there's no shortage of ways to describe it! Share with your students these idioms about weather. Then have each student choose one expression to illustrate. Display the completed drawings on a bulletin board titled "Watch Out For Wild Weather!"

- It's raining cats and dogs.
- The fog is as thick as pea soup.
- It's hot enough to fry an egg on the sidewalk.
- Jack Frost is nipping at your nose.
- The wind is howling.
- It's as cool as a cucumber.
- April showers bring May flowers.
- It's pouring down in buckets.
- It's 92° in the shade.

It's raining cats and dogs.

WEATHER WATCHERS

A weather unit is the perfect opportunity to incorporate a graphing activity. To create a weather graph, visually divide a sheet of poster board into columns as shown. Each morning have a student volunteer look out the window and announce the current weather conditions. Have him place a self-stick note in the appropriate column of the graph. At the end of the observance period, use the resulting graph to ask students questions such as, "Were there more rainy days or sunny days?", or, "How many windy days were there altogether?" Your class will be weather-wise and graphing-great!

sunny	cloudy	partly cloudy	fog	rainy	snow	wind

Let The Wind Blow!

Are you ready for some windy weather? Share the story *Henry And Mudge And The Wild Wind* by Cynthia Rylant (Ready-To-Read® Aladdin Paperbacks, 1996). After reading the story aloud, let your class watch the wind change directions with these student-made wind vanes. To make a vane, each student will need a three-inch ball of clay; a small plastic container; two 2 1/2" poster-board triangles; a pencil with an eraser; a plastic straw; a straight pin; scissors; and a small amount of gravel. Instruct the student to assemble her wind vane as follows:

1. Cut two one-inch slits across from each other in each end of the straw. Assemble the straw into an arrow by inserting the triangles into the slits as shown.
2. Attach the resulting arrow to the pencil by pushing the pin through the straw and securing it to the eraser.
3. Press the ball of clay into the bottom of the container. Place the pencil into the clay.
4. Fill the rest of the container with gravel.

Find a place outside for your students to keep their wind vanes. Provide time for your class to observe the wind directions throughout the week; then have them discuss their findings.

1. It is moving air.
2. It blows leaves.
3. It can make a Kite fly.

What's The Weather?

The Wind!

What's The Weather?

Weather Riddles

Your students will enjoy making *and* solving this guessing-game bulletin board. Have each student fold a sheet of white construction paper so that a two-inch strip is visible at the bottom. Across the strip have her use a crayon to write "What's The Weather?" Next have her choose a weather condition and write three clues about it on the top flap of her paper. Then have her unfold the paper, and illustrate and label the weather condition in the resulting space. Staple the completed projects to a bulletin board so the clues are visible but the pictures are concealed by the flaps. Provide time for students to read the clues and try to predict the weather conditions waiting inside.

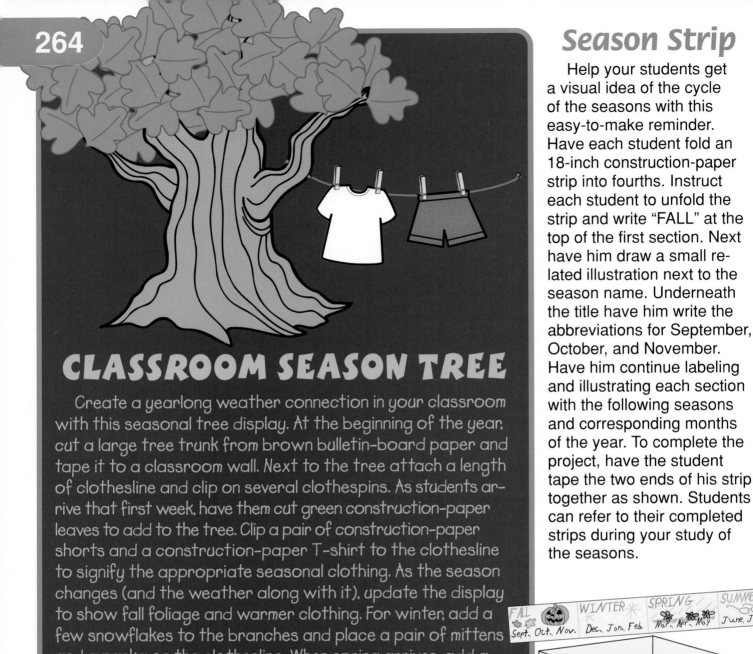

CLASSROOM SEASON TREE

Create a yearlong weather connection in your classroom with this seasonal tree display. At the beginning of the year, cut a large tree trunk from brown bulletin-board paper and tape it to a classroom wall. Next to the tree attach a length of clothesline and clip on several clothespins. As students arrive that first week, have them cut green construction-paper leaves to add to the tree. Clip a pair of construction-paper shorts and a construction-paper T-shirt to the clothesline to signify the appropriate seasonal clothing. As the season changes (and the weather along with it), update the display to show fall foliage and warmer clothing. For winter, add a few snowflakes to the branches and place a pair of mittens and a parka on the clothesline. When spring arrives, add a few flowers around the base of the tree and place a bird's nest among the branches. Your students will cheer as the winter clothing is replaced by lighter jackets and the season of outdoor activities returns!

Season Strip

Help your students get a visual idea of the cycle of the seasons with this easy-to-make reminder. Have each student fold an 18-inch construction-paper strip into fourths. Instruct each student to unfold the strip and write "FALL" at the top of the first section. Next have him draw a small related illustration next to the season name. Underneath the title have him write the abbreviations for September, October, and November. Have him continue labeling and illustrating each section with the following seasons and corresponding months of the year. To complete the project, have the student tape the two ends of his strip together as shown. Students can refer to their completed strips during your study of the seasons.

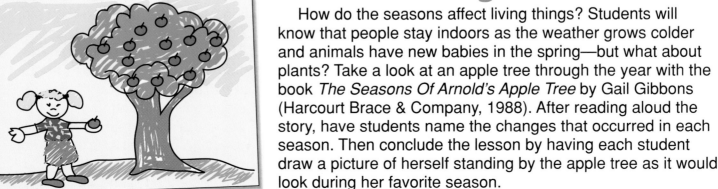

All Through The Year

How do the seasons affect living things? Students will know that people stay indoors as the weather grows colder and animals have new babies in the spring—but what about plants? Take a look at an apple tree through the year with the book *The Seasons Of Arnold's Apple Tree* by Gail Gibbons (Harcourt Brace & Company, 1988). After reading aloud the story, have students name the changes that occurred in each season. Then conclude the lesson by having each student draw a picture of herself standing by the apple tree as it would look during her favorite season.

Seasonal Symphony

Incorporate music into your study of the seasons. Find recorded music that suggests the sound of rain, thunder, wind, or other weather conditions. (Antonio Vivaldi's *Four Seasons* is a good choice.) Have the students close their eyes while they listen to the recording. Then give each student a sheet of drawing paper and crayons. Play the music a second time while students illustrate the weather scenes they imagine the music is portraying. Invite student volunteers to display their drawings and explain why they depicted the weather as they did.

Take A Seasonal Tour

This small-group project is the perfect culmination for a study of the seasons. Divide the class into four groups and assign each group a different season. On a large piece of white bulletin-board paper, have each group use markers to design a mural about its assigned season. Instruct the students to draw a landscape that shows an appropriate scene of their season. Next have each student complete a copy of the seasonal tour brochure (page 272) for her season. On the back of the brochure, have her draw a scene for her season. Then instruct each student how to fold the brochure into thirds. Tape the completed murals to a classroom wall. Then have each group use its brochures as it gives a guided tour of its season for the class. Encourage each group to dress in seasonally appropriate clothes for the occasion. What a whirlwind tour of a changing year!

Super Seasonal Selections

Put these books about weather and seasons in your classroom forecast.

Heat Wave At Mud Flat • by James Stevenson • (Greenwillow Books, 1997)
When The Earth Wakes • by Ani Rucki • (Scholastic Inc., 1998)
What Will The Weather Be? • by Lynda DeWitt • (HarperCollins Children's Books, 1993)
Tell Me A Season • by Mary M. Siddals • (Houghton Mifflin Company, 1997)
A Year In The City • by Kathy Henderson • (Candlewick Press, 1996)
Four Stories For Four Seasons • by Tomie dePaola • (Simon & Schuster Books For Young Readers, 1994)

Insights On INSECTS

Explore the worlds of beetles, butterflies, and other bugs with these interesting insect investigations.

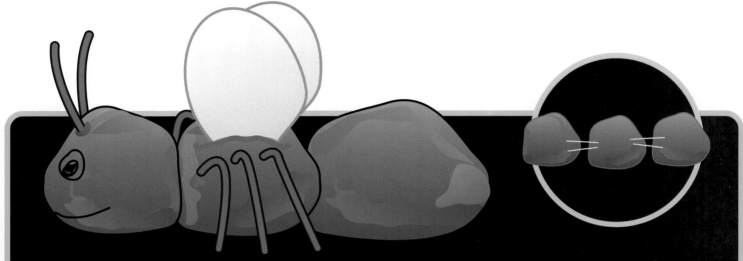

BUILD A BUG

Review the basics of bug body parts with this anatomy activity. Remind students that the body of an insect has three sections: the *head*—where eyes, antennae, and jaws are found; the *thorax*—where legs and wings are attached; and the *abdomen*—where food is digested and eggs are produced. Then have each student make a clay bug. To make a bug, a student uses toothpicks to connect three 1-inch clay balls as shown. (The balls represent the head, thorax, and abdomen of the insect, respectively.) Next he attaches two 2-inch pipe-cleaner pieces to the head for antennae and six 2-inch pipe-cleaner pieces into the thorax for the legs. Then he inserts two 2-inch construction-paper circles into the top of the thorax to create wings. For a finishing touch, he uses the point of his pencil to etch eyes into the head. No doubt your entomologists will go buggy over this idea!

Metamorphosis Models

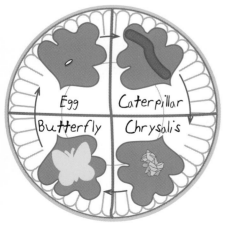

This tactile project will help youngsters understand the changes a butterfly experiences from egg to adult insect. To make a metamorphosis model, a student uses a pencil and a ruler to divide a paper plate into four equal sections. Next she glues a construction-paper leaf to each section of the plate. She then labels the top left quadrant of the plate "Egg" and glues one grain of uncooked white rice to the leaf to represent an egg. Then she labels the top right quadrant "Caterpillar" and glues a three-inch pipe-cleaner piece to the leaf. In a similar manner, she labels the bottom right quadrant "Chrysalis" and glues a wadded piece of tissue paper to the edge of the leaf. Then she labels the final quadrant "Butterfly" and glues a construction-paper butterfly to the leaf. Display the completed projects on a bulletin board for students to observe during your study of insects.

Insect Or Spider?

Reinforce the difference between these creepy crawlies by having students make diagrams of the two creatures. Remind students that an insect has three main body parts, six legs, and a pair of antennae. (See "Build A Bug" on page 266.) Then make your students spider savvy as well by having each student complete a copy of the reproducible on page 273. After following the directions to draw both an insect and a spider, your students will clearly see the difference in these two buggy beings.

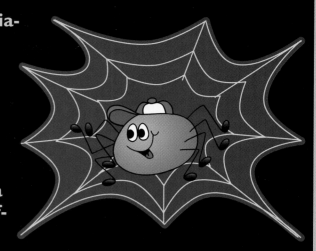

Insect Viewers

Provide your students with the opportunity to observe insects at close range with individual insect viewers. To make a viewer, each student will need a clean, transparent, two-liter bottle; an old nylon stocking; and a rubber band. Help each student cut the top off the bottle as shown. Take students outdoors to collect grass, twigs, and soil to place in their bottles. Then provide time for each student to find an insect to reside in his viewer. After the insect has been placed in the viewer, assist the student in covering the top of his bottle by securing a piece of stocking with a rubber band. Have the students observe their insects for a day or two before returning them to the area in which they were found. Conclude the activity by having each student write a paragraph about his insect observations.

Bug Off!

To culminate your study of insects, have your students play a game of Bug Off! This game is similar to Go Fish, except students try to collect pairs of insects to win the game. To prepare for the game, duplicate two tagboard copies of the insect cards on page 274 for each group of two players. If desired, have students color the insects before cutting the cards apart. To play, one student deals seven cards to himself and seven to the other player; then he places the remaining cards facedown to form a draw pile. Each player places all his matching pairs of insects on the table. Player 1 begins by asking Player 2 for a card to match one that he is holding. If he receives the match from Player 2, he places the pair on the table and takes another turn. If Player 2 does not have the card Player 1 requested, Player 2 says "Bug Off," and Player 1 draws a card from the pile. If he draws the card he requested, he may lay down the pair and take another turn. If he does not draw a match, he keeps the card and Player 2 takes a turn. Any time a player lays his last card on the table, he takes one card from the draw pile. When the draw pile is gone, the game ends. The player with the most pairs wins the game. After each pair completes its game, store the cards in a resealable plastic bag and place them in a learning center for students to use in their free time. Be prepared—they'll bug you to play again and again!

Name _____

Complete.

I Grow And Change

Date	Self-Portrait	Height	Favorite Things (books, games, foods)	Signature

©1998 The Education Center, Inc. • *The Mailbox® Superbook* • *Grade 2* • TEC451

Note To The Teacher: Use with "Student Study" on page 254.

An Extraordinary Egg

Complete.

	Guess	Check
Inside the egg is a(n) _____.		
It takes _____ days/ months to hatch.		
When it hatches it will look like this:		
When it is an adult it will look like this:		

More facts about how the animal grows:

_____

_____

_____

_____

_____

_____

Note To The Teacher: Use with "Which Came First?" on page 258.

We're The Same, Yet Different

Write answers to tell about yourself.
Find someone with the same answer.
Then find someone with a different answer.

	Me	**Someone Who's The Same**	**Someone Who's Different**
Eye color			
Hair color			
Number of brothers and sisters			
Freckles?			
Age			
Favorite season			
Favorite holiday			
Favorite sport			

Note To The Teacher: Use with "Same And Different" on page 260.

Animal Attributes

Animals can be put into different groups. Four such groups are **mammals, reptiles, birds,** and **fish.**

Write two animals that belong in each group.

Mammals
- warm-blooded
- have lungs
- have hair or fur

1. _____

2. _____

Reptiles
- cold-blooded
- have lungs
- have scaly skin

1. _____

2. _____

Birds
- warm-blooded
- have lungs
- have feathers

1. _____

2. _____

Fish
- cold-blooded
- have gills
- most have fins

1. _____

2. _____

Bonus Box: On the back of this paper, draw a picture of your favorite animal. Then write the group to which your animal belongs.

Welcome To Our Season!

The name of our season is _____.

There are many things to see and do during this season.

In our season you can see _____, _____, and _____.

Here is a picture of something to see during our season.

[ ]

In our season you can _____, _____, and _____.

Here is a picture of something to do during our season.

[ ]

To dress for our season, you should wear _____, _____, and _____.

Here is a picture of something to wear during our season.

[ ]

272

©1998 The Education Center, Inc. • The Mailbox® Superbook • Grade 2 • TEC451

Note To The Teacher: Use with "Take A Seasonal Tour" on page 265.

Insect Or Spider?

Follow the directions to learn about the differences between insects and spiders.

Insects

Insects have three body parts: a head, a thorax, and an abdomen.

Draw three circles to make an insect's body.
Draw two antennae and two eyes on the head.
Add six legs, three on each side of the thorax.
Draw two wings on the thorax.

Spiders

Spiders have two main body parts: a head and an abdomen.

Draw two circles to make a spider's body.
Draw eight legs, four on each side of the head.
Draw two rows of four eyes on the head.

Look at your drawings.
Write two sentences that tell how insects and spiders are different.

1. _____ .

2. _____ .

©1998 The Education Center, Inc. • _The Mailbox® Superbook_ • _Grade 2_ • TEC451 • Key p. 319

Note To The Teacher: Use with "Insect Or Spider?" on page 267.

Patterns

Use with "Bug Off!" on page 267.

ant	butterfly
grasshopper	praying mantis
ladybug	bee
fly	dragonfly
mosquito	wasp

HEALTH & SAFETY

Fair Play

Instill the virtue of fairness as you promote fair behaviors! Write "fairness" on the chalkboard. Encourage youngsters to give examples of times when they were treated fairly or unfairly. Next write the words "We play fair!" in large block letters on a sheet of one-inch graph paper as shown. When you see a student exhibiting an act of fairness, color a block under the first letter on the graph paper. When the remaining letter-blocks have been colored, treat youngsters to a "Fair-Play Party." On a designated day, invite students to bring from home their favorite board games to play at school. Continue this activity throughout the year to promote positive student behaviors. If desired enlist students' help in planning other fair-play activities for the parties. Now that's fair play!

Cooperative-Group Work

Here's a great cooperative-group activity that illustrates the importance of responsibility! Duplicate one copy of the task cards on page 285 onto construction paper for each group of four students. Also duplicate one copy of the evaluation form on page 285 for each student. Divide your youngsters into groups of four, and distribute a set of task cards to each group. Tell students that each group will work together to complete a cut-and-paste activity, and each group member will do *only* one step in the activity. Assign each group member a different task; then have each group work together to complete its activity. After the groups have completed the activities, have each group share how well its members worked together. Distribute the evaluation forms; then instruct each youngster to complete the form. Use the evaluation forms for additional cooperative-group activities throughout the year!

OUR WALL OF FAME!

Reinforce respect and perseverance with this one-of-a-kind idea! Invite students to think of the characteristics of individuals in various Halls Of Fame as you share some information from the box shown. List students' responses on chart paper. Then enlist students' help in creating a classroom Hall Of Fame wall. Assign each student a different classmate's name. Ask youngsters to think about why their nominees deserve a place on the wall; then invite each youngster to make a medal for his nominee. To make a medal, a student writes a story about his nominee on a precut circle of writing paper. He glues the circle to a slightly larger construction-paper circle. Finally he punches a hole at the top of the medal, threads a length of yarn through the hole, and ties the yarn's ends. After youngsters share their stories with their classmates, use tacks to suspend the medals on a bulletin board with the title "Our Wall Of Fame!"

My friend Susan King deserves a place on the Wall Of Fame. She is nice to everybody. She likes to do things for you. Susan always thinks about what other people are feeling. She is a good friend to everyone.

* **George Washington, Abraham Lincoln,** and **Benjamin Franklin** were inducted into the Hall Of Fame For Great Americans in 1900.
* **Babe Ruth** was inducted into the National Baseball Hall Of Fame in 1936.
* **The Beatles** were inducted into the Rock And Roll Hall Of Fame in 1988.

SPECIAL KIDS!

Bolster self-esteem when you present youngsters with this special certificate! For each student duplicate a copy of the certificate on page 286 onto colored paper. Write a student's name on the line provided; then glue a picture of the youngster to the middle of the certificate. If desired present the certificates after sharing Nancy Carlson's book *I Like Me!* (Viking Penguin, 1988). Your youngsters are sure to be all smiles when they receive this special recognition!

Citizenship Booklets

Here's a flag-waving idea for understanding citizenship! Ask your youngsters to brainstorm examples of good citizenship in the classroom. List their ideas on the chalkboard. Then have students create these citizenship booklets. To make a booklet, a student staples four white 9" x 12" sheets of white construction paper along the left edge. He then glues a 2" x 15" strip of tagboard atop the staples as shown. He writes the title "My Citizenship Book" on the front cover; then he decorates the cover as a flag. To complete his booklet, he copies, completes, and illustrates the phrase "Citizenship is" on each remaining booklet page. Invite youngsters to take their booklets home to share with their families. Now that's a great way to learn about citizenship!

A GIVING TREE

Encourage your youngsters to give to others when they help create this special tree. Cut a large tree from bulletin-board paper. Mount the tree on a wall with the title "Our Giving Tree." Then read aloud *The Giving Tree* by Shel Silverstein (HarperCollins Children's Books, 1964). After sharing the book, have students discuss the acts of kindness displayed by the tree. Then, on a 2" x 3" piece of white paper, have each student write a sentence about something she could give of herself, such as love, laughter, or kindness. She glues her sentence near the bottom of a four-inch square of gift wrap; then she attaches a mini self-sticking bow to the top. Invite students to share their sentences with their classmates. Then tape the gifts to the paper tree for a "tree-mendous" display that everyone will enjoy!

"Hones-tea"

Encourage youngsters to make truthful decisions when you host an "Hones-tea." Share your favorite version of the fable *The Boy Who Cried Wolf.* Invite youngsters to discuss how the boy's dishonest behaviors got him into trouble. Then have each student write about a time someone was dishonest with her. Serve "tea" (fruit punch) for youngsters to sip as they write their stories. Invite students to share their stories with their classmates. No doubt your students will realize that honesty is *always* the best policy!

Dental Health

A Mouthful Of Knowledge

Help your students understand the placement and uses of their teeth with this hands-on activity. Label four 9" x 12" sheets of construction paper "incisors," two sheets "canines," and four sheets "molars." To begin, involve youngsters in a discussion about some of these interesting facts about teeth:

- Teeth are the hardest part of the human body; they are located in the upper and lower jaws.
- Teeth play an important role in chewing food and in speech.
- Humans have two sets of teeth: baby teeth and permanent teeth.
- There are 20 baby teeth, ten in each jaw. There are three different kinds of teeth:
  — *Incisors* are biting teeth located at the front of the jaw. Incisors are sharp teeth that cut food.
  — *Canines* also bite into food. Canines rip and tear food; they are located at the sides of the jaw.
  — *Molars* grind food. They are located at the back of the jaw.

After discussing the toothy facts, randomly distribute the sheets of labeled paper to ten students. Have the youngsters stand in a U-shape at the front of the room according to the name of the tooth on their papers. Next ask each student to name and describe the purpose of his tooth. Collect the cards and redistribute them to ten new students until each child has had a turn. What a great way for students to gain a mouthful of knowledge!

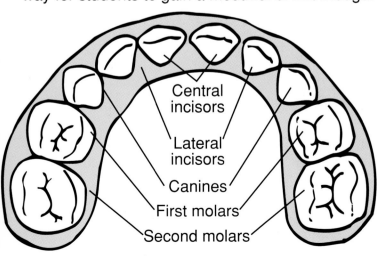

Central incisors
Lateral incisors
Canines
First molars
Second molars

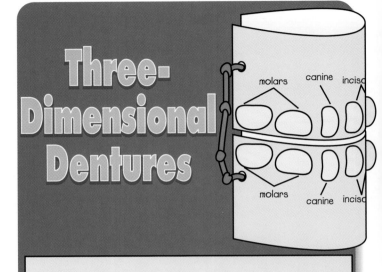

Three-Dimensional Dentures

lima beans navy beans lima beans

Youngsters will love to make these three-dimensional dentures as they learn about the placement of their teeth. Cut two 2" x 5" strips of tagboard and obtain 12 navy beans and 8 lima beans for each student. After reviewing the different kinds of teeth, have each youngster make a three-dimensional model of a child's mouth. First a student colors the strips pink to represent the gums. Next he glues the lima beans (molars) and the navy beans (incisors and canine teeth) along the bottom of each strip as shown. When the glue has dried, he labels each tooth with its appropriate name. He then punches a hole above the molars at the ends of both strips. Holding the strips so the teeth touch, thread a length of yarn through the holes on one side of the mouth model and tie the top jaw to the lower jaw; then repeat the procedure on the other side. Now that's an activity any youngster will want to sink his teeth into!

Toothy Terminology

Help students identify the parts of a tooth with this "tooth-erific" idea! Duplicate one copy of the tooth pattern on page 287 for each student. Prepare a class chart that identifies the parts of a tooth (as shown). Refer to the chart as you share the following information with the class:

- **Cementum:** lies over the dentin of the tooth's root.
- **Crown:** the part of the tooth that you can see.
- **Dentin:** a yellow substance, harder than bone, that makes up most of the tooth.
- **Enamel:** a hard substance that covers the tooth and lies over the dentin.
- **Nerves:** enter the tooth through the pulp.
- **Pulp:** the innermost layer of the tooth.
- **Root:** the part that holds the tooth to the bone.

Next have each student make a two-dimensional tooth model. To make a model, a student cuts out her tooth pattern and glues it to a 9" x 12" sheet of construction paper. Next she draws, colors, and labels each part of the tooth (cementum, crown, dentin, enamel, pulp, and root) as shown. She then glues various lengths of white dental floss inside the pulp cavity to represent the nerves of the tooth. To complete her project, she draws a pink gum line next to the tooth. Collect the projects and mount them on a bulletin board with the title "Toothy Terminology."

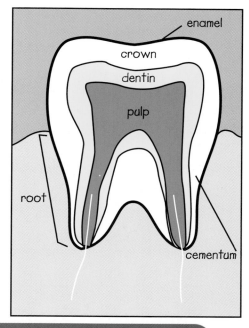

Acid Attack

Conduct a class experiment to determine why brushing is so important. Tell students that dentists recommend brushing your teeth after each meal. Then show students a hard-boiled egg. Explain to the youngsters that the hard shell protects the egg-the same way enamel protects their teeth. To begin the experiment, pour two cups of vinegar into a large jar. Place the egg into the jar, replace the lid, and put it in a safe location for student observation. Ask youngsters to predict what they think will happen to the egg. Write the students' responses on a sheet of chart paper. When two days have passed, gently remove the egg from the jar. Ask students to examine the egg and compare their predictions with the results. Tell the students that the vinegar caused the shell of the egg to break down and become soft, the same way tooth enamel is damaged by acid and bacteria in the mouth. Brushing every day is the only way to keep this from happening. If desired have each student write about the experiment. You can count on plenty of toothbrushing from now on!

Molar Mobiles

As a culminating activity, have students create molar mobiles. Duplicate four copies of the tooth pattern (page 287) onto white construction paper for each student. After a review of dental health, a student writes and illustrates one dental-health tip on each tooth pattern; then she cuts out the patterns. She staples the top corners of the cutouts together as shown. Next the student punches a hole at the top of each tooth; then she ties a 12-inch length of dental floss at each punched hole. To complete the project, she gathers the four strings at the top and ties the strings together. If time allows, have each youngster share her mobile with her classmates. Then suspend the mobiles around the room for all to enjoy!

Nutrition

Food-Pyramid Fun!

Introduce youngsters to the Food Guide Pyramid with this one-of-a-kind idea! Discuss with students the six sections of the food pyramid (see the illustration); then ask students to give examples of foods for each group. Tell students that their daily meals should include foods from each group. Ask each youngster to bring to school several canned food labels and the front panels of food boxes. When these have been collected, challenge the class to sort them according to the Food Guide Pyramid. Help students determine that some foods may fit into more than one section of the pyramid. Collect the sorted labels; then mount them on a prepared food pyramid similar to the one shown. Now, that's a great way to learn about the Food Guide Pyramid!

Fats, Sugars, Oils, etc. (use sparingly)

Milk, Yogurt, and Cheese Group (2-3 servings)

Meat, Poultry, Fish, Dried Beans, Eggs, and Nuts Group (2-3 servings)

Fruit Group (2-4 servings)

Vegetable Group (3-5 servings)

Bread, Cereal, Rice, and Pasta Group (6-11 servings)

The Very Healthy Caterpillar

Turn your youngsters on to good nutrition when you read Eric Carle's *The Very Hungry Caterpillar* (Scholastic Inc., 1987). After sharing the book, ask your students to name the foods the caterpillar ate; then list each food on the chalkboard. Challenge youngsters to decide which foods are healthful choices. Then enlist the students' help in creating a very healthy caterpillar display. Divide students into groups of two or three. Have each group cut pictures of healthful foods from magazines; then instruct them to glue the pictures to a large tagboard oval. Arrange the ovals in the shape of a giant caterpillar. Add desired paper caterpillar characteristics, such as antennae and legs, and the title "The Very Healthy Caterpillar" for a colorfully nutritious display!

A Food Sort

Your students will love playing this game to review the Food Guide Pyramid! For each student cut out one magazine picture of a food item. (Be sure to include foods from each food group.) Glue each picture to a separate 3" x 5" card. Label one area of your classroom for each of the six food groups. To play the game, distribute one card to each student. The student decides which group his food belongs in; then he stands next to the sign in his selected area. Once youngsters have sorted themselves accordingly, invite students to discuss the different food items that belong in their groups. Collect the cards, redistribute them to your students, and play the game again!

Blast Off With Good Nutrition!

Encourage students to eat nutritious, healthful meals with this far-out idea! Make four copies of the rocket pattern on page 287; then label each one with a different name: "Team 1," "Team 2," "Team 3," and "Team 4." Cover and decorate a bulletin board like the one shown; then use a marker to draw evenly spaced squares (the same size as the rockets) between the Earth and Moon. Place the rockets in the four squares closest to the Earth. Next assign each student to one of the four teams. Every day have each student list one nutritious meal that she has eaten in the last 24 hours on a scrap piece of paper. Challenge her to name the food group (fats, oils, and sweets excluded) for at least three items on her list. Move each team's rocket one square for each team member who ate a nutritious meal. Continue moving the rockets until each team has reached the Moon. Then reward students with a nutritious snack, like carrot sticks or apple slices. You'll be surprised how fast your youngsters will blast off toward good nutrition!

Tasting Party

Encourage picky eaters to sample different foods when you have a classroom tasting party! Ask parent volunteers to send in a variety of healthful foods, including cheeses, vegetables, and fruits. Cut the foods into bite-size pieces and insert a toothpick into each one. Invite each student to select a few of the foods, taste them, and record her reactions on a checklist similar to the one shown. Then have each youngster write about her favorite food. If desired graph students' favorite foods and discuss the outcome of the graph with the class. Time to start tasting!

Name	Molly	
Food	Liked	Didn't Like
cheese	X	
kiwi	X	
eggplant		X
grape	X	
broccoli		X
cauliflower	X	

What Is Nutritious?

Set the stage for good nutrition with this informative idea. Ask students to bring from home several nutrition labels from a variety of food containers. When an ample supply has been brought in, invite students to participate in any or all of the following activities:

Divide students into small groups and distribute four or five labels to each group. Challenge students to find the grams of fat, sugar, and salt (sodium) per serving in each food item. Then have each group share its findings with the rest of the class.

Challenge youngsters to determine how nutritious a food is by comparing calories and vitamins. Have each student select a different food nutrition label. Invite him to look up the calories per serving and the percentage of each vitamin on his label. Ask him to decide if he thinks his food is nutritious; then have him write a few sentences about his conclusions. Mount the food labels and the sentences on a bulletin board for all to enjoy!

Use this visual activity to make students more aware of the sugar they consume daily. Select three or four nutrition labels from your students' favorite cereals. Enlist the students' help in measuring out the grams of sugar per serving listed on each label. Place the measured sugar into individual self-sealing bags. Then ask youngsters to discuss the results as a class. If desired place additional labels and bags of sugar at a center for further student investigation.

FIRE SAFETY

Fire-Safety Fun!

Introduce your youngsters to fire-safety equipment by sharing *Fire Fighters: A To Z* by Jean Johnson (Walker Publishing Company, Inc.; 1985). This alphabet book uses black-and-white photos to show firefighters in their working environment with their equipment. After reading the book aloud, distribute one copy of the sheet on page 288 to each student. Lead your youngsters in a discussion of the firefighter equipment on the sheet; then invite each student to make an informative flip book. To make a book, a student folds a 12" x 18" sheet of drawing paper in half (to 6" x 18") and makes four equally spaced cuts in the top layer as shown. He then chooses four pieces of equipment from his sheet, colors them, and cuts them out. He glues each cutout atop a different flap; then, under each flap, he writes a short description about each piece of equipment. What a fun way to learn about fire-safety equipment!

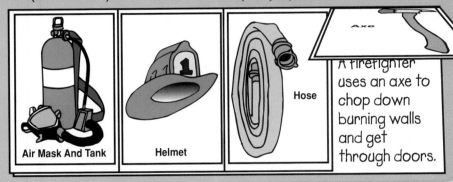

Air Mask And Tank

Helmet

Hose

Axe

A firefighter uses an axe to chop down burning walls and get through doors.

Crawl To Safety

Use this idea to emphasize to your youngsters that crawling is the best way to escape a burning room or building. Ask students to brainstorm what they should do in case of a fire. List their responses on the chalkboard. Explain that youngsters should always crawl low out of a smoke-filled room. When there is fire, smoke and gases rise, so the cleaner air is nearest the floor. By crawling to escape the fire, they will breathe cleaner air. Have a student volunteer demonstrate the correct way to crawl low. Then set up a variety of obstacles for students to crawl around or under, such as tables, desks, and chairs. Dim the classroom lights, and have two or three volunteers crawl around the obstacles to the door. Encourage your students to practice this crawling technique with their family members.

The Great Escape

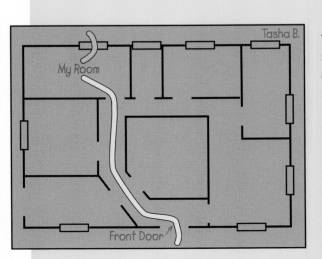

Tasha B.

My Room

Front Door

Planning fire-escape routes is a great way to reinforce fire safety. Tell youngsters that in case of a fire, they should always have two safe routes out of a burning residence or building. Then ask students to determine two safe ways to get out of the classroom. (If desired have your youngsters practice walking along each route.) Next have each youngster determine two safe routes out of her home. First a student draws a floor plan of her home on a 9" x 12" piece of tagboard. She then lightly traces two safe escape routes from a desired starting point. She glues a length of colored yarn atop the first route; then she glues a different-colored length of yarn atop the second route. If desired have youngsters share their escape plans in small groups. Now that's a great way to save a life!

"Rock," Drop, And Roll!

This activity teaches youngsters what to do should their clothes ever catch fire. Explain to your students that fire needs air to burn. Tell them that when a fire is smothered, air cannot help it burn. Ask students if they know what to do if their clothing catches fire. Have a volunteer demonstrate the *stop, drop,* and *roll* technique. Then have your class practice these important movements. Take students to an open area or room (such as a playground or gym); then ask them to spread out. Next explain to the youngsters that when they hear music playing, they are to begin dancing around in their space. When the music stops, each student should *stop, drop,* and *roll.* Then play the music. Vary the intervals and rate at which you start and stop the music. Now let's "Rock, Drop, And Roll!"

Safe At Home

Help your youngsters understand that smoke detectors are an important part of fire safety. Take your class on a short walk around the school. On your walk, point out the school's sprinkler system and smoke detectors. When you return to the classroom, explain to students that smoke detectors warn people that there is smoke or a fire. Tell them that all homes should have at least one smoke detector on each floor. As a homework assignment, have your youngsters survey their homes for smoke detectors. The next day discuss the survey results with the class. If desired contact local business organizations and ask for their help in donating smoke detectors and batteries to families in need.

Books About Fighting Fires

Share these additional titles about fire safety:
- *Fighting Fires* by Susan Kuklin (Simon & Schuster Books For Young Readers, 1993)
- *Community Helpers: Fire Fighters* by Dee Ready (Bridgestone Books, 1997)
- *Fire Trucks* by Hope Irvin Marston (Cobblehill Books, 1996)
- *Fire Fighters* by Jon Kirkwood (The Millbrook Press, Inc.; 1997)

Mrs. O'Leary's cow started the Great Chicago Fire in 1871. She accidentally knocked over a lantern. It was her fault.

Blame It On The Cow!

Relive the legend of the Great Chicago Fire of 1871 when you share *"Fire! Fire!" Said Mrs. McGuire* by Bill Martin, Jr., (Harcourt Brace & Company, 1996). After reading the book, involve students in a discussion about the role the cow played in starting the fire. Then have youngsters write their own versions of the famous legend. On a cow-shaped cutout with writing lines, have each student write a story about Mrs. O'Leary's cow and its role in the great fire. Staple the cows to a bulletin board with the title "Blame It On The Cow!" To complete the display, include the facts shown about the Great Chicago Fire.

- The Great Chicago Fire took place after a very dry summer in 1871.
- Legend has it that a cow owned by Mrs. Patrick O'Leary tipped over a lantern that ignited the fire.
- The fire was spread by very strong winds.
- Many families were driven from their homes by the flames.
- The Great Chicago Fire burned for more than 24 hours.
- When the fire finally ceased to burn, at least 300 people had died and more than 90,000 people were homeless.

Safety Tip Number...

Your youngsters are sure to chuckle and learn a lot of important safety tips, too, when you read *Officer Buckle And Gloria* by Peggy Rathmann (Scholastic Inc., 1995). In this delightful tale, a hardworking—but boring—police officer who gives safety lectures is upstaged by a dynamic dog. After reading the story, encourage youngsters to discuss why it is important to be safe. Then share the safety-tip stars on the beginning and ending pages of the book. Challenge students to brainstorm additional safety tips. Number and list each tip on the chalkboard as it is shared. Next invite each youngster to make a safety-tip star. Assign each student a different tip from the list. To make a star, a student copies his tip onto a yellow star cutout as shown and illustrates it as desired. He draws a line of glue along the edge of his star, sprinkles gold glitter atop the glue line, and then shakes off the excess glitter. When the projects are dry, mount them on a bulletin board with the title "Super Safety Tips!" What a great way to promote safe student behavior!

Safety Tip #12: Always swim with a buddy.

Bus Safety

Have your students spread the importance of bus safety with these informative guides. Ask youngsters to discuss why it is important to practice bus safety. Then have students brainstorm bus-safety rules. List their ideas on the chalkboard. To make a guide, a student folds a 9" x 12" sheet of yellow construction paper horizontally in half. He then trims the corners to create a bus shape (as shown) and adds black construction-paper wheels to the bottom. On the inside he lists important bus-safety rules; then he illustrates them as desired. To complete his guide, he adds the title "Bus Safety" and desired decorations to the front cover. Next pair each child with a student from a younger class. Invite him to share his guide with his partner. Your students are sure to receive a good lesson about bus safety *and* experience the joys of sharing information with others!

1. Always listen to the bus driver.
2. Talk in a quiet voice on the bus.
3. Always stay in your seat.
4. Never throw or put anything out the window.
5. Always walk three feet from the bus.
6. Wait for the bus to stop before you get on.

Bus Safety

Keith

Stranger Danger

Help students learn the dangers of strangers with this problem-solving activity. Remind students that a stranger is anyone whom they do not know well or do not know at all, and that they should *always* be careful of strangers. Then share the following stranger safety rules with your students:

* A stranger can appear to be a nice, friendly person.
* Even if a stranger knows your name, he is still a stranger.
* Never tell a stranger your name, address, or telephone number.
* Never go to a stranger's car or go to a stranger in a public place, even if he asks nicely.
* Never unlock or open your door to a stranger.
* Never believe a stranger who tells you that your parents have sent him to pick you up.
* Never go for a walk with a stranger who tells you that he needs to look for something.
* Never accept *anything* from a stranger.
* Never tell a stranger that you are home alone.
* Beware of a stranger who asks you for directions. A stranger should *never* ask a child for help. He should ask other adults.

Ask students if they would know what to do if they were approached by a stranger. Then have youngsters act out situations that may involve strangers. Write a number of different decision-making scenarios on index cards. Place the cards in an empty container. Have a group of two or three students draw a card from the container and act out the situation for the class. Then invite students to discuss the situation as a class. When appropriate ask another small group of students to select a card. Repeat the process until all of the cards have been drawn. Now your youngsters will know what to do if a stranger should ever approach them.

Use the task cards and the evaluation form with "Cooperative-Group Work" on page 276.

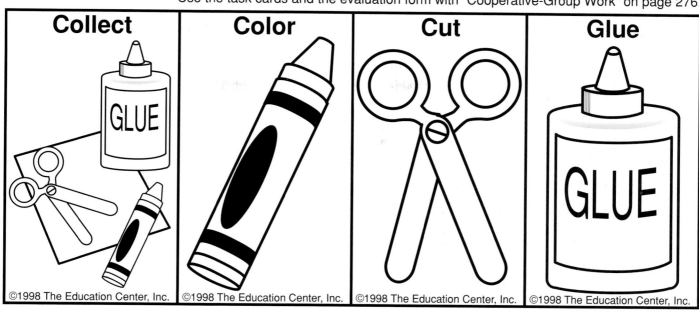

Collect	Color	Cut	Glue

©1998 The Education Center, Inc.   ©1998 The Education Center, Inc.   ©1998 The Education Center, Inc.   ©1998 The Education Center, Inc.

Name _____

How Did I Do?

I performed my task well.

My group was pleased with how I worked.

One thing I will work on next time is _____

_____

_____.

Certificate
Use with "Special Kids!" on page 276.

This is to certify that

Glue photo here.

is a

SPECIAL KID!

©1998 The Education Center, Inc. • The Mailbox® Superbook • Grade 2 • TEC451

Patterns

Use with "Toothy Terminology" and "Molar Mobiles" on page 279.

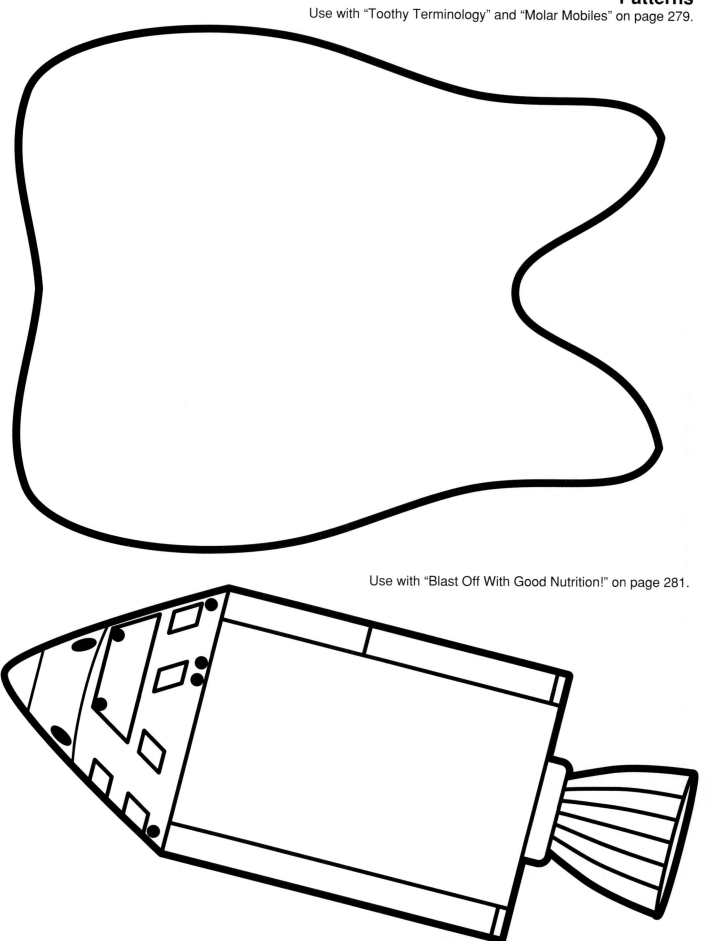

Use with "Blast Off With Good Nutrition!" on page 281.

Patterns
Use with "Fire-Safety Fun!" on page 282.

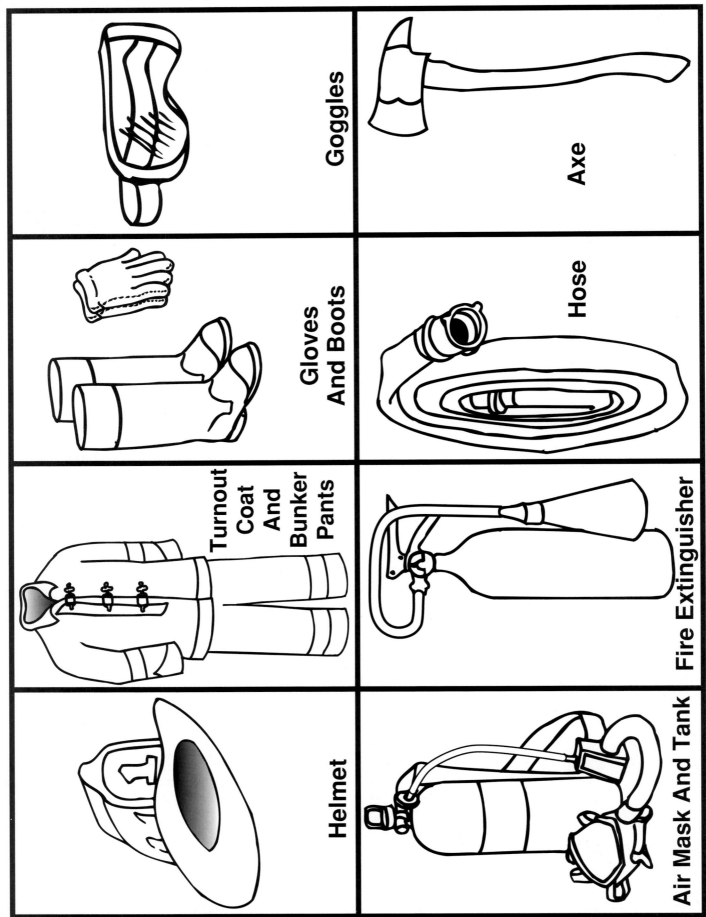

Goggles

Axe

Gloves And Boots

Hose

Turnout Coat And Bunker Pants

Fire Extinguisher

Helmet

Air Mask And Tank

HOLIDAY & SEASONAL

Get-Acquainted Activity

Early in the school year, help students get over the hurdle of new introductions with this easy-to-implement idea. On an index card, have each student write one statement about herself that she would like everyone to know. Ask children not to sign their names. Place the cards in a container. When you have a few extra minutes, draw a card from the container and read it aloud. Have children guess who wrote the statement; then ask the child to come forward and elaborate on her statement if desired. This gives each student an opportunity to tell something about herself that others may not know.

I collect butterflies.

I went to China to visit my uncle.

I help my mom raise show dogs.

Grand Locations

Use this Grandparents Day activity to incorporate map skills into your lessons. Post a U.S. map on a bulletin board in your classroom. Assist each student in inserting pushpins in the locations where his grandparents live. As an added activity, have each student write to his grandparents and request postcards from their homes. Surround the map with the postcards that are received.

GRANDPARENT SING-ALONG

Teach your students the words to some easy-to-learn songs, such as "You Are My Sunshine" or "I've Been Working On The Railroad." If desired, enlist the assistance of your music teacher for piano or guitar accompaniment. Then have each student invite his grandparents to visit your classroom for a special sing-along. For a quieter moment after the singing, read aloud *Song And Dance Man* by Karen Ackerman. Grandparents will enjoy this trip down memory lane, and students will enjoy the time with their relatives.

Pumpkin Patch Pleasers

When a student completes an assignment, encourage him to tiptoe to the pumpkin patch for some extra learning. To create the patch, cut several pumpkin shapes from orange tagboard. On each shape, write an activity for students to complete independently. (See the sample selection below.) Glue a craft stick to each pumpkin; then insert the stick into a large clay pot filled with potting soil. Place the pot on a table in a central location in your classroom. When a student visits the pumpkin patch, have him select a stick and complete the activity.

Suggested Pumpkin Patch Activities

- Draw a pumpkin on a sheet of paper, and design a jack-o'-lantern face.
- Read a story with the word *pumpkin* in the title.
- Count and list all the orange things you see in the room.
- List words that begin with *p*.
- Write a story about eating orange foods.
- Write a recipe that has pumpkin as an ingredient.

Pumpkin Patch

Write an ending to this story: "One dark and stormy night..."

Halloween Writers

Let the ghosts and ghouls of Halloween inspire your students to become holiday writers. To begin, write a student-generated list of Halloween-related words on a large ghost-shaped cutout. Next, on a sheet of orange paper, have each child use the words from the list to write a Halloween story. If desired, provide students with story titles (similar to the ones shown) for inspiration. Invite students to decorate the borders of their completed stories with Halloween stickers. Then, for added fun, gather students in a circle, turn off the lights, and encourage your youngsters to read their "spooktacular" stories!

candy
ghost
Halloween
scary
dark

The Ghost That Was Afraid

The Night I Met Gus The Ghost

Alone At The Pumpkin Patch

Facts Of A Feather

Turkeys and math facts—perfect companions for creating a Thanksgiving bulletin board. Cover a display area with yellow bulletin-board paper and a fall border. Make several turkey bodies, each from two sizes of brown construction-paper circles as shown. Laminate the turkeys and staple them to the board so that feathers can later be placed behind the bodies. For each turkey, cut six feathers from a variety of colored construction paper and laminate them. Next write a two-digit number on each turkey and a different math fact equaling that number on each of six feathers. Store all the feathers in a Press-On Pocket in the corner of the board. A student solves the fact on each feather and pins it behind its corresponding turkey. Change the answers and number sentences throughout the Thanksgiving season for additional math practice. Gobble! Gobble!

$7 + 11$

$18 + 0$

$5 + 13$

$6 + 12$

$9 + 9$

18

$7 + 5$

$12 + 0$

$2 + 10$

$6 + 6$

$9 + 3$

$10 + 8$

12

15

WINTER

Stocking Traditions

Create this fun display to share the tale of a holiday legend. Design a bulletin board to look like a fireplace. Then share the following legend of how the Christmas stocking came to be:

It is said that one Christmas Eve someone hung a wet stocking on the fireplace mantel to dry. As St. Nicholas happened by, he accidentally dropped some gold pieces down the chimney. Coincidentally, they fell into the drying stocking. This began the tradition of stockings being hung by the fireplace for Santa to fill with treats.

Using a template, each child traces two stocking shapes from white construction paper. He cuts out the stockings before personalizing one stocking cutout as desired. He glues the decorated stocking cutout—sides and bottom only—to the other stocking so that a pocket is formed. After the glue dries, hang the stockings on the bulletin board. Add candy canes and foil-wrapped chocolate coins to each stocking before returning it to its owner.

AND THE STOCKINGS WERE HUNG

Mike Angela Terry

Hanukkah Latkes

For a special treat during Hanukkah, read aloud the story *Grandma's Latkes* by Malka Drucker (Harcourt Brace & Company, 1992). Students will enjoy hearing the history of this holiday, and will especially enjoy the recipe for potato latkes found in the back of the book. Gather the supplies to make the treats in your classroom, or make them in advance and reheat them to serve to your students.

Dr. Martin Luther King

KWANZAA

One of the important elements of a Kwanzaa celebration is recognizing ancestors. This is done through the use of a *kikombe cha umoja,* or unity cup. Each member of a family drinks from the special cup to symbolize honor, praise, and commitment to his ancestors. Recreate a similar activity to recognize a significant African-American. Decorate a plastic cup with designs using Kwanzaa colors (red, black, and green). Use a permanent marker to write the name of a significant African-American on the cup. Share stories about the person; then, on a slip of paper, have each student write why the honoree is important. Collect all the students' comments in the cup and read a few of the statements each day of your Kwanzaa celebration. If desired, have each child create a cup of his own and select a person to research. Have him write several comments for his cup; then display all the cups on a classroom table for everyone to read.

WINTER WRITING WONDERLAND

Here's a great way to get your students writing about a cool subject—snow! Read aloud a snowy story, such as *Snowy Day* by Ezra J. Keats (Scholastic Inc., 1993), *Elmer In The Snow* by David McKee (Morrow Junior Books, 1995), or *The Snow Lambs* by Debi Gliori (Scholastic Inc., 1996). After discussing the book, ask students to brainstorm a list of snow-related words. (If you live in a warm climate, provide photographs of snowy conditions.) Record students' responses on a large sheet of bulletin-board paper cut to the shape of a snow shovel. Then, on a sheet of writing paper, have each child write a snow story, using some words from the list as inspiration. Remind each student to include a beginning, a middle, and an ending in his story. After the student completes his story, have him illustrate a scene from his story on a sheet of light blue construction paper. To complete the illustration, have him repeatedly hole-punch a scrap piece of white paper and randomly glue the resulting snowflakes to his paper. Mount each story with its corresponding picture; then add the snow shovel and the title "Winter Writing Wonderland." The result—a blizzard of your students' best writing.

blizzard
chilly
freezing
ice
snow
flurry

blanket
storm
cold
winter
sleet
slippery

New Year's Goals

Welcome your students back to school after the New Year's holiday with this inspiring idea. Write a self-improvement goal for the new year and post it on a prominent bulletin board. Explain to students why you chose this goal and what you plan to do to accomplish it. Next have each student write a self-improvement goal on a blank sheet of paper cut into the shape of a party hat; then have her glue it atop a slightly larger sheet of festive gift wrap and trim the edges as shown. Post the resulting party hats on a bulletin board and add a title. To create an especially festive mood, attach New Year's party hats, horns, and inflated balloons to the border of the display. Students will love this three-dimensional display!

I am going to read at home every night. Dee Dee

Recycled Calendars

Don't slip into the new year without reusing all the outdated calendars from the previous year. These timeless treasures can serve many purposes in your classroom. After asking students to bring in their discarded calendars, try the following creative projects:

- Place the pictures or photographs in a writing center. Encourage students to select a picture as inspiration for a creative writing assignments.

- Laminate the dated pages for use in a math center. Have students use wipe-off markers to write math equations equal to each number. Or have students write the corresponding Roman numeral in each calendar square.

- Cut apart dated squares after laminating to use as number cards for various projects or games.

- Laminate each month and have students place them in chronological order.

African-American Study

Use this unique report form to help students learn about accomplished African-Americans. After studying several famous African-Americans, have each child select one on which to do a report. Then give each student a 5 1/2" x 9" sheet of colored construction paper to fold in half. On one side of the folded paper, have the student write the name of his chosen African-American. On the other side of the paper, have him write an explanation as to why this person is considered famous. Glue students' folded papers to lengths of ribbon as shown. Then suspend the ribbons throughout your classroom and invite students to read about these famous African-Americans during their spare time.

Harriet Tubman

She escaped from slavery and was a conductor on the Underground Railroad.

IF I WERE PRESIDENT

President Aikman

If I were president I would make it a law that everyone must recycle.

Salute past and present presidents with these unique projects. Discuss with students the importance of the president's job and the major accomplishments of a few previous presidents. Then have each child imagine she is president, and have her write what she would like to accomplish on a sheet of blank paper. Have her glue her writing to a 9" x 12" sheet of construction paper. Next have her trace a large oval template on a 9" x 12" sheet of drawing paper. Then have her draw a presidential portrait of herself inside the oval. (Remind students that you have to be at least 35 years old to be the president.) Instruct her to cut out the oval and mount it on the other side of the construction-paper sheet. To complete the project, have her write her name on a yellow construction-paper strip and glue it beneath her portrait. Hole-punch the top of each project, thread a length of yarn through the hole, and tie the yarn's ends. Suspend the projects throughout the classroom to celebrate Presidents' Day.

GROUNDHOG HONORS

Dig into these fun activities on February 2 to honor the weather-predicting groundhog—also known as a woodchuck.

 Begin with a tongue-twisting rendition of the time-honored tongue twister, "How Much Wood Would A Woodchuck Chuck."

 Share a tale of the groundhog legend, such as *It's Groundhog Day!* by Steven Kroll (Holiday House, Inc.; 1987).

 Have students brainstorm groundhog-related words, such as burrow, hibernate, and shadow. List students' responses on a word bank. Have students use the words for writing woodchuck poetry.

 Combine a math and science lesson by having students measure their shadows.

 Culminate the day with groundhog cupcakes. To make a cupcake, a student inserts two vanilla wafers into a frosted cupcake. Then she adds chocolate-covered candies for eyes and a nose, and two miniature marshmallows for teeth.

PUZZLED HEARTS

A framed picture makes a special gift for anytime, but especially for Valentine's Day. In advance collect several discarded puzzles with pieces missing. For each student cut a heart-shaped frame (as shown below) from tagboard. Have each student glue puzzle pieces to the frame—adding a second layer after the first for added dimension. When the glue has dried, spray-paint each of the frames red. After the paint dries, spray each frame with a protective coat of clear acrylic. Have each child tape a school photograph behind the opening of his frame. Next have him glue a heart-shaped tagboard backing behind the photo. To complete the gift, secure a piece of self-sticking magnetic tape to the back of each frame. The recipients of these special frames are sure to express their heartfelt thanks.

SPRING

THE COLORS OF SPRING

Here's an easy way to get spring off to a colorful start while teaching your students about plants. Fill three tall, clear glasses with water and add ten drops of different-colored food coloring to each glass. Cut a few inches from the stems of three white carnations, and place one carnation in each of the glasses. Ask students to predict what might happen to the flowers. The next day have students observe the colorful flowers and write comments about the changes. This quick science lesson is sure to brighten your students' day.

Green Graphing

Celebrate the color green with this graphing activity. On a large sheet of bulletin-board paper, list several statements about green objects. Provide each child with several shamrock stickers. Read each statement and have each child, in turn, place a sticker next to each statement on the graph that applies to her. Have students use the completed graph to answer questions during a class discussion. Think green!

I am wearing green.	🍀 🍀 🍀 🍀 🍀
I live in a green house.	🍀
I have a green pencil.	🍀 🍀 🍀 🍀
My family has a green car.	🍀 🍀 🍀
I use a green toothbrush.	🍀 🍀
I like green Jell-O®.	🍀 🍀 🍀 🍀 🍀
I like green beans.	🍀 🍀 🍀 🍀 🍀
I have a green pet.	🍀
My favorite color is green.	🍀 🍀 🍀

St. Patrick's Snakes

To pay tribute to the legend of St. Patrick's driving the snakes from Ireland, have your students create these colorful snakes. On a sheet of white construction paper, have each child draw a random design with crayons and then fill in each space with a bright color of crayon or marker. When the page is filled with color, have the child turn the paper over and draw a snake on the back. After cutting out the snake, he should glue it onto a sheet of green construction paper. To complete the design, have each student add a wiggle eye to his snake. Display these snazzy snakes in your classroom for a colorful St. Patrick's Day celebration.

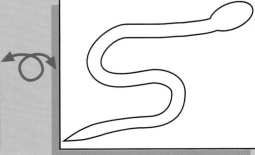

Colored-Egg Creations

What's Easter without colored eggs? Try this interesting twist on traditional colored eggs. In a small bowl, mix four tablespoons of light corn syrup with four drops of food coloring and stir. Repeat several times to make bowls of several different colors. Give each child a hard-cooked egg (prepared in advance). Have her dip her finger into one color of the mixture and then spread it on her egg. After she wipes her finger on a paper towel, have her select a different color to finish painting her egg. Let the eggs dry for at least three hours before moving them. Have each child take her egg home for an Easter display. (Remind students not to eat their eggs, as they may not have been properly refrigerated. Encourage them to discard the eggs after the holiday.)

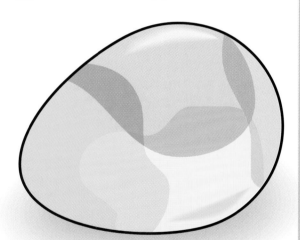

Basket Bonus

Be ready to take advantage of a few free minutes by preparing a basketful of bonus-time activities. Write several short activities (similar to the ones shown) on separate slips of paper. Fold each slip and place it inside a separate plastic egg. Place the eggs in a basket filled with cellophane grass. When you have a few spare minutes, open an egg and read aloud the activity for students to complete.

Name animals that have fur.
Name animals that lay eggs.
Name things bunnies can do.
Name kinds of Easter candy.
Name things you find in an Easter basket.
Name words that begin with *h,* like *hop.*

Name famous bunnies.

Paper Pals

Start a simple recycling effort right in your classroom in honor of Earth Day (April 22). Designate a box where students can put used paper. When they need a blank sheet, encourage them to use the back of a used piece from the box. Find a nearby recycling center that accepts paper and plan a field trip when your paper box is full. Interview the school custodian to see whether he notices less trash leaving your classroom. This class effort will help everyone see the value in recycling.

WE'RE PAPER PALS!

WE RECYCLE!

Springtime May Baskets

Many people think of May Day (May 1) as a time to celebrate spring as well as deliver May baskets to friends and family. Your students can combine these two traditions by creating these festive floral baskets to fill with treats and deliver to loved ones. In advance collect a large assortment of recycled plastic and silk flowers and a class supply of berry baskets. To make a basket, a student twists two bright-colored pipe cleaners together and attaches the ends to opposite sides of a basket to form a handle. Next he pokes a few flowers into the basket, and you secure them with hot glue. When the glue has dried, have each child write a special springtime message on an index card and place it in his basket along with a small bag of popcorn and candy treats. Just the fun part remains—delivering the baskets! Happy May Day!

Cinco de Mayo is a Mexican holiday celebrated on May 5 to commemorate an important Mexican military victory that took place on that date in 1862. This celebration lends itself to an interesting study of Mexican culture, and it wouldn't be complete without also studying the Mexican language. Teach your students the number words from one to ten in Spanish. (If you have Spanish-speaking students in your class, enlist their help in teaching the other students.) After a little practice, have your students use the Spanish number words to answer math problems. Announce or write a problem that equals an answer from one to ten; then ask a student volunteer to solve the problem using a newly learned Spanish number word. If desired, divide your class into two teams to create a competition. This fun activity is as easy as *uno, dos, tres!*

UNO ONE	**DOS** TWO	**TRES** THREE	**CUATRO** FOUR	**CINCO** FIVE
SEIS SIX	**SIETE** SEVEN	**OCHO** EIGHT	**NUEVE** NINE	**DIEZ** TEN

Memorial Day Memories

Remind students that Memorial Day is an American patriotic holiday that honors those who have died while serving our country in times of war. It is celebrated on the last Monday in May. People decorate graves, attend parades, and fly their flags at half-mast until noon to show their respect for members of the armed services who faithfully served our country. To extend students' knowledge of this holiday, create a bulletin-board display featuring pictures of military personnel, medals, and monuments. Encourage students to contribute pictures of friends and family members who have served in the armed forces. For a follow-up, invite a veteran or active-duty military person to speak to your students about his experiences. No doubt these activities will leave your students with a greater appreciation for the holiday!

"FANtastic" Mom

Your students will love making these Mother's Day fans as much as their moms will enjoy receiving them! In advance obtain several discarded wallpaper sample books and cut an assortment of 8" x 14" sheets from the books. Also cut a class supply of 12-inch lengths of ribbon. To make a fan, a child accordion-folds a wallpaper sheet and staples one end to create a fan. Next she ties a bow with a length of ribbon. Then you hot-glue the bow to her fan. She then designs a card to accompany her gift that says "Mom, you're FANtastic!" Your students' mothers will be delighted with their fanciful Mother's Day presents!

Mom, you're FANtastic!

Mom's Homework

Challenge your students' moms to find their best qualities by completing this Mother's Day word search. Have your students brainstorm characteristics of their mothers. Write students' responses on the chalkboard. Next distribute a copy of the grid on page 316 to each student. To make a word search, a student selects a word from the chalkboard and writes it at the bottom of his paper. Then he writes the word in the grid horizontally or vertically—one capital letter per box. He repeats the process until he has eight words in his puzzle. After checking his work, he fills in the remaining boxes with random capital letters. Have students take their puzzles home for their mothers to complete. No more searching for the perfect Mother's Day gift!

Mother's Day Munchies

Your students will enjoy making this special treat to show their moms how much they're loved. Purchase heart-shaped sugar cookies from a local bakery, or bake them in advance. (If desired, let your students assist with the cookie baking.) Purchase tubes of frosting in a variety of colors. Create a sample to show students basic decorating tips; then have each child decorate a cookie for her mother. Don't forget to have sandwich bags and ribbon on hand for wrapping your students' edible gifts.

End Of The Year

HAVE A BALL!

Celebrate the end of the school year with your students by throwing a beach ball—party, that is! On the day of the event, invite your students to dress in summer attire (sandals, shorts, and t-shirts). Greet each child at the door with a big "Aloha!" and a plastic lei. Then treat them to some or all of the following fun festivities:

 Read seashore stories.

 Do the limbo.

 Have students brainstorm beach vocabulary to use when writing original stories.

 Dance or play Musical Chairs to beach tunes.

 Eat watermelon.

 Watch a travel video for a tropical destination.

What a fun way to cast off from the school year and sail into summer!

Summer Senses

Try this sensible idea for getting your students to write during the summer. Assist each child in creating a blank book by stapling several sheets of blank paper between two construction-paper covers. Have her title the book "Summer Senses." On each page of the book, have each child draw a different summer activity she is planning, such as swimming, playing ball, or bicycling. Then challenge each student to write about each of the events as it occurs during the summer. Encourage her to include details about how things smell, taste, sound, feel, and look. Your students will have a sensational summer project when the book is complete.

Summer School Box

Chances are you've been collecting many things throughout the school year that have educational value, such as left-over reproducible sheets, unused workbooks, and bonus storybooks from book orders. Try this idea to rid your room of these recyclables while putting smiles on your students' faces. Have each child bring a shoebox to school and decorate it with summer scenes or postcards. While students are out of the room, randomly fill the shoeboxes with the materials you've collected. If desired, enclose skill sheets that are specific to each child's educational needs. This is also a perfect place for a class photograph and a special note from you. Put the lids on all the boxes and seal each one with a rubber band. Place a note on top of each box that says "Do not open until summer!" Then distribute the boxes on the last day of school. Your students will enjoy opening their end-of-the-year surprises and working on their special lessons well after the school year has ended.

When I go swimming, the water is wet and cold. I can hear the waves crashing to the shore. The water tastes salty. I try not to taste it.

This interesting twist on traditional show-and-tell will delight your students and may just help their parents with summer vacation planning as well. Ask each child to gather pictures, brochures, and souvenirs from a previous vacation. Have him prepare a brief presentation to tell the other students about his travels. After all the students have shared their information, display the vacation items on a classroom table. Notify parents of a special vacation preview event happening in your classroom and invite them to attend. Have students stand or sit near their vacation memorabilia as parents walk through to view the displays. Encourage parents to ask students questions regarding their vacations. After personally speaking to each young traveler, parents will have new information for making some informed vacation decisions for their families.

SUMMER OR BUST!

This idea will have your students bursting with excitement for summer! To prepare, write a different summertime activity on a paper strip for each student. Roll each strip and tuck it into a balloon; inflate each balloon and tie it. Have each student select a balloon, pop it, and pantomime the activity written on his paper strip. Have the remaining students guess the activity. Continue the fun until each child has had a chance to participate. No doubt some summer excitement will pop up in your classroom while you share this event!

drinking milk shakes

riding my bike

going to the pool

eating a hot dog

Wrap Up The School Year

Prepare this eye-catching door decoration for your students' last week of school. Cover your classroom door with bright-colored bulletin-board paper, and add a large bow. Then write the message "Time To Wrap Up Another Year!" During the final week, encourage your students to use markers to write special memories of the school year on the paper. Students are sure to smile as they read and remember.

Name _____

A Bushel Of Addition

Add.

1. 8
   + 8
   ___

2. 5
   + 6
   ___

3. 4
   + 8
   ___

4. 6
   + 6
   ___

5. 6
   + 7
   ___

6. 8
   + 7
   ___

7. 9
   + 5
   ___

8. 6
   + 9
   ___

Draw a basket for these apples.
Add.
Color.

9. 5
   + 8
   ___

10. 4
    + 7
    ___

11. 8
    + 6
    ___

12. 7
    + 5
    ___

13. 8
    + 9
    ___

14. 9
    + 9
    ___

Interview A Grandparent

Ask a grandparent these questions.
Write the answer on the line.

1. When were you born? _____ _____, _____
                              (month)   (day)   (year)

2. What games did you play when you were my age?

    _____

3. What subject did you like best when you were in school?

    _____

4. What is your favorite food?

    _____

5. What job or jobs did you have as an adult?

    _____

6. What hobbies do you have now?

    _____

Draw a picture of your grandparent.
Draw something you learned from the interview.

Safety Is In The Bag

Cut apart the sentences at the bottom of the page. Glue only the trick-or-treating safety rules onto the bag.

Walk on the sidewalk.	Cross the street without looking.
Have your parents check the candy before eating it.	Be polite.
Wear dark clothing.	Go to houses of people you know.
Wear makeup instead of a mask.	Walk with an adult.
Go to a strange house alone.	Carry a flashlight.

Tackling The Alphabet

Glue the footballs onto the field in alphabetical order.

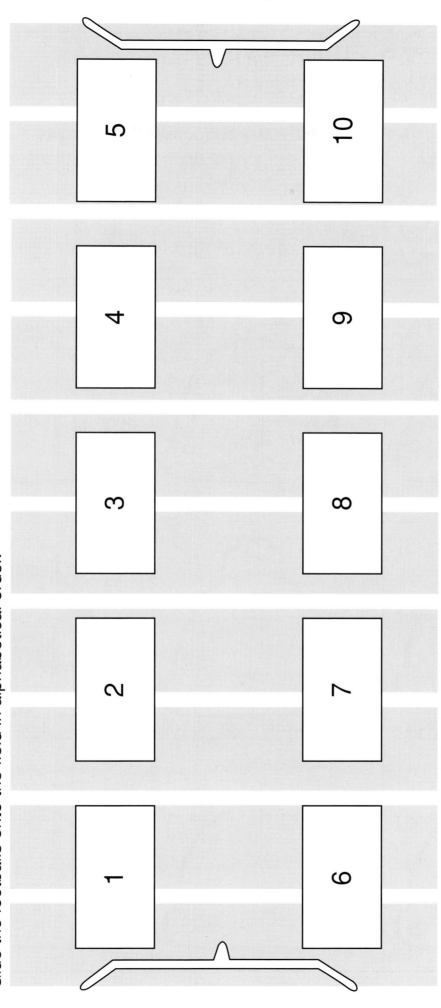

| 5 | 4 | 3 | 2 | 1 |

| 10 | 9 | 8 | 7 | 6 |

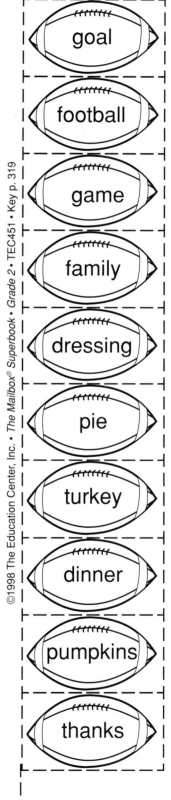

- goal
- football
- game
- family
- dressing
- pie
- turkey
- dinner
- pumpkins
- thanks

©1998 The Education Center, Inc. • *The Mailbox*® *Superbook* • *Grade 2* • TEC451 • Key p. 319

Which Hat?

Kate lost her hat. Use the clues to find her hat.

- My hat does not have spots.
- My hat does not have stripes.
- My hat has squares.
- My hat does not have a ball on top.

Color Kate's hat.

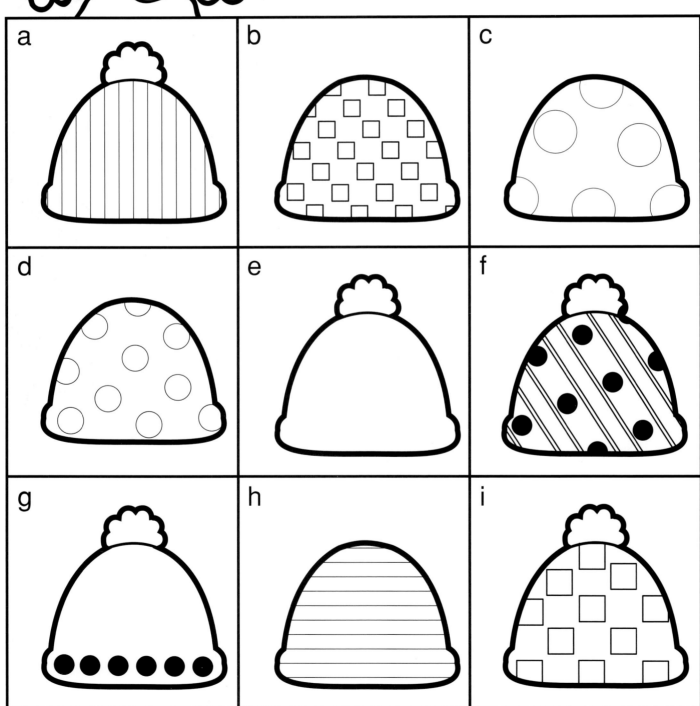

©1998 The Education Center, Inc. • *The Mailbox® Superbook • Grade 2 • TEC451 • Key p. 319*

Name _____

Stocking Stuffers

Write each missing number.

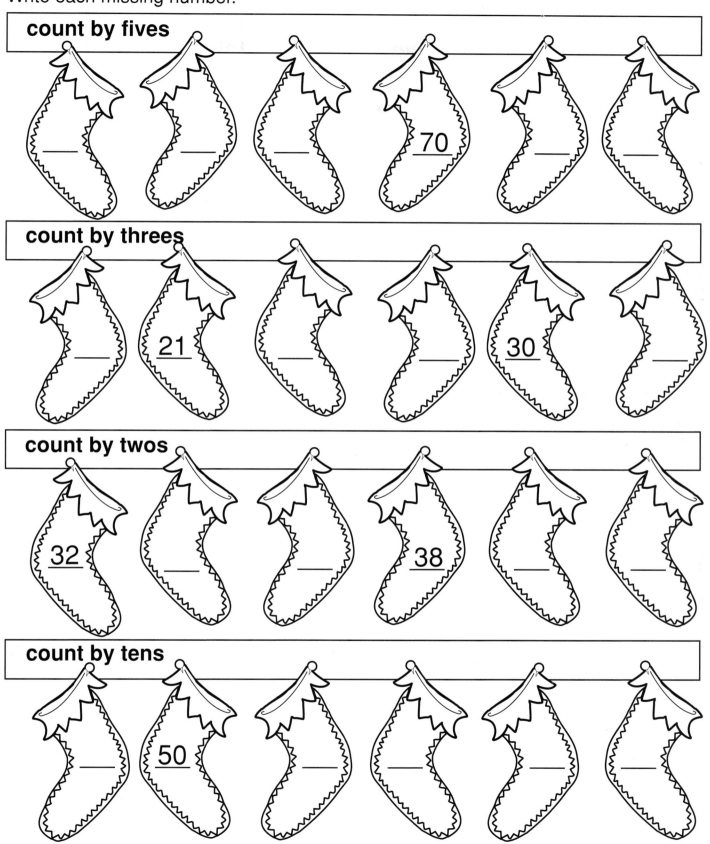

count by fives
___ ___ ___ 70 ___ ___

count by threes
___ 21 ___ ___ 30 ___

count by twos
32 ___ ___ 38 ___ ___

count by tens
___ 50 ___ ___ ___ ___

Bonus Box: Color all the **even**-numbered stockings.

Hanukkah Lights

Add. Cut the answers apart and glue each one in the right place.
There is one extra.

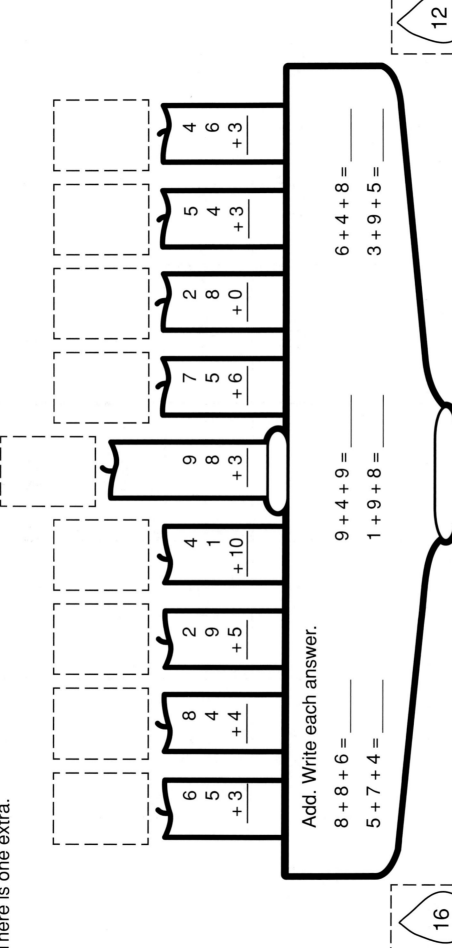

$$6 + 4 + 8 = \underline{\hspace{1cm}}$$

$$3 + 9 + 5 = \underline{\hspace{1cm}}$$

$$9 + 4 + 9 = \underline{\hspace{1cm}}$$

$$1 + 9 + 8 = \underline{\hspace{1cm}}$$

Add. Write each answer.

$$8 + 8 + 6 = \underline{\hspace{1cm}}$$

$$5 + 7 + 4 = \underline{\hspace{1cm}}$$

$$\begin{array}{r} 4 \\ 6 \\ +\ 3 \\ \hline \end{array}$$

$$\begin{array}{r} 5 \\ 4 \\ +\ 3 \\ \hline \end{array}$$

$$\begin{array}{r} 2 \\ 8 \\ +\ 0 \\ \hline \end{array}$$

$$\begin{array}{r} 7 \\ 5 \\ +\ 6 \\ \hline \end{array}$$

$$\begin{array}{r} 9 \\ 8 \\ +\ 3 \\ \hline \end{array}$$

$$\begin{array}{r} 4 \\ 1 \\ +\ 10 \\ \hline \end{array}$$

$$\begin{array}{r} 2 \\ 9 \\ +\ 5 \\ \hline \end{array}$$

$$\begin{array}{r} 8 \\ 4 \\ +\ 4 \\ \hline \end{array}$$

$$\begin{array}{r} 6 \\ 5 \\ +\ 3 \\ \hline \end{array}$$

12   19

13

18

10

16

15

14

16

20

Making A Mkeka

Find the numeral 8 in each number.
Color. Use the code.

color code:

ones place = red
tens place = green
hundreds place = black

318	787	238	381	528	484
482	850	387	801	289	870
698	782	548	681	468	586
984	832	487	860	385	807
278	583	158	485	938	189
					728

A **mkeka** is a straw mat. It's used in Kwanzaa celebrations.

Noisy New Year's

African-American Accomplishments

Read each historical accomplishment.
Cross out each lowercase letter that should be capitalized.
Write the correct capital letter above each crossed-out letter.

R   P
1. rosa parks was arrested, which formally began the civil rights movement.

2. martin luther king, jr., led more than 200,000 people in a protest march in washington, d.c.

3. jackie robinson played baseball with the brooklyn dodgers.

4. harriet beecher stowe wrote the book *uncle tom's cabin.*

5. george washington carver made more than 300 products from peanuts.

6. elijah mccoy invented the lawn sprinkler and the ironing board.

7. thurgood marshall became the first african-american judge to serve on the united states supreme court.

8. benjamin banneker built the first clock to be built in america.

Bonus Box: Choose a famous Black American from the underlined names. Read about the person. On the back of this sheet, write a paragraph describing the person.

Name _____

Sweet Treat

CUTIE PIE   BE MINE

Solve each valentine word problem.

Talos got 16 pieces of candy from his mother. He gave 6 pieces to his brother. How many pieces of candy did he have left? _____ C	Zach got 13 valentines. 6 valentines had gum. How many did not have gum? _____ L	Dan walked 6 blocks on one street and 8 blocks on another street to deliver valentines. How many blocks did he walk? _____ O
Kayla went to a Valentine's Day party. There were 14 boys and 8 girls at the party. How many more boys than girls were there? _____ C	Kate got 14 valentines. Meg got 15 valentines. How many valentines did the girls get altogether? _____ H	Lisa got a necklace with 7 diamonds, 5 rubies, and 10 emeralds in it for Valentine's Day. How many jewels were in her necklace? _____ A
Rob ate 7 red, 4 yellow, and 6 pink candy hearts. How many candy hearts did Rob eat in all? _____ O	Sue got 12 heart stickers and 7 flower stickers to use on valentines. How many stickers did she have in all? _____ E	Cathy got 12 valentines, and Mac got 8 valentines. How many more valentines did Cathy get than Mac? _____ T

Write the letter that matches each answer to discover a yummy valentine gift.

6   29   14   10   17   7   22   4   19

Spring Vowels

Write the missing vowels in each springtime word.
Cross off each vowel in the answer box.

Answer Box

e	a	i	a	i	i	e
e	e	e	i	e	e	a
e	u	o	a	u	i	i

1. fl__w__r

2. s__ __ds

3. g__rd__n

4. s__nsh__n__

5. __n__m__ls

6. r__ __n

7. k__t__s

8. __ns__cts

9. b__nn__ __ __s

Compound Coins

Write each compound word on the pot of gold.

treasure

rainbow

green

clover

luck

pot

horseshoe

smile

wishbone

coins

butterfly

gold

leprechaun

sunshine

dust

holiday

doghouse

cloudburst

Bonus Box: On the back of this sheet, write a story using all of the compound words.

Easter Fun

Find these Easter words in the puzzle.
Use the word list.
The words may be across or down.

Word List

basket	friends
bunny	fun
candy	grass
chick	holiday
chocolate	hunt
Easter	spring
eggs	

F	R	I	E	N	D	S	C	P
A	G	R	A	S	S	I	H	N
C	B	A	S	K	E	T	O	F
H	U	N	N	E	G	G	C	U
I	N	N	A	R	S	G	O	N
C	N	A	R	S	S	T	L	E
K	Y	H	O	L	I	D	A	Y
R	E	C	A	N	D	Y	T	G
S	P	R	I	N	G	G	E	S

Use a yellow crayon to color any letters in the puzzle that were not used.
Study the letters for something fun to do at Easter time. (**Hint:** Read the letters in order from left to right.)
Copy the message on the lines below.

Homework For Mom

Word Bank

_____ _____ _____ _____

_____ _____ _____ _____

Thinkin' Like A Third Grader

Read. Write.

1. My favorite **subject** in second grade was _____.

   In third grade, I might like _____.

2. My favorite **outdoor game** in second grade was _____.

   In third grade, I might like to play _____.

3. My favorite **stories** in second grade were about _____.

   In third grade, I might like stories about _____.

4. My good **friend** in second grade was _____.

   In third grade, I might like _____.

5. My favorite **food** while I was in second grade was _____.

   In third grade, I might like to eat _____.

6. My favorite **place to visit** while I was in second grade was _____.

   In third grade, I might like to go _____.

Draw.

This is what I look like at the end of second grade.	This is what I might look like when I'm in third grade.

Seasonal Clip Art

Answer Keys

Page 227
1. 3 inches
2. 5 inches
3. 1 inch
4. 4 inches
5. 2 inches

Page 248

Page 273

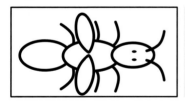 

Possible Answers:
1. Insects have three body parts and spiders have two body parts.
2. Spiders have eight legs and insects have six legs.

Page 302
Student-drawn picture of a basket under the apples.

1. 16		8. 15
2. 11		9. 13
3. 12		10. 11
4. 12		11. 14
5. 13		12. 12
6. 15		13. 17
7. 14		14. 18

Page 304
Walk with an adult.
Go to houses of people you know.
Walk on the sidewalk.
Have your parents check the candy before eating it.
Carry a flashlight.
Be polite.
Wear makeup instead of a mask.

Page 305

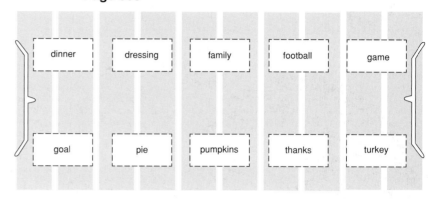

Page 306
b

Page 307

55	60	65	70	75	80
18	21	24	27	30	33
32	34	36	38	40	42
40	50	60	70	80	90

Page 308

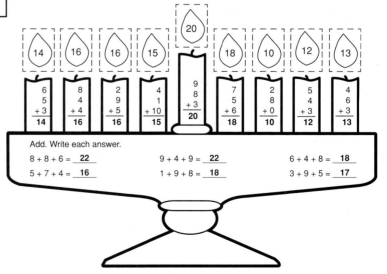

Answer Keys

Page 309

red	green	red	green	red	green	red
green	black	green	black	green	black	green
red	green	red	green	red	green	red
green	black	green	black	green	black	green
red	green	red	green	red	green	red

Page 311

1. rosa parks was arrested, which formally began the civil rights movement.
   _{R P}

2. martin luther king, jr., led more than 200,000 people in a protest march in washington, d.c.
   _{M L K J}
   _{W D C}

3. jackie robinson played baseball with the brooklyn dodgers.
   _{J R B D}

4. harriet beecher stowe wrote the book uncle tom's cabin.
   _{H B S U T C}

5. george washington carver made more than 300 products from peanuts.
   _{G W C}

6. elijah mccoy invented the lawn sprinkler and the ironing board.
   _{E M}

7. thurgood marshall became the first african-american judge to serve on the united states supreme court.
   _{T M A A}
   _{U S S C}

8. benjamin banneker built the first clock to be built in america.
   _{B B A}

Page 312

10 **C**	7 **L**	14 **O**
6 **C**	29 **H**	22 **A**
17 **O**	19 **E**	4 **T**

C H O C O L A T E
6 29 14 10 17 7 22 4 19

Page 313

1. flower
2. seeds
3. garden
4. sunshine
5. animals
6. rain
7. kites
8. insects
9. bunnies

Page 314

rainbow
wishbone
horseshoe
sunshine
doghouse
cloudburst
butterfly

Page 315

F	R	I	E	N	D	S	C	P
A	G	R	A	S	S	I	H	N
C	B	A	S	K	E	T	O	F
H	U	N	T	T	G	I	C	U
I	N	N	E	G	G	E	O	N
C	N	A	R	S	S	T	L	E
K	Y	H	O	L	I	D	A	Y
R	E	C	A	N	D	Y	T	G
S	P	R	I	N	G	G	E	S

PAINTING EASTER EGGS